The Complete Guide
to
RUGBY
WORLD CUP

Pegasus Publishing

The Complete Guide to Rugby World Cup

Adapted by Tracy Rockwell

First Published in Australia in 2015 (ebook)
This first printed edition published in 2019
By Pegasus Publishing (NSW)
PO Box 980, Edgecliff, NSW, 2027

Orders: pegasuspublishing@iinet.net.au
www.pegasuspublishing.com.au

ISBN: 978-1-925909-07-4

Introductory Images

Front Cover: 'Webb Ellis Cup' by Roman.b (2011). Available at https://en.wikipedia.org/wiki/Webb_Ellis_Cup#/media/File:Rugby_World_Cup_Trophy.jpg under Copyleft: This work of art is free; you can redistribute it and/or modify it according to terms of the Free Art License.

Title Page: 'Official 2007 RWC balls before quarter-final between South Africa and Fiji' by gepiblu (7 Oct 2007). Available at https://commons.wikimedia.org/wiki/File:2007_Rugby_World_Cup_balls.jpg under the Creative Commons Attribution-Share Alike 2.0 Generic license.

Page 7: 'Paul O'Connell in action for Ireland (v Argentina)' by Paolo Camera (30 Sep 2007). Available at https://commons.wikimedia.org/wiki/File:Paul_0%27Connell_Ireland_Rugby.jpg under the Creative Commons Attribution 2.0 Generic license.

Page 8: 'Haka' by Alessio Bragadini (14 Nov 2009). Available at https://commons.wikimedia.org/wiki/File:Haka.jpq under the Creative Commons Attribution-Share Alike 2.0 Generic license.

The Complete Guide to Rugby World Cup
[eBook Version]
ISBN: 978-0-9942014-2-3

An earlier, but now updated eBook version of this book was first published in 2015, which can be downloaded on iPhone, iPad or iMac from Apple iBooks at:
https://books.apple.com/us/book/the-complete-guide-to-rugby-world-cup/

The Complete Guide
to
RUGBY
WORLD CUP

Adapted
by
Tracy Rockwell

Pegasus Publishing

CONTENTS

Paul O'Connell in action for Ireland v Argentina, during the 2007 Rugby World Cup.

Haka! The traditional ancestral Maori war cry is a pre-game ritual for the All Blacks.

FOREWORD

The 'The Complete Guide To Rugby World Cup' is an essential companion for the pinnacle quadrennial tournament of world rugby. This essential compilation is a collection of concise but detailed information explicitly focused on the Rugby World Cup. The comprehensive guidebook details the history of the sport of rugby from its fragile beginnings through to the inception of the competition that was specifically designed to produce just one world champion, the Rugby World Cup.

The 'The Complete Guide To Rugby World Cup' lists every coach and every player from the past and present. The book reveals the tournament grounds and venues, from the most humble to the most magnificent. Search the results of each and every one of Rugby World Cup's matches to, including all the pool matches, all the knock-out matches, and of course all the drama and spectacle of the semi-finals, and finals of each and every tournament to date. Read the individual match statistics, the try scorers and kickers for every one of Rugby World Cup matches contested. At the ground or watching on television at home, the 'The Complete Guide To Rugby World Cup' makes for your essential tournament compendium.

WORLD RUGBY CUP
Champions

1987 - New Zealand

Pos	#	Player	Pos	#	Player
FB	15	John Gallagher	LL	4	Murray Pierce
RW	14	John Kirwan	TP	3	John Drake
OC	13	Joe Stanley	HK	2	Sean Fitzpatrick
IC	12	Warwick Taylor	LP	1	Steve McDowall
LW	11	Craig Green	R	16	Bernie McCahill
FH	10	Grant Fox	R	17	Frano Botica
SH	9	David Kirk (c)	R	18	Bruce Deans
N8	8	Wayne Shelford	R	19	Zinzan Brooke
OF	7	Michael Jones	R	20	Richard Loe
BF	6	Alan Whetton	R	21	Andy Dalton
RL	5	Gary Whetton	Coach		Brian Lochore

1991 - Australia

Pos	#	Player	Pos	#	Player
FB	15	Marty Roebuck	LL	4	Rod McCall
RW	14	Bob Egerton	TP	3	Ewen McKenzie
OC	13	Jason Little	HK	2	Phil Kearns
IC	12	Tim Horan	LP	1	Tony Daly
LW	11	David Campese	R	16	Jeff Miller
FH	10	Michael Lynagh	R	17	Steve Cutler
SH	9	Nick Farr-Jones (c)	R	18	Dan Crowley
N8	8	Troy Coker	R	19	Cameron Lillicrap
OF	7	Viliami Ofahengaue	R	20	Brendan Nasser
BF	6	Simon Poidevin	R	21	Anthony Herbert
RL	5	John Eales	R	22	Peter Slattery
			Coach		Bob Dwyer

1995 - South Africa

Pos	#	Player	Pos	#	Player
FB	15	André Joubert	LL	4	Kobus Wiese
RW	14	James Small (off 97')	TP	3	Balie Swart (off 68')
OC	13	Japie Mulder	HK	2	Chris Rossouw
IC	12	Hennie le Roux	LP	1	Os du Randt
LW	11	Chester Williams	R	16	Naka Drotské
FH	10	Joel Stransky	R	17	Garry Pagel (on 68')
SH	9	Joost van der Westhuizen	R	18	Rudolf Straeuli (on 90')
N8	8	Mark Andrews (off 90')	R	19	Johan Roux
OF	7	Ruben Kruger	R	20	Brendan Venter (on 97')
BF	6	Francois Pienaar (c)	R	21	Gavin Johnson
RL	5	Hannes Strydom	Coach:		Kitch Christie

1999 - Australia

Pos	#	Player	Pos	#	Player
FB	15	Matt Burke	LL	4	David Giffin
RW	14	Ben Tune	TP	3	Andrew Blades
OC	13	Dan Herbert (off 46')	HK	2	Michael Foley (off 76')
IC	12	Tim Horan (off 79')	LP	1	Richard Harry
LW	11	Joe Roff	R	16	Nathan Grey (on 79')
FH	10	Stephen Larkham	R	17	Jason Little (on 46')
SH	9	George Gregan (off 79')	R	18	Chris Whitaker (on 79')
N8	8	Toutai Kefu	R	19	Owen Finegan (on 55')
OF	7	David Wilson	R	20	Mark Connors
BF	6	Matt Cockbain (off 55')	R	21	Dan Crowley
RL	5	John Eales (c)	R	22	Jeremy Paul (on 76')
			Coach:		Rod McQueen

2003 - England

Pos	#	Player	Pos	#	Player
FB	15	Josh Lewsey (off 85')	LL	4	Martin Johnson (c)
RW	14	Jason Robinson	TP	3	Phil Vickery (off 86')
OC	12	Mike Tindall (off 79')	HK	2	Steve Thompson
IC	13	Will Greenwood	LP	1	Trevor Woodman
LW	11	Ben Cohen	R	16	Dorian West
FH	10	Jonny Wilkinson	R	17	Jason Leonard (on 86')
SH	9	Matt Dawson	R	18	Martin Corry
N8	8	Lawrence Dallaglio	R	19	Lewis Moody (on 93')
OF	7	Neil Back	R	20	Kyran Bracken
BF	6	Richard Hill (off 93')	R	21	Mike Catt (on 79')
RL	5	Ben Kay	R	22	Iain Balshaw (on 85')
			Coach:		Sir Clive Woodward

2007 - South Africa

Pos	#	Player	Pos	#	Player
FB	15	Percy Montgomery	LL	4	Bakkies Botha
RW	14	JP Pietersen	TP	3	CJ van der Linde
OC	13	Jaque Fourie	HK	2	John Smit (c) (BB 72' to 77')
IC	12	Francois Steyn	LP	1	Os du Randt
LW	11	Bryan Habana	R	16	Bismarck du Plessis (72'-77')
FH	10	Butch James	R	17	Jannie du Plessis
SH	9	Fourie du Preez	R	18	Johann Muller
N8	8	Danie Rossouw (off 72')	R	19	Wikus van Heerden (on 72')
BF	7	Juan Smith	R	20	Ruan Pienaar
OF	6	Schalk Burger	R	21	Andre Pretorius
RL	5	Victor Matfield	R	22	Wynand Olivier
			Coach:		Jake White

2011 - New Zealand

Pos	#	Player	Pos	#	Player
FB	15	Israel Dagg	LL	4	Brad Thorn
RW	14	Cory Jane	TP	3	Owen Franks
OC	13	Conrad Smith	HK	2	Keven Mealamu (off 49')
IC	12	Ma'a Nonu (off 76')	LP	1	Tony Woodcock
LW	11	Richard Kahui	R	16	Andrew Hore (on 49')
FH	10	Aaron Cruden (off 34')	R	17	Ben Franks
SH	9	Piri Weepu (off 50')	R	18	Ali Williams (on 49')
N8	8	Kieran Read	R	19	Adam Thomson
OF	7	Richie McCaw (c)	R	20	Andy Ellis (on 50')
BF	6	Jerome Kaino	R	21	Stephen Donald (on 34')
RL	5	Sam Whitelock (off 49')	R	22	Sonny Bill Williams (on 76')
			Coach:		Graham Henry

2015 - New Zealand

Pos	#	Player	Pos	#	Player
FB	15	Ben Smith (S-52' to 62')	TP	3	Owen Franks (off 54')
RW	14	Nehe Milner-Skudder (off 65')	HK	2	Dane Coles (off 65')
OC	13	Conrad Smith (off 40')	LP	1	Joe Moody (off 59')
IC	12	Ma'a Nonu	R	16	Keven Mealamu (on 65')
LW	11	Julian Savea	R	17	Ben Franks (on 59')
FH	10	Dan Carter	R	18	Charlie Faumuina (on 54')
SH	9	Aaron Smith (off 71')	R	19	Victor Vito (on 71')
N8	8	Kieran Read	R	20	Sam Cane (on 80')
OF	7	Richie McCaw (c) (off 80')	R	21	Tawera Kerr-Barlow (on 71')
BF	6	Jerome Kaino (off 71')	R	22	Beauden Barrett (on 65')
RL	5	Sam Whitelock	R	23	Sonny Bill Williams (on 40')
LL	4	Brodie Retallick	Coach:		Steve Hansen

2019 -

Pos	#	Player	Pos	#	Player
FB	15		LL	4	
RW	14		TP	3	
OC	13		HK	2	
IC	12		LP	1	
LW	11		R	16	
FH	10		R	17	
SH	9		R	18	
N8	8		R	19	
BF	7		R	20	
OF	6		R	21	
RL	5		Coach:		

2023 -

Pos	#	Player	Pos	#	Player
FB	15		LL	4	
RW	14		TP	3	
OC	13		HK	2	
IC	12		LP	1	
LW	11		R	16	
FH	10		R	17	
SH	9		R	18	
N8	8		R	19	
BF	7		R	20	
OF	6		R	21	
RL	5		Coach:		

AUSTRALIAN TEAM
190

E WALLABIES.

1. 1908/09 Australian Rugby Team

NEW ZEALAND TEAM, 1884.

O'DONNELL. UDY. ROBERTSON. ALLAN. E. MILLTON. RYAN. WILSON.
TAIAROA. CARTER. DUMBELL. BRADDON. HELMORE. WEBB. SLEIGH, Man
DAVY. W. MILLTON, *Captain*.
LECKY. WARBRICK. ROBERTS.

2. New Zealand Rugby Team, 1884.

The history of rugby union follows from various football games played long before the 19th century, but it was not until the middle of that century that rules were formulated and codified. The code of football later known as rugby union can be traced to three events: the first set of written rules in 1845, the Blackheath Club's decision to leave the Football Association in 1863 and the formation of the Rugby Football Union in 1871. The code was originally known simply as "rugby football". It was not until a schism in 1895, over the payment of players, which resulted in the formation of the separate code of rugby league, that the name "rugby union" was used to differentiate the original rugby code. For most of its history rugby was a strictly amateur football code, and the sport's administrators frequently imposed bans and restrictions on players who they viewed as professional. It was not until 1995 that rugby union was declared an 'open' game, and thus professionalism was sanctioned by the code's governing body World Rugby.

Antecedents of Rugby

Although rugby football was codified at Rugby School, many rugby playing countries had pre-existing football games not dissimilar to rugby.

Forms of traditional football similar to rugby have been played throughout Europe and beyond. Many of these involved handling of the ball, and scrummaging formations. For example, New Zealand had 'kiorahi', Australia 'marn grook', Japan 'kemari', Georgia 'lelo burti', the Scottish Borders 'Jeddart Ba' and Cornwall 'cornish hurling', Central Italy 'calcio fiorentino', South Wales 'cnapan', East Anglia 'campball' and Ireland had 'caid', an ancestor of gaelic football.

The first detailed description of what was almost certainly football in England was given by William FitzStephen between about 1174-1183. He described the activities of London youths during the annual festival of Shrove Tuesday:

"After lunch all the youth of the city go out into the fields to take part in a ball game. The students of each school have their own ball; the workers from each city craft are also carrying their balls. Older citizens, fathers, and wealthy citizens come on horseback to watch their juniors competing, and to relive their own youth vicariously. You can see their inner passions aroused as they watch the action and get caught up in the fun being had by the carefree adolescents."

Numerous attempts were made to ban football games, particularly the most rowdy and disruptive forms. This was especially the case in England, and in other parts of Europe during the Middle

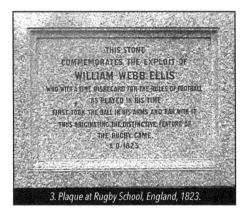

3. Plaque at Rugby School, England, 1823.

Ages and early modern period. Between 1324 and 1667, in England alone, football was banned by more than 30 royal and local laws. The need to repeatedly proclaim such laws demonstrated the difficulty in enforcing bans on popular games. King Edward II was so troubled by the unruliness of football in London that, on 13 April 1314, he issued a proclamation banning it:

"For as much as there is great noise in the city caused by hustling over large balls from which many evils may arise which God forbid; we command and forbid, on behalf of the King, on pain of imprisonment, such game to be used in the city in the future."

In 1531, Sir Thomas Elyot wrote that: "English footeballe is nothinge but beastlie furie and extreme violence."

Football games that included ball carrying continued to be played over the century, right up to the time of William Webb Ellis' alleged invention.

Rugby History

Playing football has been a long tradition in England and versions of football had probably been played at Rugby School for 200 years before three boys published the first set of written rules in 1845. The rules had always been determined by the pupils instead of the masters and they were frequently modified with each new intake. Rule changes, such as the legality of carrying or running with the ball, were often agreed shortly before the commencement of a game. There were thus no formal rules for football during the time that William Webb Ellis was at the school (1816-25) and the story of the boy "who with a fine disregard for the rules of football as played in his time, first took the ball in his arms and ran with it" in 1823 is apocryphal. The story first appeared in 1876, some four years after the death of Webb Ellis, and is attributed to a local antiquarian and former Rugbeian Matthew Bloxam. Bloxam was not a contemporary of Webb Ellis and vaguely quoted an unnamed person as informing him of the incident that had supposedly happened 53 years earlier. The story has been dismissed as unlikely since an official investigation by the Old Rugbeian Society in 1895. However, the cup for the Rugby World Cup is named the Webb Ellis trophy in his honour, and a plaque at the school commemorates the "achievement".

Rugby football has strong claims to the world's first and oldest "football club", the

Guy's Hospital Football Club, formed in London in 1843, by old boys from Rugby School. Around the anglosphere, a number of other clubs formed to play games based on the Rugby School rules. One of these, Dublin University Football Club, founded in 1854, has arguably become the world's oldest surviving football club in any code. The Blackheath Rugby Club, in London, founded in 1858 is the oldest surviving non-university/school rugby club. Cheltenham College 1844, Sherborne School 1846 and Durham School 1854 are the oldest documented school's clubs. Francis Crombie and Alexander Crombie introduced rugby into Scotland via Durham School in 1850.

Formation of the Rugby Union

On 4th December 1870, Edwin Ash of Richmond and Benjamin Burns of Blackheath published a letter in The Times suggesting that...

"those who play the rugby-type game should meet to form a code of practice as various clubs play to rules which differ from others, which makes the game difficult to play"

On 26th January 1871, a meeting attended by representatives from 21 clubs was held in London at the Pall Mall restaurant.

The 21 clubs and schools (all from London or the Home Counties) attended the meeting: Addison, Belsize Park, Blackheath (represented by Burns and Frederick Stokes the latter becoming the first captain of England), Civil

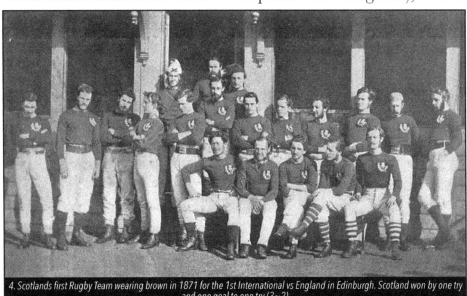

4. Scotlands first Rugby Team wearing brown in 1871 for the 1st International vs England in Edinburgh. Scotland won by one try and one goal to one try (3~2).

Service, Clapham Rovers, Flamingoes, Gipsies, Guy's Hospital, Harlequins, King's College, Lausanne, The Law Club, Marlborough Nomads, Mohicans, Queen's House, Ravenscourt Park, Richmond, St Paul's, Wellington College, West Kent, and Wimbledon Hornets. The one notable omission was the Wasps who "In true rugby fashion ... turned up at the wrong pub, on the wrong day, at the wrong time and so forfeited their right to be called Founder Members".

As a result of this meeting, the Rugby Football Union (RFU) was founded. Algernon Rutter was elected as the first president of the RFU and Edwin Ash was elected as treasurer. Three lawyers, who were Rugby School alumni (Rutter, Holmes and L. J. Maton), drew up the first laws of the game, and these were approved in June 1871.

First International Game

The first international football game resulted from a challenge issued in the sporting weekly Bell's Weekly on 8th December 1870 and signed by the captains of five Scottish clubs, inviting any team "selected from the whole of England" to a 20-a-side game to be played under the Rugby rules. The game was played at Raeburn Place, Edinburgh, the home ground of Edinburgh Academicals, on 27 March 1871.

This is not only the first international rugby match, but the first international of any form of football because, despite the fact that three England v Scotland fixtures had already been played according to Association Football rules at The Oval, London, in 1870 and 1871, these are not considered full internationals by RFU as the players competing in the Scotland team were London-based players who claimed a Scottish family connection rather than being truly Scottish players.

The English team wore all white with a red rose on their shirts and the Scots wore brown shirts with a thistle and white cricket flannels. The England team was captained by Frederick Stokes of Blackheath, that representing Scotland was led by Francis Moncrieff, and the umpire was Hely Hutchinson Almond, headmaster of Loretto College.

The game, played over two halves, each of 50 minutes, was won by Scotland, who scored a goal with a successful conversion kick after grounding the ball over the goal line (permitting them to

5. Australian Rugby Team, 1899.

'try' to kick a goal). Both sides achieved a further 'try' each, but failed to convert them to goals as the kicks were missed (see also 'Method of Scoring and Points'). Angus Buchanan of Royal High School FP and Edinburgh University RFC was the first man to score a try in international rugby.

In a return match at the Kennington Oval, London, in 1872, England managed to defeat the Scots.

Rugby and the Empire

According to the Australian Rugby Union, rugby football was an extremely early introduction to Australia, with games of the primitive code being played in the early to mid-19th century, and the first formal team, Sydney University Football Club being set up in 1864. In 1869, Newington College was the first Australian school to play rugby in a match against the University of Sydney. From this beginning, the first metropolitan competition in Australia developed, formally beginning in 1874. This was organised by the Southern Rugby Union, which was administered by the rugby union at Twickenham, in England. Administration was given over to the Southern Rugby Union in 1881.

Introduction to New Zealand came later, but formal development took place around the same time as Australia. Christchurch Football Club, was founded in 1863 and is now a Rugby Football Club; however they did not 'change' to Rugby Football rules until after the 1868 formation of the Nelson Rugby Football Club. Rugby football was first introduced to New Zealand in 1870 by Charles John Monro, son of the then-Speaker of the House of Representatives, David Monro. He encountered the game while studying at Christ's College Finchley, in East Finchley, London, England, and on his return introduced the game to Nelson College, who played the first rugby union match against Nelson football club on 14th May. By the following year, the game had been formalised in Wellington, and subsequently rugby was taken up in Wanganui and Auckland in 1873 and Hamilton in 1874. It is thought that by the mid-1870s, the game had been taken up by the majority of the colony.

When Canon George Ogilvie became headmaster of Diocesan College in Cape Town, South Africa in 1861, he introduced the game of football, as played at Winchester College. This version of football, which included handling of the ball, is seen as the beginnings of rugby in South Africa. In around 1875 rugby began to be played in the Cape Colony, the following year the first rugby (as opposed to Winchester football) club was formed. Former England international William Henry Milton arrived in Cape Town in 1878. He joined the Villagers club and started playing and preaching rugby. By the end of that year, Cape Town had all but abandoned the Winchester game in favour of rugby. In 1883, the Stellenbosch club was formed in the predominantly Boer farming district outside Cape Town and rugby was enthusiastically adopted by the young Boer farmers. As British and Boer migrated to the interior, they helped spread the game from the Cape colony through the Eastern Cape, and Natal, and along the gold and diamond routes to Kimberley and Johannesburg. However, for a number of years, South African rugby would be hindered by systemic racial segregation.

Early forms of rugby football were being played in Canada from 1823 onwards, in east Canadian towns such as Halifax, Montreal and Toronto. Rugby football proper in Canada dates to the 1860's. Introduction of the game and its early growth is usually credited to settlers from Britain and the British army and navy in Halifax, Nova Scotia and Esquimalt, British Columbia. In 1864, the first recorded game of rugby in Canada took place in Montreal, Quebec amongst artillery men. It is most likely that rugby got its start in British Columbia in the late 1860's or early 1870's, when brief mentions of "football" appeared in print. Canadian rugby however, soon faced stiff competition from Canadian football.

Influence on other Football Codes

Rugby league and association football were not the only early competitors to rugby union. In the late 19th century, a number of 'national' football codes emerged around the world, including Australian rules football (originating in Australia), Gaelic football (Ireland), and the gridiron codes of American Football and the slightly different Canadian football.

6. FC 1880 Frankfurt at the 1900 Olympic Games.

Some of these codes took direct influence from rugby union or rugby football, but all of these involved kicking and carrying the ball towards posts, meaning that they were in direct competition with rugby union. While American, Canadian, and Australian rules football are professional, and so competed for rugby union players' economic attentions, Gaelic football has remained staunchly amateur. The former three also use an oblong ball, superficially similar in appearance to a rugby football.

Tom Wills, the founder of Australian rules football, was educated at Rugby School. In Melbourne in 1858, he umpired and played in several football matches using experimental rules. It was reported that "exceptions were taken... to some of the Rugby regulations", and on 17th May 1859 Wills chaired a meeting to incorporate the Melbourne Football Club in which the club's rules (later the laws of Australian Football) were written down for the first time. While Wills was a fan of the rugby rules, his intentions were clear that he favoured rules that suited the drier and harder Australian fields. Geoffrey Blainey, Leonie Sandercock, Ian Turner and Sean Fagan have all written in support for the theory that rugby football was one of the primary influences on Australian rules football along with other games emanating from English public schools.

American football resulted from several major divergences from rugby from 1869 onwards, most notably the rule changes instituted by Walter Camp, considered the 'Father of American Football'. Among these important changes were the introduction of the line of scrimmage and of down-and-distance rules. Later developments such as the forward pass, and professionalism in American football made it diverge even further from its rugby origins.

Michael Cusack, one of the founders of the Gaelic Athletic Association, had been known as a rugby player in Ireland, and was involved with the game at Blackrock College and Clongowes Wood College. Cusack was a native Irishman who had been concerned with the decline of Irish football codes. Cusack, along with others, codified Gaelic football in 1887. The GAA retained some hostility to rugby and soccer until recent years, through its Rule

7. A photograph of a rugby game between France and Germany at the 1900 Summer Olympic Games.

42, which prohibits the use of GAA property for games with interests in conflict with the interests of the GAA such games are referred to by some as "garrison games" or "foreign sports". In practice, the rule has only been applied to the sports of soccer, and rugby, which were perceived to be rivals to the playing of Gaelic games.

Not all such codes were successful like Swedish football, which was created from a mixture of rugby and soccer rules, but was overtaken by soccer.

International Appeal

By the end of the 19th century, rugby football and rugby union had spread far and wide. This diversification was by no means confined to the British Empire.

Rugby football was an early arrival in Germany. The first German rugby team existed at Neuenheim College, now called Heidelberg College in Heidelberg. Around 1850, the game started to attract the attention of the students. Students under the guidance of the teacher Edward Hill Ullrich were the ones who then founded the rugby department of the Heidelberger Ruderklub von 1872 Heidelberger Flaggenklub (HRK 1872) was established in 1891, which today claims to be the oldest German rugby club. The oldest still existing rugby department within a club is that of DSV 78 Hannover, formed in 1878 by Ferdinand-Wilhelm Fricke. German rugby has traditionally been centred on Heidelberg and Hanover, but has spread over the entire country in recent decades.

In the United States, rugby football-like games were being played very early. For example, Princeton University students played a game called "ballown" in 1820. All of these games remained largely "mob" style games, with huge numbers of players attempting to advance the ball into a goal area, often by any means necessary. By the 1840's, Harvard, Yale and Princeton were all playing rugby football stemming partly from Americans who had been educated in English schools.

However in 1862, Yale dealt rugby a major blow by banning it for being too violent and dangerous. Unfortunately, American football's growth came at exactly the point at which rugby was beginning to establish itself in the States. In 1869, the first game of American football was played between Princeton and Rutgers with rules substantially identical to rugby. However by 1882, the rule innovations of Walter Camp, like the snap and downs, had distinguished the American game from rugby.

Rugby union also reached South America early, a continent with few British colonies. The first rugby union match in Argentina was played in 1873, the game having been brought to South America by the British. In 1886 Buenos Aires Football Club played Rosario Athletic Club in Buenos Aires. Early Argentinian rugby was not immune to political problems either. An 1890 game in Buenos Aires resulted in both teams, and all 2,500 spectators being arrested. National president Juarez Celman was particularly paranoid after the Revolution of the Park in the city earlier in the year, and the police had suspected that the match was in fact a political meeting. Rugby reached neighbouring Uruguay early, but it is disputed just how early. Cricket clubs were the incubators of rugby in South America, although rugby has survived much better in these countries than has cricket. It has been claimed that Montevideo Cricket Club (MVCC) played rugby football as early as 1865, but the first certain match was between Uruguayans and British members of the MVCC in 1880. The MVCC claims to be the oldest rugby club outside Europe.

Rugby also appears to have been the first (non-indigenous) football code to be played in Russia, around a decade before the introduction of association football. Mr Hopper, a Scotsman who worked in Moscow arranged a match in the 1880's and the first soccer match was in 1892. In 1886 however, the Russian police clamped down on rugby because they considered it brutal, and liable to incite demonstrations and riots.

International Rugby Football Board

In 1884, England had a disagreement with Scotland over a try that England had scored but that the referee disallowed citing a foul by Scotland. England argued that the referee should have played advantage and that, as they made the Law, if they said it was a try then it was. The International Rugby Football Board (IRFB) was formed by Scotland, Ireland and Wales in 1886, but England refused to join since they believed that they should have greater representation on the board because they had a greater number of clubs. They also refused to accept that the IRFB should be the recognised law maker of the game.

The IRFB agreed that the member countries would not play England until the RFU agreed to join and accept that the IRFB would oversee the games between the home unions. England finally agreed to join in 1890. In 1930, it was agreed between the members that all future matches would be played under the laws of the IRFB. In 1997, the IRFB moved its headquarters from London to Dublin and a year later it changed its name to

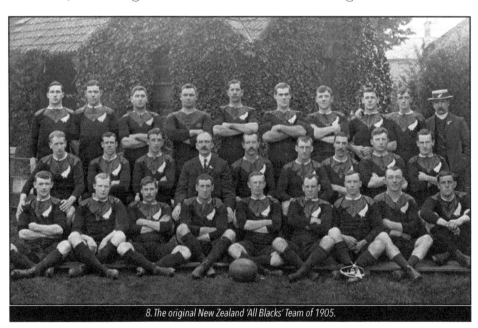

8. The original New Zealand 'All Blacks' Team of 1905.

Historic Rugby Photo Gallery

9.1 The first England Rugby Union team prior to their match v Scotland in 1871.

9.3 New Zealand native rugby union team, prior to a match against Middlesex at Lord Sheffields Park on the 20th October 1888.

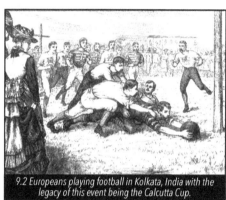

9.2 Europeans playing football in Kolkata, India with the legacy of this event being the Calcutta Cup.

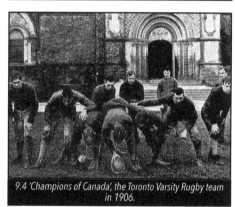

9.4 'Champions of Canada', the Toronto Varsity Rugby team in 1906.

SOUTH AFRICAN RUGBY FOOTBALL TEAM 1906

Matsburg.   Jackson.   Neill.   Brookes. Reid.   Millar. De Melker. Marlthize. J.Le Roup.   Mare.
Loubser. Dauell.   Burger.   Raaff.   Mc Carden. D. Ross. Morkel. Burmeister.
T.D. Morkel.   Carolin.   W.S. Morkel.   P. Le Roux   Stegmann.

9.5 The 1906 South African Rugby Union team.

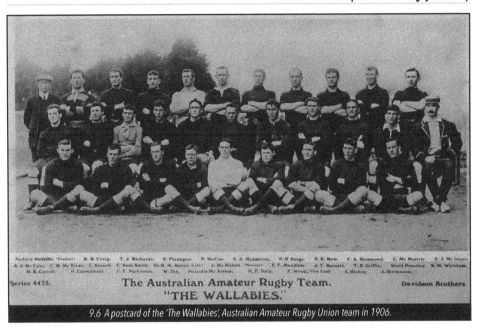

9.6 A postcard of the 'The Wallabies', Australian Amateur Rugby Union team in 1906.

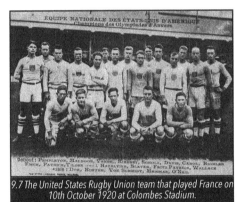

9.7 The United States Rugby Union team that played France on 10th October 1920 at Colombes Stadium.

9.9 Rugby match between France and the United States team at the 1924 Summer Olympics.

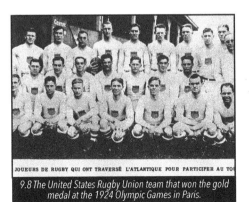

9.8 The United States Rugby Union team that won the gold medal at the 1924 Olympic Games in Paris.

9.10 Enormous crowd watching a rugby union match at Athletic Park, Wellington New Zealand about 1930.

9.11 The South African 'Springboks' tour squad to Australia and New Zealand in 1937.

9.14 The Italian Rugby Union team line up v France for the 1974 FIRA Trophy at Stadio Flaminio in Rome. The French won the match 16~9.

9.12 A 'Springbok' passes the ball to a team mate v Australia during the 1937 tour.

9.13 The forward line of Argentina (Los Pumas) in 1970: Garcia Yanez, Handley and Foster.

the International Rugby Board (IRB) and in 2014, it changed its name again to the current World Rugby (WR).

Summer Olympic Games

Pierre de Coubertin, the revivor of the modern Olympics, introduced rugby union to the Summer Olympics at the 1900 games in Paris. Coubertin had previous associations with the game, refereeing the first French domestic championship as well as France's first international. France, the German Empire and Great Britain all entered teams in the 1900 games (Great Britain was represented by Moseley RFC, Germany by the SC 1880 Frankfurt). France won gold by defeating both opponents. The rugby event drew the largest crowd at that particular games. Rugby was next played at the 1908 Olympic Games in London. A Wallaby team on tour in the

United Kingdom took part in the event and won the gold by defeating Great Britain who were represented by a team from Cornwall. The United States won the next event, at the 1920 Summer Olympics, defeating the French. The Americans repeated their achievement at the 1924 Summer Olympics in Paris, again defeating France in a tournament marred by controversies surrounding the rivalry between the two teams. Though rugby had attracted bigger crowds than the Track and Field events in 1924, it was dropped from the next Games and has not been included since.

In October 2009, the International Olympic Committee voted to return a form of rugby to the Olympics, when rugby sevens for both men and women were contested at the Rio de Janeiro in 2016.

The 1900's and Early 1910's

Between 1905 and 1908, all three major Southern Hemisphere rugby countries sent their first touring teams to the Northern Hemisphere, with New Zealand in 1905, followed by South Africa in 1906 and then Australia in 1908. All three teams brought new styles of play, fitness levels and tactics, and were far more successful than critics had expected. The New Zealand 1905 touring team performed a 'haka' before each match, leading Welsh Rugby Union administrator Tom Williams to suggest that Wales player Teddy Morgan lead the crowd in singing the Welsh National Anthem, 'Hen Wlad Fy Nhadau', as a response. After Morgan began singing, the crowd joined in, the first time a national anthem was sung at the start of a sporting event. In 1905, France played England in its first international match.

World War I

The horrific bloodshed and suffering of World War I affected all sports, including rugby union. The Five Nations Championship was suspended in 1915 and was not resumed until 1920, though in Britain in 1919 a tournament was arranged between Forces teams, and it was won by the New Zealand Army.

One hundred and thirty-three international players were killed during World War I. The Queensland Rugby Union was disbanded after the war and was not reformed until 1929. NSW took responsibility for rugby union in Australia until the formation of the ARU in 1949.

10. Rugby Union match at the Inter-Allied games of 1919 with Romania vs France, at the Stade de Colombes, France.

The 1920's

As 1923 approached, there were discussions of a combined England and Wales XV playing a Scottish-Irish team in celebration of when William Webb Ellis picked up the football and ran with it in 1823. The planned game was controversial in that there was a disagreement over whether it should be held at Rugby School, or be played at Twickenham, where an obviously larger crowd could witness the match. In the end, the match was contested at Rugby School.

The 1930's

For many years, there had been suspicion that the governing body of French rugby union, the French Rugby Federation (FFR) was allowing the abuse of the rules on amateurism, and in 1931 the French Rugby Union was suspended from playing against the other IRFB nations. As a result, Federation Internationale de Rugby Amateur (FIRA) was founded in 1932.

In 1934, the Association was formed at the instigation of the French. It was designed to organise rugby union outside the authority of the International Rugby Football Board (as it was known at the time). The founder members were Italy, Romania, Netherlands, Catalonia, Portugal, Czechoslovakia, and

Sweden. In the 1990's, the organisation recognised the IRB as the governing body of rugby union worldwide and in 1999 changed its name to the Association of European Rugby (FIRA), an organisation to promote and rule over rugby union in the European area. The organisation changed its name again in 2014 to Rugby Europe.

Until its eventual merger with the IRB, Rugby Europe was the most multinational rugby organisation in the world, partly because the IRB had concentrated on the Five Nations, Tri Nations, and from 1987 the Rugby World Cup, competitions. Rugby Europe has generally been a positive force in spreading the sport beyond the 'Anglosphere'.

In 1931 Lord Bledisloe, the Governor General of New Zealand, donated a trophy for competition between Australia and New Zealand. The 'Bledisloe Cup' became one of the great rivalries in international rugby union.

Following the suspension of the French Rugby Federation (FFR) in 1931, many French players turned to rugby league, which soon became the dominant game in France, particularly in the south west of the country.

In 1934, the Federation Internationale de Rugby Amateur (FIRA) was formed at the instigation of the French. It was designed to organise rugby union outside the authority of the IRB. In the 1990's, the organisation recognised the IRB as the governing body of rugby union world wide and later changed its name twice, in 1999 to FIRA Association of European Rugby, and in 2014 to Rugby Europe. Today, Rugby Europe promotes and rules over rugby union in the European region.

In 1939, the FFR was invited to send a team to the Five Nations Championship for the following season, but when war was declared, international rugby was suspended. Tragically, some 88 international rugby union football players were to be killed during the five years of World War II.

World War II

During World War II, the RFU temporarily lifted its ban on rugby league players, many of whom played in the eight 'internationals' between England and Scotland that were played by Armed Services teams under the rugby union code. The authorities also allowed the playing of two

"Rugby League v Rugby Union" fixtures as fund-raisers for the war effort. The rugby league team (which included some pre-war professionals) won both matches, which were held under union rules.

After the defeat of France in 1940, the French Rugby Union authorities worked with the German collaborating Vichy regime to re-establish the dominance of their sport. Rugby union's amateur ethos appealed to the occupier's view of the purity of sport. Rugby league, along with other professional sports, was banned. Many players and officials of the sport were punished, and all of the assets of the Rugby League and its clubs were handed over to the Union. The consequences of this action reverberate to this day, as these assets were never returned. Although the ban on rugby league was lifted, it was prevented from calling itself 'rugby' until the mid-1980's, having to use the name 'Jeu a Treize' (game of 13) in reference to the number of players in a rugby league side.

Post-War 1940's and 50's

In 1947, the Five Nations Championship resumed with France taking part. In 1948, the worth of a drop goal was reduced from four to three points. In 1949, the Australian

11. Marcelo Pascual diving in goal v the Junior Springboks, for Las Pumas' first great International rugby victory (1965).

Rugby Union was formed and took over the administration of the game in Australia from the New South Wales Rugby Union.

The 1960's

During the 1960's, there was stronger and stronger condemnation of the racist apartheid regime in South Africa. This racism extended to rugby union, and the sport soon found itself involved in its most serious controversy since 1895. By 1969, the 'Halt All Racist Tours' campaign group had been set up in New Zealand. Everywhere the Springboks toured they received a boisterous reception from anti-apartheid protesters.

The 1970's

The year 1970 saw the invention of mini rugby, a form of the game still used to train children today. In 1971, Scotland appointed Bill Dickinson as their head coach, after years of avoidance, as it was their belief that rugby should remain an amateur sport. The 1971 Springbok tour to Australia was famous for its political protests against South Africa's apartheid system. The 1970's were a golden era for Wales with the team capturing five 'Five Nations' titles and

dominating the Lions selections throughout the decade. In the middle of the decade, after overseeing the rise in popularity of rugby union in the United States, member bodies met in Chicago in 1975 and formed the United States of America Rugby Football Union, known today as USA Rugby.

The 1980's

The 1981 Springbok Tour to New Zealand was also marked by political protests and is still referred to by New Zealanders as 'The Tour'. The tour divided New Zealand society and rugby lost some of its prestige, which was not restored until New Zealand won the inaugural 1987 Rugby World Cup. In 1983, the WRFU (Women's Rugby Football Union) was formed, with 12 inaugural clubs, the body being responsible for women's rugby in England, Wales, Scotland and Ireland.

In 1984 one of the greatest Wallaby teams completed their first grand slam, defeating all four nations of the British Isles, and announcing their emergence as a power in world rugby. But these individual rugby test matches and tours were erratic and irregular, and there came a call for a world championship... a World Cup!

Photograph of an early rugby match in the United States.

Professionalism

On 26th August 1995, the International Rugby Board declared rugby union an 'open' game and thus removed all restrictions on payments or benefits to those connected with the game. It did this because of a committee conclusion that to do so was the only way to end the hypocrisy of 'shamateurism' and to keep control of rugby union.

Professionalism opened the door for the emergence of a new rugby generation in Italy. The Italian domestic leagues had attracted a degree of tax relief in the 1990's, and were able to attract both strong corporate sponsorship and also high quality coaches and players with recent Italian heritage from Australia and Argentina. These improvements led to a national team capable of competing with the national teams of the British Isles, proven by a famous victory against Ireland in 1995. Lobbying was successful to have Italy included in the century-old tournament for the top European rugby nations which became the 'Six Nations' championship in the year 2000.

The Birth of Rugby World Cup

The first Rugby World Cup was played in 1987. New Zealand hosted the tournament with some games, including both semi-finals, being held in Australia. The New Zealand All Blacks defeated France in the inaugural final. The remainder of this book details each of those Rugby World Cup tournaments from 1987 to 2015, and previews the 2019 tournament.

CREDITS

TEXT

This article uses material from the Wikipedia article https://en.wikipedia.org/wiki/History_of_rugby_union which is released under the http://creativecommons.org/licenses/by-sa/3.0/ Creative Commons Attribution-Share-Alike License 3.0.

IMAGES

1. 'The Australian Wallabies 1908-09. This image (or other media file) is in the public domain because its copyright has expired

2. '1884 All Black Team In Australia' by Unknown Author (1884). Available at http://rugby-pioneers.blogs.com/rugby/2011/09/all-not-so-blacks-1884.html This New Zealand work is in the public domain in New Zealand, because its copyright has expired or it is not subject to copyright.

3. 'Plaque of the Rugby School in memory of William Webb Ellis who is said to have invented the rugby sport by G-Man (6 Nov 2003). Available at https://commons.wikimedia.org/wiki/File:WWEplaque_700.jpg The copyright holder of this work, releases this work into the public domain.

4. 'Scotland national rugby union team for the 1st international match against England in Edinburgh' by Unknown (1871). Available at https://commons.wikimedia.org/wiki/File:Scotland_rugbyteam_1871.jpg This image (or other media file) is in the public domain because its copyright has expired and its author is anonymous.

5. '1899 Australian rugby union team' by Unknown (1899). Available at https://commons.wikimedia.org/wiki/File:1899_Australian_Team.jpg This image is of Australian origin and is now in the public domain because its term of copyright has expired.

6. FC 1880 Frankfurt at the 1900 Olympic Games. This image (or other media file) is in the public domain because its copyright has expired.

7. A photograph of a rugby game between France and Germany at the 1900 Summer Olympics. This image (or other media file) is in the public domain because its copyright has expired.

8. 'All Blacks rugby union team that toured the United Kingdom in 1905-6' by E. Kelley (1905). Available at https://upload.wikimedia.org/wikipedia/commons/8/81/Original_allblacks.jpg This New Zealand work is in the public domain in New Zealand because its copyright has expired or it is not subject to copyright.

9.01 Photo of the first ever England national rugby union team, before their game v. Scotland. This image (or other media file) is in the public domain because its copyright has expired.

9.02 Europeans playing rugby football in Kolkata, India; the main legacy of this development was the Calcutta Cup. This image (or other media file) is in the public domain because its copyright has expired.

9.03 'New Zealand native rugby union team, prior to a match against Middlesex at Lord Sheffield's Park on 20 October 1888.'by Author Unknown (1888). Uploaded by Greg Ryan (1993) and available at https://upload.wikimedia.org/wikipedia/commons/f/f6/StateLibQld_1_188931_New_Zeal_and_native_Rugby_Union_team%2C_prior_to_a_match_at_Lord_Sheffield%27s_Park_in_1888.jpg This New Zealand work is in the public domain in New Zealand, because its copyright has expired or it is not subject to copyright.

9.04 Toronto Varsity Rugby Team, circa 1906, "Champions of Canada". This image (or other media file) is in the public domain because its copyright has expired.

9.05 'The 1906 South Africa rugby union team.' by Scott & Co. Studio (1906). Available at https://en.wikipedia.org/wiki/South_Africa_national_rugby_union_team#/media/File:South_africa_rugby_team_1906.jpg This work was first published in South Africa and is now in the public domain because its copyright protection has expired by virtue of the Copyright Act No. 98 of 1978, amended 2002.

9.06 Australian Wallabies Postcard, 1906. This image (or other media file) is in the public domain because its copyright has expired.

9.07 'The United States rugby union team that played France on 10 October 1920 at Colombes Stadium' by Unknown Author (1920). Available at https://upload.wikimedia.org/wikipedia/commons/9/96/USA_rugby_team_for_the_octob_er_1920_test_match_vs_France.jpg This image (or other media file) is in the public domain because its copyright has expired and its author is anonymous.

9.08 'The USA national rugby union team that won the Gold Medal at the 1924 Summer Olympics' by Unknown Author (1 May 1924). Available at https://upload.wikimedia.org/wikipedia/commons/e/e1/USA_1924_rugby_team.jpg This image (or other media file) is in the public domain because its copyright has expired and its author is anonymous.

9.09 'Rugby match between France and the U.S. team at the 1924 Summer Olympics in Paris' by Unknown [maybe Armand Noyer] (1924). Available at https://commons.wikimedia.org/wiki/File:1924_France_vs_USA_rugby_match.jpg This image (or other media file) is in the public domain because its copyright has expired.

9.10 Crowd watching a rugby match at Athletic Park Wellington, ca 1930. This image (or other media file) is in the public domain because its copyright has expired.

9.11 'The Springbok tour squad to Australia and New Zealand' by Unknown Author (1937). Available at https://upload.wikimedia.org/wikipedia/commons/5/50/1937_span_011.jpg This work was first published in South Africa and is now in the public domain because its copyright protection has expired by virtue of the Copyright Act No. 98 of 1978, amended 2002.

9.12 'Springboks v. Australia, 1937 A Springbok passes the ball to his team mate' by Sunday Truth (1937). Available at https://commons.wikimedia.org/wiki/File:StateLibQld_1_105568_Springboks_v._Australi_a._1937.jpg This image is of Australian origin and is now in the public domain because its term of copyright has expired. According to the Australian Copyright Council (ACC), ACC Information Sheet G023v16 (Duration of copyright) (Feb 2012).

9.13 'Argentina national rugby union team (Los Pumas) forward line in 1970: García Yáñez, Handley and Foster' by Unknown (1970). Available at https://commons.wikimedia.org/wiki/File:Los_pumas_1970.jpg This image is in the public domain because the copyright of this photograph, registered in Argentina, has expired.

9.14 'The lineup of the Italy national rugby union team vs France, 1974–75 FIRA Trophy. Stadio Flaminio in Rome. France won 16-9' by Unknown Author (15 Feb 1975). Available at https://commons.wikimedia.org/wiki/File:Italy_Rugby_ITA_-_FRA_1975.jpg This photograph is in the public domain in Italy because it was first published in Italy and its term of copyright has expired.

10. 'Rugby union match at the Inter-Allied Games of 1919: Romania vs. France (France up by 48 to 5). Stade de Colombes (Stade Olympique Yves-du-Manoir), Colombes, France' by Agence Rol (22 Jun 1919). Available at https://commons.wikimedia.org/wiki/File:Stade_de_Colombes,_22.06.1919,_jeux_interal_lies,_rugby,_match_France_contre_Roumanie.JPG This image from the National Library of France (BnF) is a reproduction by scanning of a bidimensional work that is now in the public domain.

11. 'Marcelo Pascual diving in the ingoal of Junior Springboks in 1965, Los Pumas' first great international victory' by El Grafico (19 Jun 1965). Available at https://commons.wikimedia.org/wiki/File:Pumas_try_1965.jpg This image is in the public domain because the copyright of this photograph, registered in Argentina, has expired.

Full terms at http://creativecommons.org/licenses/by/2.0.

1987

I RUGBY WORLD CUP

New Zealand & Australia

1987 NEW ZEALAND
1991 AUSTRALIA
1995 SOUTH AFRICA
1999 AUSTRALIA
2003 ENGLAND
2007 SOUTH AFRICA

1. The Webb Ellis Cup

I Rugby World Cup
22nd May to 20th June, 1987

2. Carisbrook Stadium, Dunedin NZ.

The 1987 Rugby World Cup was the first Rugby Union World Cup and ran from 22nd May to 20th June 1987. New Zealand and Australia agreed to co-host the tournament.

THE HOSTS

New Zealand hosted 20 matches, 17 pool stage matches, two quarter finals and the two finals. Australia as the junior partner hosted 12 matches, seven pool matches, two quarter finals and both semi-finals.

THE TEAMS

Sixteen teams competed in the inaugural tournament in New Zealand and Australia. There was no qualification for the inaugural World Cup so the tournament comprised the seven then members of the IRFB, with the remaining nine places filled by teams invited by the IRFB.

South Africa was excluded due to its pro-apartheid policies, the Soviet Union were invited but declined, and Western Samoa was controversially not invited despite them having a better international win/loss record than some of the other invited nations.

Seeded Teams

Seven teams were automatically filled by the International Rugby Football Board members including **New Zealand, Australia, England, Scotland, Ireland, Wales** and **France**. South Africa was prevented from competing because of the international boycott, which included a boycott on sports.

Invited Teams

There was no qualification process to fill the remaining nine pool positions. Instead invitations were sent out to **Argentina, Fiji, Italy, Canada, Romania, Tonga, Japan, Zimbabwe** and the **United States**. This left Western Samoa controversially excluded, despite their better playing record over some of the other teams invited. The USSR were to be invited, but they refused the invitation on political grounds, allegedly due to the continued IRFB membership of South Africa.

THE POOL STAGE

The tournament witnessed a number of one-sided matches, with the seven traditional IRFB members proving far too strong for the other teams. Half of the 24 matches across the four pools saw one team score 40 or more points. Despite this only the 'most points by an individual' statistic is recorded against this tournament.

A simple pool format was used with the 16 nations divided into four pools of four nations, with each nation playing their other pool opponents once, every nation playing three times during the pool stage.

Teams were awarded two points for a win, one for a draw and zero for a loss, with the top two nations from each pool advancing to the quarter finals. The runners-up of each pool faced the winners of a different pool in the quarter finals. The quarter final winners then moved on to the semi finals, and the semi final winners qualified for the final. The two losers of the semi finals contested the play off for 3rd place.

> **LEGEND:**
> **P** = Number of games played; **W** = Number of games won; **D** = Number of games drawn; **L** = Number of games lost; **TF** = Number of tries scored (Tries For); **PF** = Number of points scored in the game (Points For); **PA** = Number of points scored against the team (Points Against); **BP** = Bonus (pool) points ; **Pts** = Total number of (pool) points.

37

POOL 1 - TEAMS

1	AUSTRALIA	ENGLAND	JAPAN	USA
Coaches:	Alan Jones	Martin Green	Miyati Katsumi	George Hook
Players:	David Campese	Rob Andrew	Shogo Mukai	Ray Nelson
	Michael Lynagh	Kevin Simms	Nofomuli Taumoefolau	Kevin Higgins
	Andrew Slack	Richard Harding	Kojiro Yoshinaga	Gary Hein
	Matthew Burke	Marcus Rose	Eiji Kutsuki	Mike Purcell
	Peter Grigg	Mark Bailey	Shinji Onuki	Ed Fernandez
	Brett Papworth	Richard Hill	Seiji Hirao	Roy Helu Sr.
	Nick Farr-Jones	Fran Clough	Hisataka Ikuta	Joe Clarkson
	Brian Smith	Peter Williams	Mitsutake Hagimoto	Mike Saunders
	Andrew Leeds	Rory Underwood	Katsuhiro Matsuo	Mike Caulder
	Michael Cook	Jon Webb	Daijiro Murai	Dave Horton
	Roger Gould	Jon Hall	Minoru Okidoi	Dave Dickson
	Anthony Herbert	Mike Harrison (c)	Toshiro Yoshino	Tommy Vinnick
	Steve James	Jamie Salmon	Koji Yasumi	John Mickel
	William Campbell	Gareth Chilcott	Tsuyoshi Fujita	Denis Shanagher
	Steve Cutler	Wade Dooley	Takaharu Horaguchi	Jim Hmielewski
	Tom Lawton	Graham Dawe	Toshiyuki Hayashi (c)	Kevin Swords
	Andy McIntyre	Brian Moore	Atsushi Oyagi	Pat Johnson
	Simon Poidevin	Steve Bainbridge	Katsufumi Miyamoto	Rick Bailey
	Steve Tuynman	Peter Winterbottom	Sinali Latu	John Everett
	David Codey (c)	Jeff Probyn	Michihito Chida	Fred Paoli
	Troy Coker	David Egerton	Tsutomu Hirose	Ed Burlingham (c)
	Cameron Lillicrap	Gary Rees	Toshitaka Kimura	Blane Warhurst
	Jeff Miller	Dean Richards	Seiji Kurihara	Gary Lambert
	Topo Rodriguez	Nigel Redman	Yoshihiko Sakuraba	Jeff Peter
	Mark Hartill	Gary Pearce	Yasuharu Kawase	Brian Vizard
	Mark McBain	Paul Rendall	Mazaharu Aizawa	Tony Ridnell
	Ross Reynolds			Neal Brendel
				Bob Causey
				Steve Finkel
				Bill Shiflet

3. McLean Park, Napier NZ

Pool 1 Matches

The nations in Pool 1 consisted of **Australia, England, Japan** and the **United States**. It was fascinating for the crowds to watch the plucky Americans compete on the world stage in rugby, and Japan surprisingly put up a very good showing against the Wallabies (23~42).

The United States defeated Japan to avoid the bottom of the table, and Australia managed to overcome a resolute English team in the tournament opener (19~6), the result of which determined the first and second places in this pool.

4. John Kirwan, New Zealand (taken 2011).

POOL 1

1.1 Australia d. England (19~6)

23 May 1987, Concord Oval, Sydney.
Attendance: 17,896; Referee: Keith Lawrence (NZ).
Australia. Tries: Campese, Poidevin; Con: Lynagh; Pen: Lynagh (3).
England. Try: Harrison; Con: Webb.

1.2 United States d. Japan (21~18)

24 May 1987, Ballymore, Brisbane.
Referee: Guy Maurette (France).
United States. Tries: Nelson, Purcell, Lambert; Con: Nelson (3); Pen: Nelson.
Japan. Tries: Taumoefolau (2), Yoshinaga; Pen: Yoshinaga, Kutsuki.

1.3 England d. Japan (60~7)

30 May 1987, Concord Oval, Sydney.
Attendance: 4,893; Referee: René Hourquet (France).
England. Tries: Harrison (3), Underwood (2), Salmon, Richards, Redman, Rees, Simms; Con: Webb (7); Pen: Webb (2).
Japan. Try: Miyamoto; Pen: Matsuo.

1.4 Australia d. United States (47~12)

31 May 1987, Ballymore, Brisbane.
Attendance: 10,855; Referee: Brian Anderson (Scotland).
Australia. Tries: Leeds (2), Penalty try, Campese, Smith, Slack, Papworth, Codey; Con: Lynagh (6); Pen: Lynagh.
United States. Try: Nelson; Con: Nelson; Pen: Nelson; Drop: Horton.

1.5 England d. United States (34~6)

3 June 1987, Concord Oval, Sydney.
Attendance: 8,785; Referee: Kerry Fitzgerald (Australia).
England. Tries: Winterbottom (2), Harrison, Dooley; Con: Webb (3); Pen: Webb (4).
United States. Try: Purcell; Con: Nelson.

1.6 Australia d. Japan (42~23)

3 June 1987, Concord Oval, Sydney.
Attendance: 8,785; Referee: Jim Fleming (Scotland).
Australia. Tries: Slack (2), Burke (2), Tuynman, Grigg, Hartill, Campese; Con: Lynagh (5).
Japan. Tries: Kutsuki (2), Fujita; Con: Okidoi; Pen: Okidoi (2); Drop: Okidoi.

Results	P	W	D	L	PF	PA	Pts
Australia	3	3	0	0	108	41	6
England	3	2	0	1	100	32	4
USA	3	1	0	2	39	99	2
Japan	3	0	0	3	48	123	0

5. Rugby Park, Hamilton NZ.

POOL 2 - TEAMS

2	CANADA	IRELAND	TONGA	WALES
Coaches:	Gary Johnston	Mick Doyle Jim Davidson		Tony Gray
Players:	Ian Hyde-Lay	Michael Bradley	Asa Amone	Bleddyn Bowen
	John L Lecky	Keith Crossan	Soane Asi	Malcolm Dacey
	Spence McTavish	Paul Dean	Tali Ete'aki	Jonathan Davies
	Pat Palmer	Tony Doyle	Quddus Fielea	John Devereux
	Gareth Rees	David Irwin	Talai Fifita	Ieuan Evans
	Ian Stuart	Mike Kiernan	Talanoa Kitelei'aho	Ray Giles
	Dave Tucker	Hugo MacNeill	Alamoni Liava'a	Adrian Hadley
	Paul Vaesen	Brendan Mullin	Samiu Mohi	Kevin Hopkins
	Tom Woods	Philip Rainey	Manu Vunipola	Robert Jones
	Mark Wyatt	Trevor Ringland	Maliu Filise	Mark Ring
	Bruce Breen	Paul Haycock	Kasi Fine	Paul Thorburn
	Ross Breen	Tony Ward	Kini Fotu	Mark Titley
	Mark Cardinal	Willie Anderson	Amoni Fungavaka	Glen Webbe
	Glen Ennis	Nigel Carr (*)	Talia'uli Liava'a	Steve Blackmore
	Eddie Evans	Paul Collins	Viliami Lutua	Anthony Buchanan
	Rob Frame	Des Fitzgerald	Takai Makisi	Richie Collins
	Hans de Goede	Neil Francis	Soakai Motu'apuaka	Phil Davies
	Steve Gray	Jim Glennon	Latu Vaeno	Stuart Evans
	Bill Handson	Terry Kingston	Leneki Vaipulu	William James
	Ro Hindson	Job Langbroek	Fakahau Valu (c)	Paul Moriarty
	Randy McKellar	Donal Lenihan (c)	Liose Tahaafe	Bob Norster
	Roy Radu	Phillip Matthews	Polutele Tu'ihalamaka	Alan Phillips
	Karl Svoboda	John MacDonald	Mofuiki Tu'ingafasi	Kevin Phillips
	Ron van den Brink	J. J. McCoy	Hakatoa Tupou	John Rawlins
		Derek McGrath	Taipaleti Tu'uta	Huw Richards
		Philip Orr		Gareth Roberts
		Steve Smith		Steve Sutton
		Brian Spillane		Richard Webster
				Jeff Whitefoot
				Dai Young

POOL 2

2.1 Canada d. Tonga (37~4)

24 May 1987, McLean Park, Napier.
Referee: Clive Norling (Wales).
Canada. Tries: Palmer (2), Vaesen (2), Stuart, Frame, Penalty try; Con: Wyatt (2), Gareth Rees; Pen: Rees.
Tonga. Try: Valu.

2.2 Wales d. Ireland (13~6)

25 May 1987, Athletic Park, Wellington.
Referee: Kerry Fitzgerald (Australia).
Wales. Try: Ring; Pen: Thorburn; Drop: Davies (2).
Ireland. Pen: Kiernan (2).

2.3 Wales d. Tonga (29~16)

29 May 1987, Showgrounds Oval, Palmerston North.
Referee: David Bishop (New Zealand).
Wales. Tries: Webbe (3), Hadley; Con: Thorburn (2); Pen: Thorburn (2); Drop: Davies.
Tonga. Tries: Fielea, Fifita; Con: Liava'a; Pen Liava'a, Amone.

2.4 Ireland d. Canada (46~19)

30 May 1987, Carisbrook, Dunedin.
Referee: Fred Howard (England).
Ireland. Tries: Crossan (2), Bradley, Spillane, Ringland, MacNeill; Con: Kiernan (5); Pen: Kiernan (2); Drop: Ward, Kiernan.
Canada. Try: Cardinal; Pen: Rees (3); Wyatt; Drop: Rees.

2.5 Wales d. Canada (40~9)

3 June 1987, Rugby Park, Invercargill.
Referee: David Bishop (New Zealand).
Wales. Tries: Evans (4), Devereux, Bowen, Hadley, Phillips; Con: Thorburn (4).
Canada. Pen: Rees (3).

2.6 Ireland d. Tonga (32~9)

3 June 1987, Ballymore, Brisbane.
Referee: Guy Maurette (France).
Ireland. Tries: Mullin (3), MacNeill (2); Pen: Ward (2); Con: Ward (3).
Tonga. Pen: Amone (3).

Results	P	W	D	L	PF	PA	Pts
Wales	3	3	0	0	82	31	6
Ireland	3	2	0	1	84	41	4
Canada	3	1	0	2	65	90	2
Tonga	3	0	0	3	29	98	0

Pool 2 Matches

The nations in Pool 2 consisted of **Canada, Ireland, Tonga** and **Wales**. The Canadians played some very entertaining rugby and managed to score eight tries in their three pool games, while Tonga showed some occasional touches of absolute brilliance.

Canada resoundly defeated Tonga (37~4) to avoid the wooden spoon. But once again there were no real surprises as the matches in this group also played out according to recent form with both Wales and Ireland progressing to the quarter finals.

6. Canadian fans get behind their team.

POOL 3 - TEAMS

3	ARGENTINA	FIJI	ITALY	NEW ZEALAND
Coaches:	*Hector Silva* *Angel Guastella*		*Marco Bollesan*	*Brian Lochore*
Players:	Guillermo Angaut	Severo K. Waqanibau	Daniele Tebaldi	Kieran Crowley
	Marcelo Campo	Serupepeli Tuvula	Massimo Mascioletti	Grant Fox
	Diego Cuesta Silva	Epineri Naituku	Fabio Gaetaniello	John Gallagher
	Fabio Gomez	Tomasi Cama	Stefano Barba	Craig Green
	Juan Lanza	Kavekini Nalaga	Marcello Cuttitta	David Kirk (c)
	Pedro Lanza	Willie Rokowailoa	Oscar Collodo	John Kirwan
	Julian Manuele	Pauliasi Tabulutu	Fulvio Lorigiola	Bernie McCahill
	Rafael Madero	Paula Nawalu	Alessandro Ghini	Joe Stanley
	Hugo Porta (c)	Jone Kubu	Rodolfo Ambrosio	Warwick Taylor
	Sebastián Salvat	Sirilo Lovokuru	Sergio Zorzi	Terry Wright
	Fabian Turnes	Sairusi Naituku	Serafino Ghizzoni	Frano Botica
	Martín Yangüela	Salacieli Naivilawasa	Guido Rossi	Bruce Deans
	Jorge Allen	Rusiate Namoro	Antonio Galeazzo	Albert Anderson
	Eliseo Branca	Koli Rokoroi (c)	Tito Lupini	Zinzan Brooke
	Sergio Carossio	Ilaitia Savai	Mauro Gardin	Mark Brooke-Cowden
	Julio Clement	Peceli Gale	Antonio Colella	John Drake
	Diego Cash	Manasa Qoro	Mario Pavin	Andy Earl
	Roberto Cobelo	John Sanday	Marzio Innocenti (c)	Sean Fitzpatrick
	Serafin Dengra	Epali Rakai	Gianni Zanon	Michael Jones
	Gustavo Milano	Livai Kididromo	Stefano Romagnoli	Richard Loe
	Luis Molina	Samu Vunivalu	Franco Berni	Steve McDowell
	Fernando Morel		Raffaele Dolfato	Murray Pierce
	Jose Mostany			Wayne Shelford
	Alejandro Schiavio			Alan Whetton
	Hugo Torres			Gary Whetton
	Gabriel Travaglini			

7. Showgrounds Oval, Palmerston North (now FMG Stadium) NZ.

POOL 3

3.1 New Zealand d. Italy (70~6)

22 May 1987, Eden Park, Auckland.
Attendance: 20,000; Referee: Bob Fordham (Australia).
New Zealand. Tries: Kirwan (2), Kirk (2), Green (2), Penalty try, Jones, Taylor, McDowell, Stanley, Whetton; Con: Fox (8); Pen: Fox (2).
Italy. Pen: Collodo; Drop: Collodo.

3.2 Fiji d. Argentina (28~9)

24 May 1987, Rugby Park, Hamilton.
Referee: Jim Fleming (Scotland).
Fiji. Tries: Gale, Naivilawasa, Nalaga, Savai; Con: Koroduadua (2), Rokowailoa; Pen: Koroduadua (2).
Argentina. Try: Penalty try; Con: Porta; Pen: Porta.

3.3 New Zealand d. Fiji (74~13)

27 May 1987, Lancaster Park, Christchurch.
Attendance: 26,000; Referee: Derek Bevan (Wales).
New Zealand. Tries: Gallagher (4), Green (4), Kirk, Kirwan, Penalty try, Whetton; Con: Fox (10); Pen: Fox (2).
Fiji. Try: Cama; Pen: Koroduadua (3).

3.4 Argentina d. Italy (25~16)

28 May 1987, Lancaster Park, Christchurch.
Referee: Roger Quittenton (England).
Argentina. Tries: Lanza, Gómez. Con: Porta; Pen: Porta (5).
Italy. Tries: Innocenti, Cuttitta; Con: Collodo; Pen: Collodo (2).

3.5 Italy d. Fiji (18~15)

31 May 1987, Carisbrook, Dunedin.
Referee: Keith Lawrence (New Zealand).
Italy. Tries: Cuttitta, Cucchiella, Mascioletti; Pen: Collodo; Drop: Collodo.
Fiji. Try: Naivilawasa; Con: Koroduadua; Pen: Koroduadua (2); Drop: Quro.

3.6 New Zealand d. Argentina (46~15)

1 June 1987, Athletic Park, Wellington.
Attendance: 35,000; Referee: Roger Quittenton (England).
New Zealand. Tries: Kirk, Brooke, Stanley, Earl, Crowley, Whetton; Con: Fox (2); Pen: Fox (6).
Argentina. Try: Lanza; Con: Porta; Pen: Porta (3).

Results	P	W	D	L	PF	PA	Pts
New Zealand	3	3	0	0	190	34	6
Fiji	3	1	0	2	56	101	2
Italy	3	1	0	2	40	110	2
Argentina	3	1	0	2	49	90	2

8. Sean Fitzpatrick, New Zealand (taken 2008).

Pool 3 Matches

The nations in Pool 3 consisted of **Argentina, Fiji, Italy** and **New Zealand**. The All Blacks, which included such rugby greats as Sean Fitzpatrick, John Kirwan, Grant Fox and Michael Jones, were in a class all of their own.

It was fascinating to watch the other three evenly placed teams fight it out for second place. Fiji defeated Argentina, who defeated Italy, who defeated Fiji. But the entertaining Fijians took out the other quarter final berth on points.

9. Rugby Park, Invercargill NZ.

POOL 4 - TEAMS

4	FRANCE	ROMANIA	SCOTLAND	ZIMBABWE
Coaches:	Jacques Fouroux		Derrick Grant	
Players:	Marc Andrieu	Vasile Ion	Richard Cramb	Andy Ferreira
	Pierre Berbizier	Marcel Toader	Matthew Duncan	Pete Kaulback
	Serge Blanco	Vasile David	Gavin Hastings	Richard Tsimba
	Eric Bonneval	Stefan Tofan	Scott Hastings	Campbell Graham
	Didier Camberabero	Adrian Lungu	Keith Robertson	Eric Barrett
	Denis Charvet	Romeo Bezuscu	John Rutherford	Craig Brown
	Patrick Esteve	Mircea Paraschiv (c)	Alan Tait	Malcolm Jellicoe (c)
	Jean-Baptiste Lafond	Liviu Hodorca	Iwan Tukalo	Andre Buitendag
	Patrice Lagisquet	Adrian Pilotschi	Douglas Wyllie	Shawn Graham
	Guy Laporte	Florea Opris	Finlay Calder	Marthinus Grobler
	Franck Mesnel	Vasile Ilca	J. Campbell-Lamerton	Errol Bredenkamp
	Rodolphe Modin	Vasile Pascu	Colin Deans (c)	Jumbo Davidson
	Philippe Sella	Nicolae Veres	John Jeffrey	Keith Bell
	Louis Armary	Laurentiu Constantin	Roy Laidlaw	George Elcome
	Alain Carminati	Ene Necula	Iain Milne	Lance Bray
	Éric Champ	Gheorghie Dumitru	Greg Oliver	Andy Tucker
	Jean Condom	Cristian Raducanu	Iain Paxton	Tom Sawyer
	Philippe Dintrans	Florica Murariu	Norman Rowan	Michael Martin
	Daniel Dubroca (c)	Haralambie Dumitras	David Sole	Rod Gray
	Dominique Erbani	Gheorghe Leonte	Alan Tomes	Dirk Buitendag
	JP Garuet-Lempirou	Emilian Grigore	Derek Turnbull	Mark Neill
	Francis Haget		Derek White	Neville Kloppers
	Jean-Luc Joinel			Alex Nicholls
	Alain Lorieux			
	Pascal Ondarts			
	Laurent Rodriguez			
	Jean-Louis Tolot			

POOL 4

4.1 Romania d. Zimbabwe (21~20)

23 May 1987, Eden Park, Auckland
Referee: Stephen Hilditch (Ireland).
Romania. Tries: Paraschiv, Toader, Hodorca; Pen: Alexandru (3).
Zimbabwe. Tries: Tsimba (2), Neill; Con: Ferreira; Pen: Ferreira (2).

4.2 France dr. Scotland (20~20)

23 May 1987, Lancaster Park, Christchurch.
Referee: Fred Howard (England).
France. Tries: Sella, Berbizier, Blanco; Con: Blanco; Pen: Blanco (2).
Scotland. Tries: White, Duncan; Pen: Hastings (4).

4.3 France d. Romania (55~12)

28 May 1987, Athletic Park, Wellington.
Referee: Bob Fordham (Australia).
France. Tries: Lagisquet (2), Charvet (2), Sella, Andrieu, Camberabero, Erbani, Laporte; Co: Laporte (8); Pen: Laporte.
Romania. Pen: Bezuscu (4).

4.4 Scotland d. Zimbabwe (60~21)

30 May 1987, Athletic Park, Wellington.
Referee: David Burnett (Ireland).
Scotland. Tries: Tait (2), Tukalo (2), Duncan (2), Paxton (2), Oliver, Hastings, Jeffrey; Con: Hastings (8).
Zimbabwe. Try: Buitendag; Con: Grobler; Pen: Grobler (5).

4.5 Scotland d. Romania (55~28)

2 June 1987, Carisbrook, Dunedin.
Referee: Stephen Hilditch (Ireland).
Scotland. Tries: Jeffrey (3), Tait (2), Hastings (2), Duncan, Tukalo; Con: Hastings (8); Pen: Hastings.
Romania. Tries: Murariu (2), Toader; Con: Alexandru, Ion; Pen: Alexandru (3).

4.6 France d. Zimbabwe (70~12)

2 June 1987, Eden Park, Auckland.
Referee: Derek Bevan (Wales).
France. Tries: Modin (3), Camberabero (3), Charvet (2), Rodriguez (2), Dubroca, Esteve, Laporte; Con: Camberabero (9).
Zimbabwe. Try: Kaulbach; Con: Grobler; Pen: Grobler (2).

Results	P	W	D	L	PF	PA	Pts
France	3	2	1	0	145	44	5
Scotland	3	2	1	0	135	69	5
Romania	3	1	0	2	61	130	2
Zimbabwe	3	0	0	3	53	151	0

10. Serge Blanco, France (taken 2010).

Pool 4 Matches

The nations in Pool 4 consisted of **France, Romania, Scotland** and **Zimbabwe**. Although Scotland had lost to France in the 1987 Five Nations Tournament, they managed to salvage a draw against the 'tricolours', but finished 2nd in the pool on points.

Both the Romanian and Zimbabwian teams were outclassed allowing 130 and 151 points against them respectively, but they had at least made an appearance on the world rugby stage.

11. Lancaster Park Stadium, Christchurch.

THE PLAYOFFS

Quarter Finals

The crossover format of the four quarter finals saw New Zealand rampage over Scotland (30~3) to firm as tournament favourites. Australia had a difficult match, but prevailed against Ireland (33~15) with goalkicker Michael Lynagh being the difference.

France overcame a very unpredictable Fiji (31~16) to gain the first semifinal berth. But the outstanding performance of Wales in defeating a tryless England (16~3), and scoring three of their own in the process was a tournament highlight.

QUARTER FINALS

QF1 New Zealand d. Scotland (30~3)

6 June 1987, Lancaster Park, Christchurch.
Attendance: 40,000; Referee: David Burnett (Ireland).
New Zealand. Tries: Whetton, Gallagher; Con: Fox (2);
Pen: Fox (6).
Scotland. Pen: Hastings.

QF2 Australia d. Ireland (33~15)

7 June 1987, Concord Oval, Sydney.
Referee: Brian Anderson (Scotland).
Australia. Tries: Burke (2), McIntyre, Smith; Con: Lynagh (4);
Pen: Lynagh (3).
Ireland. Tries: MacNeill, Kiernan; Con: Kiernan (2); Pen: Kiernan.

QF3 France d. Fiji (31~16)

7 June 1987, Eden Park, Auckland.
Referee: Clive Norling (Wales).
France. Tries: Rodriguez (2), Lorieux, Lagisquet; Con: Laporte
(3); Pen: Laporte (2); Drop: Laporte.
Fiji. Tries: Qoro, Damu; Con: Koroduadua; Pen: Koroduadua (2).

QF4 Wales d. England (16~3)

8 June 1987, Ballymore, Brisbane.
Referee: René Hourquet (France).
Wales. Tries: Roberts, Jones, Devereux; Con: Thorburn (2).
England. Pen: Webb.

Semi Finals

Australia was highly rated to take out the inaugural trophy, but France who were the reigning Five Nations Champions were very focused on the prize. The first semi final saw a fabulous display of running rugby right from the kick-off. The lead swapped three times in the see-sawing encounter with Michael Lynagh keeping the Wallabies in the match through his kicking. But the French enthusiasm was overwhelming and their 30~24 victory culminated in a magnificent team try, which was finished off by Serge Blanco.

In the second semi final

SEMI FINALS

Semi Final 1
France d. Australia (30~24)
13 June 1987, Concord Oval, Sydney.
Attendance: 17,768; Referee: Brian Anderson (Scotland).
France. Tries: Lorieux, Sella, Lagisquet, Blanco; Con: Camberabero (4); Pen: Camberabero (2).
Australia. Tries: Campese, Codey; Con: Lynagh (2); Pen: Lynagh (3); Drop: Lynagh.

Semi Final 2
New Zealand d. Wales (49~6)
14 June 1987, Ballymore, Brisbane.
Attendance: 22,576; Referee: Kerry Fitzgerald (Australia).
New Zealand. Tries: Kirwan (2), Shelford (2), Drake, Whetton, Stanley, Brooke: Cowden; Con: Fox (7); Pen: Fox.
Wales. Try: Devereux; Con: Thorburn.

there seemed to be no stopping the All Black juggernaut as they steamrolled over a brave, but totally outplayed Wales (49~6). The Welsh could only manage

12. Concord Oval (eastern grandstand), Sydney AUS.

13. Eden Park Stadium, Auckland NZ.

one try, while New Zealand crossed their line eight times, and predictably qualified to contest the final against France.

3rd Place Playoff

The Australians who had had the World Cup in their sights for months were coming off a dispiriting loss to France in the semi final, whereas Wales weren't expected to advance this far in the tournament and saw the battle for third place as an opportunity.

Right from the kickoff it was obvious that the Welsh were determined to make something of this great opportunity. The match was evenly balanced throughout with Wales scoring three tries to Australia's two. But the somewhat dour encounter was eventually decided by kicking when Paul Thorburn converted a difficult kick from the sideline for Wales to narrowly win the game (22~21) and take third place, which remains their best ever result in the Rugby World Cup.

THE FINAL

The amazingly gifted New Zealand side, which was captained by David Kirk and included a raft of All Black greats, didn't disappoint their home crowd as they controlled the final match over a subdued French team. France were a very capable outfit, but couldn't repeat their inspirational win over Australia in the semi-final. The New Zealanders had done their homework and dominated in all aspects of the game right from the start, with Grant Fox scoring 17 of the All Blacks 29 points. It was a comprehensive performance by the All Blacks, who in defeating France (29~9) wrote their name on a brand new page of rugby history.

After witnessing a total of 32 international matches, world rugby fans (the author included) had been treated to an amazing display across the 29 days of the tournament. Despite some criticism of the mismatched results of some of the pool games, the Rugby World Cup was seen as a major success and proved that the event was here to stay.

The 1st Rugby World Cup also encouraged many other countries to affiliate with the International Rugby Football Board, which in turn led to the IRFB becoming the principal authority for administering the growing international game of rugby union worldwide.

FINALS

FINAL

New Zealand d. France (29~9)

20 June 1987, Eden Park, Auckland.
Attendance: 48,035; Referee: Kerry Fitzgerald (Australia).
New Zealand. Tries: Jones, Kirk, Kirwan; Con: Fox; Pen: Fox (4); Drop: Fox.
France. Try: Berbizier; Con: Camberabero; Pen: Camberabero.

3rd/4th Playoff

Wales d. Australia (22~21)

18 June 1987, Rotorua, New Zealand.
Referee: Fred Howard (England).
Wales. Tries: Roberts, Moriarty, Hadley; Con: Thorburn (2); Pen: Thorburn (2).
Australia. Tries: Burke, Grigg; Con: Lynagh (2); Pen: Lynagh (2); Drop: Lynagh.

CREDITS

TEXT

IMAGES

1991
II RUGBY WORLD CUP
England, Scotland, Wales, Ireland & France

1. Stade Lesdiguieres, Grenoble, France.

II Rugby World Cup

3rd October to 2nd November, 1991

2. Cardiff Arms Park, Cardiff, Wales.

The 1991 Rugby World Cup was the second edition of this tournament, and was jointly hosted by England, Scotland, Wales, Ireland and France. The 1991 tournament was the first Rugby World Cup to be staged in the northern hemisphere, with England being elected as the host of the final championship match. At that time, these were the European countries that participated in the 'Five Nations' Championship, and they all pitched in to ensure the success of the event.

THE HOSTS

The host countries shared the task with France hosting six pool matches and two quarter finals.

Wales hosted six pool matches and the 3rd/4th playoff match. Scotland and Ireland hosted three pool matches each as well as a quarter final and semi final each. England hosted six pool matches plus the competition final at Twickenham in London.

THE TEAMS

Qualifying matches were introduced for the first time as the number of aspiring entrants increased from just 16 nations four years earlier to a total of 33 countries.

Seeded Teams

The eight quarter finalists from the 1987 Rugby World Cup qualified for the top eight seeded places in the 1991 tournament, which meant that **New Zealand, France, Wales, Australia, England, Scotland, Ireland** and **Fiji** were all automatic entrants.

Qualifying Teams

The other 25 nations that vied for a place in the tournament had to qualify for the remaining eight spots through a series of qualification matches. **Zimbabwe** won the African Zone by defeating Tunisia, Morocco and the Ivory Coast. **Canada, Argentina** and the **United States** were the only entrants from the America's Zone and so all three qualified. **Italy** and **Romania** won the two hotly contested spots from the European Zone over teams from Israel, Switzerland, Denmark, Sweden, Czechoslovakia, Yugoslavia, Germany, Portugal, Spain, Belgium, Poland and the Netherlands. Finally, **Western Samoa** and **Japan** won the final two spots from the Asia/Oceania Zone over Tonga and South Korea.

THE POOL STAGE

The same pool format from 1987 was used with a minor change to the points system. The 16 nations were again divided into four pools of four nations, with each nation playing their other pool opponents once, and every nation playing three times during the pool stage.

Teams were awarded three points for a win, two for a draw and one for a loss, with the top two nations from each pool advancing to the quarter finals. The runners-up of each pool faced the winners of a different pool by way of crossovers in the quarter finals. The quarter final winners then moved on to the semi finals and the semi final winners qualified for the final. The losers of the two semi finals contested the play off for 3rd place.

POOL 1 - TEAMS

1	ENGLAND	ITALY	NEW ZEALAND	USA
Coaches:	Geoff Cooke	Bertrand Fourcade	John Hart Alex Wylie	Jim Perkins
Players:	Rob Andrew	Stefano Barba	Graeme Bachop	Barry Daily
	Will Carling (c)	Massimo Bonomi	Kieran Crowley	Mark Pidcock
	Jeremy Guscott	Stefano Bordon	Grant Fox	Chris O'Brien
	Simon Halliday	Marcello Cuttitta	Craig Innes	Mike de Jong
	Nigel Heslop	Diego Dominguez	John Kirwan	Joe Burke
	Richard Hill	Ivan Francescato	Walter Little	Kevin Higgins
	Simon Hodgkinson	Fabio Gaetaniello	Bernie McCahill	Mark Williams
	Dewi Morris	Francesco Pietrosanti	Jon Preston	Gary Hein
	Chris Oti	Daniele Tebaldi	Shayne Philpott	Eric Whittaker
	Rory Underwood	Luigi Troiani	John Timu	Ray Nelson
	Jon Webb	Paolo Vaccari	Va'aiga Tuigamala	Paul Sheehy
	Paul Ackford	Edgardo Venturi	Terry Wright	Chris Lippert
	Wade Dooley	Alessandro Bottachiari	Zinzan Brooke	Lance Manga
	Jason Leonard	Carlo Checchinato	Mark Carter	Norm Mottram
	Brian Moore	Antonio Colella	Andy Earl	Fred Paoli
	John Olver	Giambattista Croci	Sean Fitzpatrick	Tony Flay
	Gary Pearce	Massimo Cuttitta	Paul Henderson	Pat Johnson
	David Pears	Roberto Favaro	Jason Hewett	Bill Leversee
	Jeff Probyn	Massimo Giovanelli	Ian Jones	Kevin Swords (c)
	Nigel Redman	Giovanni Grespan	Michael Jones	Chuck Tunnacliffe
	Gary Rees	Carlo Orlandi	Richard Loe	Rob Farley
	Dean Richards	Giancarlo Pivetta	Steve McDowell	Shawn Lipman
	Michael Skinner	Franco Properzi	Graham Purvis	Mark Sawicki
	Mike Teague	Guido Rossi	Alan Whetton	Brian Vizard
	Peter Winterbottom	Roberto Saetti	Gary Whetton (c)	Tony Ridnell
	Paul Rendall	Gianni Zanon (c)		

3. Welford Road Stadium, Leicester, England.

Pool 1 Matches

The nations in Pool 1 consisted of **England, Italy, New Zealand** and the **United States**. The tournament opening match pitted the title holders New Zealand against the hosts England. New Zealand overturned a narrow half-time deficit to win the match and the group, with both teams qualifying for the quarter-finals after easy victories in their other matches. Italy also played a memorable match against the All Blacks, crossing for two tries.

4. Michael Jones, New Zealand (taken 2010).

POOL 1

1.1 New Zealand d. England (18~12)

3 October 1991, Twickenham Stadium, London.
Attendance: 70,000; Referee: Jim Fleming (Scotland).
New Zealand. Tries: Jones; Con: Fox; Pen: Fox (4).
England. Pen: Webb (3); Drop: Andrew.

1.2 Italy d. United States (30~9)

5 October 1991, Cross Green, Otley.
Referee: Owen Doyle (Ireland).
Italy. Tries: Barba, Francescato, Vaccari, Gaetaniello; Con: Dominguez (4); Pen: Dominguez (2).
United States. Tries: Swords; Con: Williams; Pen: Williams.

1.3 New Zealand d. United States (46~6)

8 October 1991, Kingsholm, Gloucester.
Attendance: 12,000; Referee: Efraim Sklar (Argentina).
New Zealand. Tries: Wright (3), Earl, Purvis, Timu, Tuigamala, Innes; Con: Preston (4); Pen: Preston (2).
United States. Pen: Williams (2).

1.4 England d. Italy (36~6)

8 October 1991, Twickenham Stadium, London.
Referee: Brian Anderson (Scotland).
England. Tries: Guscott (2), Underwood, Webb; Con: Webb (4); Pen: Webb (4).
Italy. Tries: Cuttitta; Con: Dominguez.

1.5 England d. United States (37~9)

11 October 1991, Twickenham Stadium, London.
Referee: Les Peard (Wales).
England. Tries: Underwood (2), Carling, Skinner, Heslop; Con: Hodgkinson (4); Pen: Hodgkinson (3).
United States. Tries: Nelson; Con: Williams; Pen: Williams.

1.6 New Zealand d. Italy (31~21)

13 October 1991, Welford Road, Leicester.
Attendance: 16,800; Referee: Kerry Fitzgerald (Australia).
New Zealand. Tries: Brooke, Innes, Tuigamala, Hewett; Con: Fox (3); Pen: Fox (3).
Italy. Tries: Cuttitta, Bonomi; Con: Dominguez (2); Pen: Dominguez (3).

Results	P	W	D	L	PF	PA	Pts
New Zealand	3	3	0	0	95	39	9
England	3	2	0	1	85	33	7
Italy	3	1	0	2	57	76	5
USA	3	0	0	3	24	113	3

55

5. Murrayfield Stadium, Edinburgh, Scotland.

POOL 2 - TEAMS

2	IRELAND	JAPAN	SCOTLAND	ZIMBABWE
Coaches:	Ciaran Fitzgerald	Hiroaki Shukuzawa	Jim Telfer	
Players:	Fergus Aherne	Takahiro Hosokawa	Gary Armstrong	Brian Currin (c)
	Jack Clarke	Terunori Masuho	Craig Chalmers	Craig Brown
	Keith Crossan	Eiji Kutsuki	Iwan Tukalo	Mark Letcher
	Vince Cunningham	Seiji Hirao (captain)	Sean Lineen	Richard Tsimba
	David Curtis	Yoshihito Yoshida	Scott Hastings	David Walters
	Simon Geoghegan	Katsuhiro Matsuo	Tony Stanger	Ralph Kuhn
	Ralph Keyes	Masami Horikoshi	Gavin Hastings	Andy Ferreira
	Brendan Mullin	Wataru Murata	Peter Dods	William Schultz
	Kenny Murphy	Yukio Motoki	Graham Shiel	Ian Noble
	Rob Saunders	Tatsuya Maeda	Douglas Wyllie	Ewan MacMillan
	Jim Staples	Osamu Ota	David Milne	Elimon Chimbima
	Des Fitzgerald	Tsuyoshi Fujita	Greig Oliver	Robin Hunter
	Neil Francis	Mazanori Takura	Graham Marshall	Brian Beattie
	Gary Halpin	Toshiyuki Hayashi	Alan Watt	Adrian Garvey
	Gordon Hamilton	Atsushi Oyagi	David Sole (c)	Michael Martin
	Terry Kingston	Ekeroma Lauaiufi	John Allan	Rob Demblon
	Donal Lenihan	Hiroyuki Kajihara	Paul Burnell	Chris Botha
	Noel Mannion	Sinali-Tui Latu	Chris Gray	Brendon Dawson
	Phillip Matthews (c)	Mazahiro Kunda	Doddie Weir	Brenton Catterall
	Nick Popplewell	Katsufumi Myiamoto	John Jeffrey	Alex Nicholls
	Steve Smith	Kazuaki Takahashi	Finlay Calder	Honeywell Nguruve
	Brian Robinson	Shuji Nakashima	Derek White	Gary Snyder
				Darren Muirhead
				Chris Roberts

POOL 2

2.1 Scotland d. Japan (47~9)

5 October 1991, Murrayfield Stadium, Edinburgh.
Referee: Ed Morrison (England).
Scotland. *Tries: S. Hastings, Stanger, Chalmers, White, Penalty Try, Tukalo, G. Hastings; Con: G. Hastings (5); Pen: G. Hastings (2); Chalmers.*
Japan. *Tries: Hosokawa; Con: Hosokawa; Drop: Hosokawa.*

2.2 Ireland d. Zimbabwe (55~11)

6 October 1991, Lansdowne Road, Dublin.
Referee: Keith Lawrence (New Zealand).
Ireland. *Tries: Robinson (4), Popplewell (2), Geoghegan, Curtis; Con: Keyes (4); Pen: Keyes (5).*
Zimbabwe. *Tries: Dawson, Schultz; Pen: Ferreira.*

2.3 Ireland d. Japan (32~16)

9 October 1991, Lansdowne Road, Dublin.
Referee: Laikini Colati (Fiji).
Ireland. *Tries: Mannion (2), O'Hara, Staples; Con: Keyes (2); Pen: Keyes (4).*
Japan. *Tries: Hayashi, Kajihara, Yoshida; Con: Hosokawa (2).*

2.4 Scotland d. Zimbabwe (51~12)

9 October 1991, Murrayfield Stadium, Edinburgh.
Referee: Don Reordan (United States).
Scotland. *Tries: Tukalo (3), Turnbull, S. Hastings, Stanger, Weir, White; Con: Dods (5); Pen: Dods (2); Drop: Wylie.*
Zimbabwe. *Tries: Garvey (2); Con: Currin (2).*

2.5 Scotland d. Ireland (24~15)

12 October 1991, Murrayfield Stadium, Edinburgh.
Referee: Fred Howard (England).
Scotland. *Tries: Shiel, Armstrong; Con: G. Hastings (2); Pen: G. Hastings (3); Drop: Chalmers.*
Ireland. *Pen: Keyes (4); Drop: Keyes.*

2.6 Japan d. Zimbabwe (52~8)

14 October 1991, Ravenhill, Belfast.
Referee: René Hourquet (France).
Japan. *Tries: Yoshida (2), Mashuho (2), Kutsuki (2), Horikoshi, Luaiufi, Matsuo; Con: Hosokawa (2); Pen: Hosokawa (4).*
Zimbabwe. *Tries: Tsimba, Nguruve.*

Results	P	W	D	L	PF	PA	Pts
Scotland	3	3	0	0	122	36	9
Ireland	3	2	0	1	102	51	7
Japan	3	1	0	2	77	87	5
Zimbabwe	3	0	0	3	31	158	3

Pool 2 Matches

The nations in Pool 2 consisted of **Scotland, Ireland, Japan** and **Zimbabwe**. The Japanese played some very entertaining rugby and managed to score 13 tries in their pool games, while Zimbabwe were outclassed for the most part.

Once again, there were no real surprises as the matches in this group also played out according to recent form with both Scotland and Ireland easily progressing to the quarter finals.

6. Gavin Hastings, Scotland (taken 2011).

POOL 3 - TEAMS

3	ARGENTINA	AUSTRALIA	WALES	WEST SAMOA
Coaches:	Luis Gradin Guillermo Lamarca	Bob Dwyer	Alan Davies	Bryan Williams
Players:	Federico Méndez	Dan Crowley	Paul Arnold	Andrew Aiolupo
	Ricardo Le Fort	Phil Kearns	Richie Collins	Brian Lima
	Luis Molina	Tony Daly	Phil Davies	To'o Vaega
	Pedro Sporleder	Ewen McKenzie	Mark Davies	Frank Bunce
	Germán Llanes	David Nucifora	Laurance Delaney	Tupo Fa'amasino
	José Santamarina	Cameron Lillicrap	Mike Griffiths	Stephen Bachop
	Pablo Garretón (captain)	John Eales	Garin Jenkins	Mathew Vaea
	Mario Carreras	Rod McCall	Emyr Lewis	Timo Tagaloa
	Gonzalo Camardón	Steve Cutler	Phil May	Tu Nu'uali'itia
	Lisandro Arbizu	Simon Poidevin	Martyn Morris	Filipo Saena
	Diego Cuesta Silva	Viliami Ofahengaue	Kevin Moseley	**Forwards**
	Hernán García Simón	Troy Coker	Ken Waters	Peter Fatialofa (c)
	Eduardo Laborde	Jeff Miller	Richard Webster	Stan To'omalatai
	Martín Terán	Brendon Nasser	Hugh Williams-Jones	Vili Alalatoa
	Guillermo del Castillo	Nick Farr-Jones (c)	Andy Booth	Mark Birtwistle
	Manuel Aguirre	Peter Slattery	Tony Clement	Mat Keenan
	Mariano Bosch	Michael Lynagh	Adrian Davies	Junior Paramore
	Pablo Buabse	Tim Horan	Arthur Emyr	Danny Kaleopa
	Francisco Irarrázaval	Jason Little	David Wyn Evans	Apollo Perelini
	Gustavo Jorge	David Campese	Ieuan Evans	Sila Vaifale
	Mariano Lombardi	Bob Egerton	Steve Ford	Pat Lam
	Agustín Zanoni	John Flett	Scott Gibbs	Eddie Ioane
	Santiago Méson	Marty Roebuck	Mike Hall	Palamia Lilomaiava
	Diego Cash	Anthony Herbert	Robert Jones	David Sio
	Guillermo Angaut		Mike Rayer	
	Matías Allen		Mark Ringer	

7. Stradey Park, Llanelli, Wales.

POOL 3

3.1 Australia d. Argentina (32~19)

4 October 1991, Stradey Park, Llanelli.
Attendance: 11,000; Referee: David Bishop (New Zealand).
Australia. *Tries: Campese (2), Horan (2), Kearns; Con: Lynagh (3); Pen: Lynagh (2).*
Argentina. *Tries: Terán (2); Con: del Castillo; Pen: del Castillo; Drop: Arbizu (2).*

3.2 Western Samoa d. Wales (16~13)

6 October 1991, National Stadium (Cardiff Arms Park), Cardiff.
Referee: Patrick Robin (France).
Western Samoa. *Tries: Vaega, Vaifale; Con: Vaea; Pen: Vaea (2).*
Wales. *Tries: Emyr, Evans; Con: Ring; Pen: Ring.*

3.3 Australia d. Western Samoa (9~3)

9 October 1991, Pontypool Park, Pontypool.
Referee: Ed Morrison (England).
Australia. *Pen: Lynagh (3).*
Western Samoa. *Pen: Vaea.*

3.4 Wales d. Argentina (16~7)

9 October 1991, National Stadium (Cardiff Arms Park), Cardiff.
Attendance: 35,000; Referee: René Hourquet (France).
Wales. *Tries: Arnold; Pen: Ring (3), Rayer.*
Argentina. *Tries: García Simón; Pen: del Castillo.*

3.5 Australia d. Wales (38~3)

12 October 1991, National Stadium (Cardiff Arms Park), Cardiff.
Referee: Keith Lawrence (New Zealand).
Australia. *Tries: Roebuck (2), Slattery, Campese, Horan, Lynagh; Con: Lynagh (4); Pen: Lynagh (2).*
Wales. *Pen: Ring.*

3.6 Western Samoa d. Argentina (35~12)

13 October 1991, Sardis Road, Pontypridd.
Attendance: 8,500; Referee: Brian Anderson (Scotland). Replaced by Jim Fleming (Scotland).
Western Samoa. *Tries: Tagaola (2), Lima (2), Bunce, Bachop; Con: Vaea (4); Pen: Vaea.*
Argentina. *Tries: Terán; Con: Arbizu; Pen: Laborde, Arbizu.*

Results	P	W	D	L	PF	PA	Pts
Australia	3	3	0	0	79	25	9
West Samoa	3	2	0	1	54	34	7
Wales	3	1	0	2	32	61	5
Argentina	3	0	0	3	38	83	3

8. Simon Poidevin, Australia (taken 2011).

Pool 3 Matches

The nations in Pool 3 consisted of **Argentina, Australia, Wales** and **Western Samoa**. With four well respected rugby nations this was a very competitive pool resulting in a number of close matches. Making their debut in the Rugby World Cup, Western Samoa produced a major shock when they defeated 1987 semi finalists Wales (16~13) in Cardiff, which resulted in Samoa qualifying for the quarter finals and the shock tournament elimination of Wales.

9. Parc Municipal des Sports, Brive, France.

POOL 4 - TEAMS

4	CANADA	FIJI	FRANCE	ROMANIA
Coaches:	Ian Bertwell		Daniel Dubroca	Peter Ianusevici
Players:	Eddie Evans	Epeli Naituivau	Pascal Ondarts	Tiberiu Brînză
	Dan Jackart	Salaceli Naivilawasa	Grégoire Lascubé	Gheorghe Leonte
	David Speirs	Mosese Taga (c)	Philippe Marocco	Gheorghe Ion
	Karl Svoboda	Samuela Domoni	Louis Armary	Constantin Stan
	Paul Szabo	Ilaitia Savai	Philippe Gimbert	Sandu Ciorascu
	Norm Hadley	Alifereti Dere Ratu	Jean-Marie Cadieu	Constantin Cojocariu
	John Robertsen	Laisenia Katonawale	Olivier Roumat	Gheorghe Dinu
	Ron van den Brink	Ifereimi Tawake	Thierry Devergie	Andrei Guranescu
	Bruce Breen	Pauliasi Taubulutu	Éric Champ	Haralambie Dumitras (c)
	Al Charron	Waisale Serevi	Abdelatif Benazzi	Neculai Nichitean
	Glen Ennis	Tomasi Lovo	Marc Cécillon	Nicolae Racean
	Gord MacKinnon	Savenaca Aria	Laurent Cabannes	George Sava
	John Graf	Noa Nadruku	Michel Courtiols	Adrian Lungu
	Chris Tynan	Fili Seru	Philippe Benetton	Catalin Sasu
	Gareth Rees	Severo K. Waqanibau	Fabien Galthié	Marian Dumitru
	Dave Lougheed	Dranivesi Baleiwei	Henri Sanz	Ioan Doja
	John Lecky	Tevita Vonolagi	Didier Camberabero	Nicolae Fulina
	Tom Woods	Tomasi Rabaka	Thierry Lacroix	Ilie Ivancuic
	Christian Stewart	Mosese Vosanibole	Philippe Sella	Cornel Gheorghe
	Steve Gray	Pita Naruma	Franck Mesnel	Mihai Foca
	Pat Palmer	Naibuka Vuli	Philippe Saint-André	Gabriel Vlad
	Scott Stewart	Peni Volavola	Jean-Baptiste Lafond	Daniel Neaga
	Mark Wyatt (c)	Kalaveti Naisoro	Patrice Lagisquet	Lician Colceriu
	Roy Radu	Opeti Turuva	Pierre Hontas	Micusor Marin
	Gary Dukelow	Max Olsson	Serge Blanco (c)	
		Aisake Nadolo	Jean-Luc Sadourny	

10. Pontypool Park, Pontypool, Wales.

POOL 4

4.1 France d. Romania (30~3)

4 October 1991, Stade de la Méditerranée, Béziers.
Referee: Les Peard (Wales).
France. Tries: Roumat, Lafond, Penalty Try, Saint-André; Con: Camberabero; Pen: Camberabero (4).
Romania. Pen: Nichitean.

4.2 Canada d. Fiji (13~3)

5 October 1991, Stade Jean Dauger, Bayonne.
Referee: Kerry Fitzgerald (Australia).
Canada. Tries: Stewart; Pen: Rees (3).
Fiji. Drop: Serevi.

4.3 France d. Fiji (33~9)

8 October 1991, Stade Lesdiguières, Grenoble.
Referee: Derek Bevan (Wales).
France. Tries: Lafond (3), Sella (2), Camberabero; Con: Camberabero (3); Pen: Camberabero.
Fiji. Tries: Naruma; Con: Koroduadua; Pen: Koroduadua.

4.4 Canada d. Romania (19~11)

9 October 1991, Stade Ernest-Wallon, Toulouse.
Referee: Sandy MacNeill (Australia).
Canada. Tries: McKinnon, Ennis; Con: Mark Wyatt; Pen: Wyatt (2); Drop: Rees.
Romania. Tries: Lungu, Sasu; Pen: Nichitean.

4.5 Romania d. Fiji (17~15)

12 October 1991, Parc Municipal des Sports, Brive.
Referee: Owen Doyle (Ireland).
Romania. Tries: Ion, Dumitras, Sasu; Con: Racean; Pen: Nichitean.
Fiji. Pen: Turuva (2); Drop: Rabaka (2), Turuva.

4.6 France d. Canada (19~13)

13 October 1991, Stade Armandie, Agen.
Referee: Stephen Hilditch (Ireland).
France. Tries: Lafond, Saint-André; Con: Camberabero; Pen: Lacroix (2), Camberabero.
Canada. Tries: Wyatt; Pen: Wyatt, Rees; Drop: Rees.

Results	P	W	D	L	PF	PA	Pts
France	3	3	0	0	82	25	9
Canada	3	2	0	1	45	33	7
Romania	3	1	0	2	31	64	5
Fiji	3	0	0	3	27	63	3

Pool 4 Matches

The nations in Pool 4 consisted of **Canada, Fiji, France** and **Romania**. Canada played amazingly well to finish second in the pool with two wins and a very close loss to France (13~19). Their performance resulted in a quarter final berth alongside France in what remains Canada's best performance in the Rugby World Cup.

Fiji didn't have a good tournament and even lost to Romania, who had definitely improved their game.

11. Parc des Princes, Paris, France.

THE PLAYOFFS

Quarter Finals

The crossover format of the four quarter finals saw England eliminate France (19~10), which also confirmed their status as 'Five Nations' champions. Scotland had an easier match than expected against Western Samoa (28~6) and also captured a semi final berth.

Australia only just escaped with a last minute try against the fighting Irish (19~18) at home at Lansdowne Park, which gave the Wallabies a real fright. And New

QUARTER FINALS

QF1 England d. France (19~10)

19 October 1991, Parc des Princes, Paris.
Referee: David Bishop (New Zealand).
England. Tries: Underwood, Carling; Con: Webb; Pen: Webb (3).
France. Tries: Lafond; Pen: Lacroix (2).

QF2 Scotland d. Western Samoa (28~6)

19 October 1991, Murrayfield Stadium, Edinburgh.
Referee: Derek Bevan (Wales).
Scotland. Tries: Jeffrey (2), Stanger; Con: Hastings (2); Pen: Hastings (4).
Western Samoa. Pen: Vaea; Drop: Bachop.

QF3 Australia d. Ireland (19~18)

20 October 1991, Lansdowne Road, Dublin
Referee: Jim Fleming (Scotland).
Australia. Tries: Campese (2), Lynagh; Con: Lynagh (2); Pen: Lynagh.
Ireland. Tries: Hamilton; Con: Keyes; Pen: Keyes (3); Drop: Keyes.

QF4 New Zealand d. Canada (29~13)

20 October 1991, Stadium Lille-Metropole, Villeneuve d'Ascq.
Attendance: 33,800; Referee: Fred Howard (England).
New Zealand. Tries: Timu (2), McCahill, Brooke, Kirwan; Con: Fox (3); Pen: Fox.
Canada. Tries: Tynan, Charron; Con: Rees; Pen: Wyatt.

Zealand eliminated the plucky Canadians (29~13) in the fourth quarter final.

Semi Finals

The old rivalry came to the fore when England lined up against Scotland in the first semi final of the 1991 Rugby World Cup. England were slight favourites, but the Scots had played wonderful rugby throughout the tournament and had a great opportunity to progress especially playing in front of their home crowd at Murrayfield. Unfortunately no tries were scored and the grueling encounter went England's way, but only by a whisker (9~6).

In the second semi final, New Zealand was stopped by a determined Australian

SEMI FINALS

Semi Final 1
England d. Scotland (9~6)
26 October 1991, Murrayfield Stadium, Edinburgh.
Referee: Kerry Fitzgerald (Australia).
England. Pen: Webb (2); Drop: Andrew.
Scotland. Pen: G. Hastings (2).

Semi Final 2
Australia d. New Zealand (16~6)
27 October 1991, Lansdowne Road, Dublin.
Attendance: 54,000; Referee: Jim Fleming (Scotland).
Australia. Tries: Campese, Horan; Con: Lynagh; Pen: Lynagh (2).
New Zealand. Pen: Fox (2).

team that was buoyed by the great support they received from the Irish crowd. The All Blacks faltered under the pressure of being both the reigning World Cup holders and Bledisloe Cup champions. The staunch defense of the Wallabies completely shut the All Blacks out (16~6), to take

12. Lansdowne Road Stadium, Dublin, Ireland.

13. Twickenham Stadium, London, England.

the match and line themselves up for a crack at the title.

3rd Place Playoff

The playoff for third place was contested between New Zealand and Scotland and played at the National Stadium at Cardiff Arms Park, in front of a crowd of 44,000 spectators on Wednesday the 30th October 1991.

The match was very evenly balanced throughout with Scotland bravely keeping the New Zealanders at bay. The All Blacks managed to score one unconverted try through the efforts of Walter Little, but otherwise couldn't breach the staunch Scottish defense. The Scots were equally repelled and also couldn't break the All Black wall, who eventually won (13~6), helped along by three penalty goals from Jon Preston.

THE FINAL

The final of the 1991 Rugby World Cup was contested between Australia and England and played at Twickenham Stadium in London, in front of a crowd of 56,000 spectators on

Saturday the 2nd November 1991. The English had played stolidly throughout the tournament, losing only narrowly to New Zealand (12~18) in the tournament opener. They had relied for the most part on their big forwards and Rob Andrew's superb kicking skills, but changed their tactics from the outset in an attempt to put the Wallabies off.

FINALS

FINAL
Australia d. England (12~6)

2 November 1991, Twickenham Stadium, London.
Attendance: 56,000; Referee: Derek Bevan (Wales).
Australia. Tries: Daly; Con: Lynagh; Pen: Lynagh (2).
England. Pen: Webb (2).

3rd/4th Playoff
New Zealand d. Scotland (13~6)

30 October 1991, National Stadium (Cardiff Arms Park), Cardiff.
Attendance: 44,000; Referee: Stephen Hilditch (Ireland).
New Zealand. Tries: Little; Pen: Preston (3).
Scotland. Pen: G. Hastings (2)

The Australians on the other hand had not dropped a game and played running rugby all tournament. Despite their great form however, the only try of the match came after Willie Ofahengaue broke through the English line, with prop Tony Daly scoring from the resulting melee.

England appealed for a penalty try after David Campcsc knockcd down a pass to prevent an English overlap, but the referee awarded a penalty kick for the infringement. The Australians held on for a deserved victory (12~6) with captain Nick Farr-Jones tightly wrapping his hands around the William Webb Ellis trophy.

Following on from the success of the inaugural 1987 Rugby World Cup, the 1991 World Cup received much increased attention worldwide and was sccn as a major global sporting event for the first time.

CREDITS

TEXT

This article uses material from the Wikipedia article https://en.wikipedia.org/wiki/1991_Rugby_World_Cup which is released under the http://creativecommons.org/licenses/by-sa/3.0/ Creative Commons Attribution-Share-Alike License 3.0.

IMAGES

1. 'Stade Lesdiguières et parc Bachelard - Grenoble' by Milky (Nov 2009). Available at https://commons.wikimedia.org/wiki/File:Stade_Lesdiguières_-_Grenoble.JPG The copyright holder of this work, releases this work into the public domain.

2. 'Entrance to Cardiff Arms Park, Cardiff, Wales' by Seth Whales (13 Nov 2007). Available at https://commons.wikimedia.org/wiki/File:Entrance_to_Cardiff_Arms_Park.jpg This work has been released into the public domain by its author, Seth Whales.

3. 'Welford Rd, Stadium... Clubhouse End Leicester Tigers Ground. Currently an open terrace with club facilities to the rear' by Michael Trolove (4 Jan 2009). Available at https://commons.wikimedia.org/wiki/File:Clubhouse_End_Leicester_Tigers_Ground_-_geograph.org.uk_-_1110784.jpg under the Creative Commons Attribution-Share Alike 2.0 Generic license.

4. 'All Black legend, Michael Jones' by US Embassy NZ (8 Sep 2011). Available at https://commons.wikimedia.org/wiki/File:Michael_Jones_2011_(cropped).jpg This image is a work of a United States Department of State employee, taken or made as part of that person's official duties. As a work of the U.S. federal government, the image is in the public domain per 17 U.S.C. § 101 and § 105 and the Department Copyright Information.

5. 'Murrayfield hosting a Scotland rugby match, this was taken at half time in the Rugby World Cup 2007' by Alistairjh (Nov 2008). Available at https://commons.wikimedia.org/wiki/File:MurrayfieldRugbyWorldCup.JPG under the Creative Commons Attribution 3.0 Unported license.

6. 'Gavin Hastings at Pipefest in Edinburgh march down the Royal Mile, 7 August 2010' by Grant Ritchie (7 Aug 2010). Available at https://commons.wikimedia.org/wiki/File:Gavin_Hastings.jpg under the Creative Commons Attribution-Share Alike 3.0 Unported license.

7. 'Stradey Park, Llanelli prior to the Magners League rugby match between Llanelli Scarlets and Glasgow Warriors' by Alexander Jones (8 Sep 2006). Available at https://commons.wikimedia.org/wiki/File:Stradey_Park.jpg The copyright holder of this work, releases this work into the public domain.

8. 'Simon Poidevin' by Heymabel (6 Sep 2010). Available at https://commons.wikimedia.org/wiki/File:Simon_Poidevin.jpg under the Creative Commons Attribution-Share Alike 3.0 Unported license.

9. 'Stade Amédée-Domenech, Brive-la-Gaillarde' by Benj05 (10 Sep 2009). Available at https://commons.wikimedia.org/wiki/File:Stade_Amédée_Domenech.JPG under the Creative Commons Attribution-Share Alike 3.0 Unported, 2.5 Generic, 2.0 Generic and 1.0 Generic license.

10. 'Pontypool Rugby Ground Pontypool Rugby Ground, seen from a hillside in the park, today hosting a horse show' by David Roberts (23 May 2009). Available at https://commons.wikimedia.org/wiki/File:Pontypool_Rugby_Ground_-_geograph.org.uk_-_1760922.jpg under the Creative Commons Attribution-Share Alike 2.0 Generic license.

11. 'Entrée du Parc des Princes' by PSGMAG.NET (15 Mar 2009). Available at https://commons.wikimedia.org/wiki/File:Entrée_Parc_des_Princes.jpg under the Creative Commons Attribution 2.0 Generic license.

12. 'Picture of old Lansdowne Road Stadium' by Unknown (Undated). Available at https://en.wikipedia.org/wiki/File:Old_Lansdowne_Road.jpg This image is a faithful digitisation of a unique historic image, and the copyright for it is most likely held by the person who created the image or the agency employing them. It is believed that the use of this image may qualify as fair use under United States copyright law. Other use of this image, on Wikipedia or elsewhere, may be copyright infringement.

13. 'Stade de Twickenham à Londres' by Tijani59 (31 Mar 2009). Available at https://commons.wikimedia.org/wiki/File:Stade_de_Twickenham_à_Londres.jpg under the Creative Commons Attribution-Share Alike 2.0 Generic license.

Full terms at http://creativecommons.org/licenses/by/2.0.

1995

III RUGBY WORLD CUP

South Africa

1. Newlands Stadium, Cape Town, South Africa.

III Rugby World Cup

25th May to 24th June, 1995

2. Ellis Park Stadium, Johannesburg, SA.

The 1995 Rugby World Cup was the third Rugby World Cup. It was hosted by South Africa, and was the first Rugby World Cup in which every match was held in the one country.

THE HOST

The 3rd Rugby World Cup was the first major sporting event to take place in South Africa following the end of apartheid. It was also the first Rugby World Cup in which South Africa was allowed to compete.

The International Rugby Football Board (IRFB) had only readmitted South Africa to international rugby competition in 1992, following negotiations to end apartheid. The 3rd Rugby World Cup would also be the last major event of rugby union's amateur era as two months after this tournament, the IRFB opened up the sport to professionalism.

With all venues being within the one country a total of nine stadiums were used for this

World Cup. Six of the nine stadiums were South African Test grounds. The four largest stadiums were used for the finals, with the final taking place at Johannesburg's Ellis Park.

THE TEAMS

Nine nations gained automatic places in the tournament, but the remaining seven positions were contested by a record 45 teams.

Seeded Teams

The eight quarter finalists from the 1991 Rugby World Cup all received automatic entry into this tournament. This meant that **Australia, England, New Zealand, Scotland, France, Ireland, Canada** and **Western Samoa** were all seeded teams. This was also the very first World Cup tournament where the host nation was also automatically accepted into the competition. Therefore, as tournament hosts, the **South Africa** side became the 9th automatically entered team.

Qualifying Teams

All the other nations that vied for a place in the tournament had to qualify for the remaining seven spots through a series of qualification matches.

Ivory Coast won the single African Zone place over Kenya, Zimbabwe, Namibia, Tunisia, Morocco and a team called the Arabian Gulf. **Argentina** won the single American Zone place over teams from Uruguay, Paraguay, Chile, Bermuda and the United States.

The European Zone had three spots up for grabs and was contested by 22 nations. **Wales, Italy** and **Romania** eventually won the hotly contested places over teams from Israel, Andorra, Luxembourg, Switzerland, Denmark, Hungary, Sweden, Czechoslovakia, Yugoslavia, Germany, Latvia, Lithuania, Portugal, Spain, Belgium, Russia, Poland, Georgia and the Netherlands.

Japan won the single Asian Zone spot over teams from Taiwan, Malaysia, Sri Lanka, South Korea, Hong Kong, Thailand, Singapore; and **Tonga** won the single Oceania Zone place over Fiji.

THE POOL STAGE

The 16 nations were again divided into four pools of four nations, with each nation playing their other pool opponents once, and every nation playing three times during the pool stage.

Teams gained three points for a win, two for a draw and one for playing, with the top two nations from each pool advancing to the quarter finals. The runners-up of each pool faced the winners of a different pool in the quarter finals crossovers. Quarter final winners moved on to the semi finals and the semi final winners qualified for the final. The losers of the two semi finals contested the play off for 3rd place.

POOL A - TEAMS

A	AUSTRALIA	CANADA	ROMANIA	SOUTH AFRICA
Coaches:	Bob Dwyer	Ian Birtwell	Mircea Paraschiv Constantin Fugigi	Kitch Christie
Players:	Matt Pini	John Graf	Vasile Brici	Os du Randt ‡
	Matt Burke	Steve Gray	Lucian Cocleriu	Balie Swart
	Daniel Herbert	David Lougheed	Ionel Rotaru	Marius Hurter
	Jason Little	Shawn Lytton	Gheorghe Solomie	Garry Pagel
	Tim Horan	Gareth Rees (c)	Adrian Lungu	Chris Rossouw
	Joe Roff	Bobby Ross	Radu Fugigi	James Dalton †
	David Campese	Winston Stanley	Romeo Gontineac	Naka Drotske ‡
	Damian Smith	Christian Stewart	Nicolae Răcean	Mark Andrews
	Michael Lynagh (c)	Scott Stewart	Ilie Ivanciuc	Kobus Wiese
	Scott Bowen	Ron Toews	Neculai Nichitean	Hannes Strydom
	George Gregan	Alan Tynan	Vasile Flutur	Krynauw Otto
	Peter Slattery	Richard Bice	Daniel Neaga	Francois Pienaar (c)
	Tim Gavin	Mark Cardinal	Cătălin Drăguceanu	Ruben Kruger
	Troy Coker	Al Charron	Tiberiu Brînză (c)	Robbie Brink
	Viliami Ofahengaue	Glen Ennis	Andrei Guranescu	Rudolph Straeuli
	Ilivasi Tabua	Eddie Evans	Alexandru Gealapu	Adriaan Richter
	David Wilson	Ian Gordon	Traian Oroian	Joost van der Westhuizen
	Rod McCall	John Hutchinson	Ovidiu Slusariuc	Johan Roux
	John Eales	Mike James	Sandu Ciorascu	Joel Stransky
	Warwick Waugh	Paul LeBlanc	Constantin Cojocariu	Hendrik le Roux
	Tony Daly	Gordon MacKinnon	Valere Tufă	Japie Mulder
	Dan Crowley	Colin McKenzie	Ionel Negreci	Brendan Venter
	Ewen McKenzie	Chris Michaluk	Vasile Lucaci	Christiaan Scholtz
	Mark Hartill	Gareth Rowlands	Gabriel Vlad	Pieter Hendriks †
	Phil Kearns	Rod Snow	Leodor Costea	Chester Williams ‡
	Michael Foley	Karl Svoboda	Gheorghe Leonte	James Small
†-banned				Andre Joubert
‡-replacement				Gavin Johnson

3. Passionate South African fans.

Pool A Matches

The nations in Pool A consisted of **Australia, Canada, Romania** and **South Africa**. The eyes of the rugby world were on the South Africans in their World Cup debut tournament opener against Australia, coming away with a win (27~18).

The Canadians played particularly well to lose by respectable margins against both Australia (11~27) and eventual champions South Africa (0~20). But as expected, the two 'tier one' nations in Australia and South Africa progressed to the quarterfinals.

4. *Joost van der Westhuizen, South Africa (taken 2014).*

POOL A

A.1 South Africa d. Australia (27~18)

25 May 1995, Newlands, Cape Town.
Referee: Derek Bevan (Wales).
South Africa. Tries: Hendriks, Stransky; Con: Stransky; Pen: Stransky (4); Drop: Stransky.
Australia. Tries: Kearns, Lynagh; Con: Lynagh; Pen: Lynagh (2).

A.2 Canada d. Romania (34~3)

26 May 1995, Boet Erasmus Stadium, Port Elizabeth.
Referee: Colin Hawke (New Zealand).
Canada. Tries: Charron, McKenzie, Snow; Con: Rees (2); Pen: Rees (4); Drop: Rees.
Romania. Pen: Nichitean.

A.3 South Africa d. Romania (21~8)

30 May 1995, Newlands, Cape Town.
Referee: Ken McCartney (Scotland).
South Africa. Tries: Richter (2); Con: Johnson; Pen: Johnson (3).
Romania. Tries: Guranescu; Pen: Ivancuic.

A.4 Australia d. Canada (27~11)

31 May 1995, Boet Erasmus Stadium, Port Elizabeth.
Referee: Patrick Robin (France).
Australia. Tries: Lynagh, Tamanivalu, Roff; Con: Lynagh (3); Pen: Lynagh (2).
Canada. Tries: Charron; Pen: Rees (2).

A.5 Australia d. Romania (42~3)

3 June 1995, Danie Craven Stadium, Stellenbosch.
Referee: Naoki Saito (Japan);
Australia. Tries: Smith, Wilson, Roff (2), Foley, Burke Con: Burke (2), Eales (4).
Romania. Pen: Ivancuic.

A.6 South Africa d. Canada (20~0)

3 June 1995, Boet Erasmus Stadium, Port Elizabeth.
Referee: David McHugh (Ireland).
South Africa. Tries: Richter (2); Con: Stransky (2); Pen: Stransky (2)
Canada. Nil.

Results	P	W	D	L	PF	PA	Pts
Sth Africa	3	3	0	0	68	26	9
Australia	3	2	0	1	87	41	7
Canada	3	1	0	2	45	50	5
Romania	3	0	0	3	14	97	3

5. Kings Park (ABSA) Stadium, Durban, SA.

POOL B - TEAMS

B	ARGENTINA	ENGLAND	ITALY	WEST SAMOA
Coaches:	Alejandro Petra Ricardo Paganini	Jack Rowell	Georges Coste	Bryan Williams
Players:	Diego Albanese	Mike Catt	Alessandro Troncon	Tupo Fa`amasino
	Agustín Pichot	Jonathan Callard	Diego Dominguez	Michael Umaga
	Rodrigo Crexell	Tony Underwood	Luigi Troiani	George Harder
	Guillermo del Castillo	Rory Underwood	Massimo Bonomi	Brian Lima
	José Cilley	Ian Hunter	Ivan Francescato	George Leaupepe
	Fernando del Castillo	Will Carling (c)	Stefano Bordon	Esera Puleitu
	Lisandro Arbizu	Jeremy Guscott	Marco Platania	Fereti Tuilagi
	Sebastián Salvat (c)	Phil de Glanville	Massimo Ravazzolo	To'o Vaega
	Francisco García	Damian Hopley	Marcello Cuttitta	Darren Kellett
	Gonzalo Camardon	Rob Andrew	Mario Gerosa	Fata Sini
	Diego Cuesta Silva	Kyran Bracken	Francesco Mazzariol	Tuetu Nu`ualiitia
	Martín Terán	Dewi Morris	Paolo Vaccari	Vaapuu Vitale
	Ezequiel Jurado	Jason Leonard	Piermassimiliano Dotto	Peter Fatialofa
	Santiago Mesón	Graham Rowntree	Massimo Cuttitta (c)	George Latu
	Matias Corral	Victor Ubogu	Franco Properzi	Michael Mika
	Marcelo Urbano	John Mallett	Giovanni Grespan	Tala Leiasamaivo
	Roberto Grau	Brian Moore	Massimo Giovanelli	Brendan Reidy
	Patricio Noriega	Graham Dawe	Mauro Dal Sie	Lio Falaniko
	Federico Mendez	Martin Bayfield	Andrea Castellani	Potu Leavasa
	Ricardo Le Fort	Martin Johnson	Roberto Favaro	Saini Lemanea
	Germán Llanes	Richard West	Mark Giacheri	Daryl Williams
	Pedro Sporleder	Tim Rodber	Pierpaolo Pedroni	Malaki Iupeli
	Nicolás Bossicovich	Dean Richards	Giambattista Croci	Junior Paramore
	Pablo Buabse	Ben Clarke	Carlo Checchinato	Sila Viafale
	Rolando Martin	Steve Ojomoh	Diego Scaglia	Pat Lam
	Cristián Viel	Neil Back	Julian Gardner	Sham Tatupu
	Martín Sugasti		Orazio Arancio	
	Sebastián Irazoqui		Andrea Sgorlon	
	José Santamarina		Massimiliano Capuzzoni	
	Agustín Macome		Moreno Trevisiol	
			Carlo Orlandi	

POOL B

B.1 Western Samoa d. Italy (42~18)

27 May 1995, Basil Kenyon Stadium, East London.
Referee: Joël Dume (France).
Western Samoa. Tries: Lima (2), Harder (3), Kellet, Tatupu;
Con: Kellet (2); Pen: Kellet (1).
Italy. Tries: Vaccari, Cuttitta; Con: Dominguez; Pen:
Dominguez; Drop: Dominguez.

B.2 England d. Argentina (24~18)

27 May 1995, Kings Park Stadium, Durban.
Referee: Jim Fleming (Scotland).
England. Pen: Andrew (6); Drop: Andrew (2).
Argentina. Tries: Arbizu, Noriega; Con: Arbizu; Pen: Arbizu (2).

B.3 Western Samoa d. Argentina (32~26)

30 May 1995, Basil Kenyon Stadium, East London.
Referee: David Bishop (New Zealand).
Western Samoa. Tries: Lam, Leaupepe, Harder; Con: Kellet;
Pen: Kellet (5).
Argentina. Tries: Penalty try, Crexell; Con: Cilley (2); Pen: Cilley (4).

B.4 England d. Italy (27~20)

31 May 1995, Kings Park Stadium, Durban.
Referee: Stephen Hilditch (Ireland).
England. Tries: R. Underwood, T. Underwood; Con: Andrew;
Pen: Andrew (5).
Italy. Tries: Cuttitta, Vaccari; Con: Dominguez (2); Pen:
Dominguez (2).

B.5 Italy d. Argentina (31~25)

4 June 1995, Basil Kenyon Stadium, East London.
Referee: Clayton Thomas (Wales).
Italy. Tries: Vaccari, Gerosa, Dominguez; Con: Dominguez (2);
Pen: Dominguez (4).
Argentina. Tries: Corral, Martin, Cilley; Con: Cilley; Pen: Cilley.

B.6 England d. Western Samoa (44~22)

4 June 1995, Kings Park Stadium, Durban.
Referee: Patrick Robin (France).
England. Tries: R. Underwood (2), Back, Penalty Try; Con:
Callard (3); Pen: Callard (5); Drop: Catt.
Western Samoa. Tries: Sini (2), Umaga; Con: Fa'amasino (2);
Pen: Fa'amasino.

Results	P	W	D	L	PF	PA	Pts
England	3	3	0	0	95	60	9
West Samoa	3	2	0	1	96	88	7
Italy	3	1	0	2	69	94	5
Argentina	3	0	0	3	69	87	3

Pool B Matches

The nations in Pool B consisted of **Argentina, England, Italy** and **Western Samoa**. Both Italy and Argentina had a job ahead of them and played brilliant rugby in this tournament, losing four of their six matches by less than seven points.

England and Western Samoa were the standout teams of this pool however, and both qualified for the quarter finals. England defeated the Samoans (44~22) in their final bruising pool encounter to gain the top pool slot.

6. Martin Johnson, England (taken 2008).

POOL C - TEAMS

C	IRELAND	JAPAN	NEW ZEALAND	WALES
Coaches:	*Gerry Murphy*	*Shō Yabu Osamu*	*Laurie Mains*	*Alex Evans*
Players:	Jim Staples	Tsutomu Matsuda	Glen Osborne	Tony Clement
	Conor O'Shea	Kiyoshi Imaizumi	Eric Rush	Adrian Davies
	Simon Geoghegan	Terunori Masuho	Jeff Wilson	David Wyn Evans
	Richard Wallace	Akira Yoshida	Marc Ellis	Ieuan Evans
	Darragh O'Mahony	Lopeti Oto	Jonah Lomu	Steve Ford
	Brendan Mullin	Seiji Hirao	Frank Bunce	Mike Hall (c)
	Jonathan Bell	Yoshihito Yoshida	Walter Little	Neil Jenkins
	Maurice Field	Yukio Motoki	Alama Ieremia	Robert Jones
	Eric Elwood	Katsuhiro Matsuo	Andrew Mehrtens	Andy Moore
	Paul Burke	Keiji Hirose	Simon Culhane	Wayne Proctor
	Niall Hogan	Masami Horikoshi	Ant Strachan	Gareth Thomas
	Michael Bradley (r)	Wataru Murata	Graeme Bachop	Justin Thomas
	Nick Popplewell	Osamu Ota	Zinzan Brooke	Mark Bennett
	John Fitzgerald	Kazuaki Takahashi	Kevin Schuler	John Davies
	Gary Halpin	Masanori Takura	Mike Brewer	Stuart Davies
	Paul Wallace	Masahiro Kunda (c)	Jamie Joseph	Ricky Evans
	Terry Kingston (c)	Eiji Hirotsu	Paul Henderson	Mike Griffiths
	Keith Wood	Kazu Hamabe	Josh Kronfeld	Jonathan Humphreys
	Neil Francis	Yoshihiko Sakuraba	Blair Larsen	Garin Jenkins
	Gabriel Fulcher	Bruce Ferguson	Ian Jones	Spencer John
	Davy Tweed	Takashi Akatsuka	Robin Brooke	Derwyn Jones
	Anthony Foley	Hiroyuki Kajihara	Craig Dowd	Emyr Lewis
	David Corkery	Sinali Latu	Olo Brown	Gareth Llewellyn
	Eddie Halvey	Ko Izawa	Richard Loe	Greg Prosser
	Denis McBride	Sione Latu	Sean Fitzpatrick (c)	Stuart Roy
	Paddy Johns	Tomoya Haneda	Norm Hewitt	Hemi Taylor

7. South African fans are amongst the most vocal of supporters.

POOL C

C.1 Wales d. Japan (57~10)

27 May 1995, Free State Stadium, Bloemfontein.
Referee: Efrahim Sklar (Argentina).
Wales. Tries: G. Thomas (3), I. Evans (2), Moore, Taylor; Con: N. Jenkins (5); Pen: N. Jenkins (4).
Japan. Tries: Ota (2).

C.2 New Zealand d. Ireland (43~19)

27 May 1995, Ellis Park, Johannesburg.
Attendance: 38,000; Referee: Wayne Erickson (Australia).
New Zealand. Tries: Lomu (2), Kronfeld, Bunce, Osborne; Con: Mehrtens (3); Pen: Mehrtens (4).
Ireland. Tries: Corkery, McBride, Halpin; Con: Elwood (2).

C.3 Ireland d. Japan (50~28)

31 May 1995, Free State Stadium, Bloemfontein.
Referee: Stef Neethling (South Africa).
Ireland. Tries: Francis, Geoghegan, Corkery, Halvey, Hogan, 2 Pen tries; Con: Burke (6); Pen: Burke.
Japan. Tries: Latu, Izawa, Hirao, Takura; Con: Yoshida (4).

C.4 New Zealand d. Wales (34~9)

31 May 1995, Ellis Park, Johannesburg.
Attendance: 45,000; Referee: Ed Morrison (England).
New Zealand. Tries: Ellis, Little, Kronfeld; Con: Mehrtens (2); Pen: Mehrtens (4); Drop: Mehrtens.
Wales. Pen: N. Jenkins (2); Drop: N. Jenkins.

C.5 New Zealand d. Japan (145~17)

4 June 1995, Free State Stadium, Bloemfontein.
Attendance: 25,000; Referee: George Gadjovic (Canada).
New Zealand. Tries: Ellis (6), Rush (3), Wilson (3), R. Brooke (2), Osborne (2), Loe, Culhane, Henderson, Dowd, Ieremia; Con: Culhane (20).
Japan. Tries: Kajihara (2); Con: Hirose (2); Pen: Hirose.

C.6 Ireland d. Wales (24~23)

4 June 1995, Ellis Park, Johannesburg.
Referee: Ian Rogers (South Africa).
Ireland. Tries: Halvey, Popplewell, McBride; Con: Elwood (3); Pen: Elwood.
Wales. Tries: Humphreys, Taylor; Con: N. Jenkins (2); Pen: N. Jenkins (2); Drop: A. Davies.

Results	P	W	D	L	PF	PA	Pts
New Zealand	3	3	0	0	222	45	9
Ireland	3	2	0	1	93	94	7
Wales	3	1	0	2	89	68	5
Japan	3	0	0	3	55	252	3

8. Agustin Pichot, Argentina (taken 2007

Pool C Matches

The nations in Pool C consisted of **Ireland, Japan, New Zealand** and **Wales**. The All Blacks, led by perennial Sean FitzPatrick came into this tournament as the top ranked team. They recorded easy wins against both Ireland and Wales and absolutely destroyed Japan (145~17).

Japan were completely outclassed, which left only one quarter final place for either Ireland or Wales. In the very last pool game Ireland scored three tries to two to scrape past Wales (24~ 23) and claim a quarterfinal berth.

9. Loftus Versfeld Stadium, Pretoria, SA.

POOL D - TEAMS

D	FRANCE	IVORY COAST	SCOTLAND	TONGA
Coaches:	Jacques Fouroux	Claude Ezoua	Jim Telfer	Fakahau Valu
Players:	Jean-Luc Sadourny	Felix Dago	Gavin Hastings (c)	Manu Vunipola
	Sébastien Viars	Frédéric Dupont	Cameron Glasgow	Akuila Mafi
	Philippe Saint-André	Aboubakar Camara	Kenny Logan	Elisi Vunipola
	Philippe Sella	Athanase Dali (c)	Craig Joiner	Pita Alatini
	Franck Mesnel	Thierry Kouame	Tony Stanger	Falanisi Manukia
	Émile Ntamack	Alfred Okou	Scott Hastings	Penieli Latu
	Thierry Lacroix	Lucien Niakou	Ian Jardin	Sione Ngauamo
	William Téchoueyres	Aboubacar Soulama	Graham Shiel	Alasika Taufa
	Christophe Deylaud	Paulin Bouazo	Craig Chalmers	Tevita Va`enuku
	Yann Delaigue	Max Brito	Bryan Redpath	Semi Taupeaafe
	Aubin Hueber	Celestin N'Gbala	David Hilton	Sateki Tu'ipulotu
	Guy Accoceberry	Victor Kouassi	John Manson	Taipe 'Isitolo
	Fabien Galthié	Jean-Baptiste Sathiq	Peter Wright	Simani Mafile'o
	Abdelatif Benazzi	Ernest Bley	Paul Burnell	Tevita Manako
	Philippe Benetton	Toussaint Djehi	Kenny Milne	Nafe Tufui
	Marc Cecillon	Jean-Pascal Ezoua	Kevin McKenzie	Mana Otai (c)
	Laurent Cabannes	Daniel Quansah	Stewart Campbell	Tu'akalau Fukofuka
	Arnaud Costes	Édouard Angoran	Damian Cronin	Etuini Talaki
	Albert Cigagna	Achille Niamien	Jeremy Richardson	Sa'ili Fe`ao
	Olivier Roumat	Ble Aka	Doddie Weir	Fe'ao Vunipola
	Olivier Brouzet	Gilbert Bado	Rob Wainwright	Fololisi Masila
	Olivier Merle	Amidou Kone	Peter Walton	Pouvalu Latukefu
	Christian Califano	Soumalia Kone	Ian Morrison	Falamani Mafi
	Philippe Gallart	Patrice Pere	Ian Smith	Willie Lose
	Jean-Michel Gonzalez	Djakaria Sanoko	Eric Peters	Ipolitio Fenukitau
	Louis Armary	Ismaila Lassissi		Toutai Kefu
	Laurent Benezech			Fili Finau
	Marc de Rougemont			Inoke Afeaki
				Danial Manu
				Feleti Fakaongo
				Feleti Mahoni
				Takau Lutua

10. Adbelatif Benazzi, France (taken 2013).

POOL D

D.1 Scotland d. Ivory Coast (89~0)

26 May 1995, Olympia Park, Rustenburg.
Referee: Felise Vito (Western Samoa).
Scotland. Tries: G. Hastings (4), Logan (2), Walton (2), Wright,
Chalmers, Stanger, Burnell, Shiel; Con: G. Hastings (9); Pen: G.
Hastings (2).
Ivory Coast. Nil.

D.2 France d. Tonga (38~10)

26 May 1995, Loftus Versfeld, Pretoria.
Referee: Steve Lander (England).
France. Tries: Lacroix (2), Hueber, Saint-André; Con: Lacroix
(3); Pen: Lacroix (3); Drop: Delaigue.
Tonga. Tries: Va'enuku; Con: Tu'ipulotu; Pen: Tu'ipulotu.

D.3 France d. Ivory Coast (54~18)

30 May 1995, Olympia Park, Rustenburg.
Referee: Han Moon-Soo (South Korea).
France. Tries: Lacroix (2), Benazzi, Téchoueyres, Viars,
Accoceberry, Saint-André, Costes; Con: Deylaud (2), Lacroix
(2); Pen: Lacroix (2).
Ivory Coast. Tries: Soulama, Camara; Con: Kouassi; Pen: Kouassi (2).

D.4 Scotland d. Tonga (41~5)

30 May 1995, Loftus Versfeld, Pretoria.
Referee: Barry Leask (Australia).
Scotland. Tries: S. Hastings, Peters, G. Hastings; Con: G.
Hastings; Pen: G. Hastings (8).
Tonga. Tries: Fenukitau.

D.5 Tonga d. Ivory Coast (29~11)

3 June 1995, Olympia Park, Rustenburg.
Referee: Don Reordan (United States).
Tonga. Tries: 'Otai, Tu'ipulotu, Latukefu; Con: Tu'ipulotu (3);
Pen: Tu'ipulotu.
Ivory Coast. Tries: Okou; Pen: Dali (2).
NB. Three minutes into this match the Ivorian winger Max Brito was crushed
beneath several other players, leaving him paralyzed below the neck.

D.6 France d. Scotland (22~19)

3 June 1995, Loftus Versfeld, Pretoria.
Referee: Wayne Erickson (Australia).
France. Tries: Ntamack; Con: Lacroix; Pen: Lacroix (5).
Scotland. Tries: Wainwright; Con: G. Hastings; Pen: G. Hastings (4).

Results	P	W	D	L	PF	PA	Pts
France	3	3	0	0	114	47	9
Scotland	3	2	0	1	149	27	7
Tonga	3	1	0	2	44	90	5
Ivory Coast	3	0	0	3	29	172	3

Pool D Matches

The nations in Pool D consisted of **France, Ivory Coast, Scotland** and **Tonga**. The tournament broadened its membership with the inclusion of a new team from the Ivory Coast, which included a number of players from French provincial teams. Tonga was making their second World Cup appearance.

Both France and Scotland however, were the standout teams in this group. Their match in the final pool encounter in Pretoria decided who was to finish first and second in the pool, with France progressing (22~19).

11. Loftus Versfeld Stadium, Pretoria, SA.

THE PLAYOFFS

Quarter Finals

The crossover format of the four quarter finals saw France dispose of Ireland (36~12) to be the first nation into the semi finals. The South Africans too, looked very strong in their demolition of Western Samoa (42~14) and were definitely improving as the tournament progressed.

England played outstanding rugby to claim a semi final berth in defeating Australia (25~22), who had been the reigning champions. The last quarter final saw New Zealand defeat a very brave Scotland (48~30) to firm as tournament favourites.

Semi Finals

The first semi final of the 1995 Rugby World Cup was a defensive tussle. An entertaining

QUARTER FINALS

QF1 France d. Ireland (36~12)

10 June 1995, Kings Park Stadium, Durban.
Referee: Ed Morrison (England).
France. Tries: Saint-André, Ntamack; Con: Lacroix; Pen: Lacroix (8).
Ireland. Pen: Elwood (4).

QF2 South Africa d. Western Samoa (42~14)

10 June 1995, Ellis Park, Johannesburg.
Referee: Jim Fleming (Scotland).
South Africa. Tries: Williams (4), Rossouw, Andrews; Con: Johnson (3); Pen: Johnson (2).
Western Samoa. Tries: Tatupu, Nu'uali'itia; Con: Fa'amasin (2).

QF3 England d. Australia (25~22)

11 June 1995, Newlands, Cape Town.
Referee: David Bishop (New Zealand).
England. Tries: T. Underwood; Con: Andrew; Pen: Andrew (5); Drop: Andrew.
Australia. Tries: Smith; Con: Lynagh; Pen: Lynagh (5).

QF4 New Zealand d. Scotland (48~30)

11 June 1995, Loftus Versfeld, Pretoria.
Attendance: 28,000; Referee: Derek Bevan (Wales).
New Zealand. Tries: Little (2), Lomu, Mehrtens, Bunce, Fitzpatrick; Con: Mehrtens (6); Pen: Mehrtens (2).
Scotland. Tries: Weir (2), S. Hastings; Con: G. Hastings (3); Pen: G. Hastings (3).

match was expected with both teams being undefeated throughout the tournament, but the contest was decided in the Springboks favour by goal kicks from Joel Stransky (19~15), with Ruben Kruger of South Africa scoring the games only try.

In the second semi final there seemed to be no stopping the All Blacks especially with their try scoring machine Jonah Lomu, who scored four tries. New Zealand crossed for six tries in the match, and Zinzan Brooke even scored a drop goal. In the second half however, England

12. Capacity attendance at the 1995 Rugby World Cup.

SEMI FINALS

Semi Final 1
South Africa d. France (19~15)

17 June 1995, Kings Park Stadium, Durban.
Referee: Derek Bevan (Wales).
South Africa. Tries: Kruger; Con: Stransky; Pen: Stransky (4).
France. Pen: Lacroix (5).

Semi Final 2
New Zealand d. England (45~29)

18 June 1995, Newlands, Cape Town
Attendance: 51,000; Referee: Stephen Hilditch (Ireland).
New Zealand. Tries: Lomu (4), Kronfeld, Bachop; Con: Mehrtens (3); Pen: Mehrtens; Drop: Brooke, Mehrtens.
England. Tries: Carling (2), R. Underwood (2),; Con: Andrew (3),; Pen: Andrew.

3rd Place Playoff

The playoff for third place was contested between England and France and played at the Loftus Versfeld Stadium in the capital Pretoria, in front of a large crowd on the 22nd June 1995.

Despite the fact that England were the 1995 'Five Nations' champions, winning the Calcutta Cup, taking the Grand Slam in the process, and defeating France (31~10) in the 'Five Nations' rounds, they couldn't rise to the occasion in Pretoria. The English and French kickers

changed tactics to somewhat stem the flow with four tries, but they couldn't match the skill and speed of New Zealand who qualified for the final (45~29).

13. Victory celebrations went on in South Africa for weeks.

scored three penalty goals apiece, but the difference was three superb, although unconverted tries to France who employed their unique running style to outscore the English (19~9).

THE FINAL

The final was contested by New Zealand and hosts South Africa. Both nations had finished undefeated at the top of their pools. Ellis Park in Johannesburg was the venue for the big game and it was refereed by Ed Morrison of England in front of 63,000 spectators.

South Africa led 9~6 at half time, and New Zealand leveled the scores at 9-all with a drop goal during the second half. Though Andrew Mehrtens almost kicked a late drop goal for the All Blacks, the score remained tied at full-time, forcing the game into extra time. Both teams scored penalty goals in the first half of extra time, but Joel Stransky booted a drop goal to grab victory and a first Rugby World Cup for South

FINALS

FINAL
South Africa d. New Zealand (15~12 xt)

24 June 1995, Ellis Park, Johannesburg.
Attendance: 63,000; Referee: Ed Morrison (England).
South Africa. *Pen: Stransky (3); Drop: Stransky (2).*
New Zealand. *Pen: Mehrtens (3); Drop: Mehrtens.*

3rd/4th Playoff
France d. England (19~9)

22 June 1995, Loftus Versfeld, Pretoria.
Referee: David Bishop (New Zealand).
France. *Tries: Olivier Roumat, Ntamack; Pen: Lacroix (3).*
England. *Pen: Andrew (3).*

Africa (15~12).

What happened after the match has become an iconic moment in the history of the sport. Nelson Mandela, wearing a Springbok rugby shirt and baseball cap, presented the William Webb Ellis Cup to South African captain Francois Pienaar to the delight of the capacity crowd. The moment is thought by some to be one of the most famous finals of any sport or code of football. The South African Mint issued a one ounce gold proof 'Protea' coin with a total mintage of just 406 pieces to commemorate the event being hosted by South Africa.

CREDITS

1999

IV RUGBY WORLD CUP

Wales

1. Millenium Stadium, Cardiff, Wales.

IV Rugby World Cup

1st October to 6th October, 1999

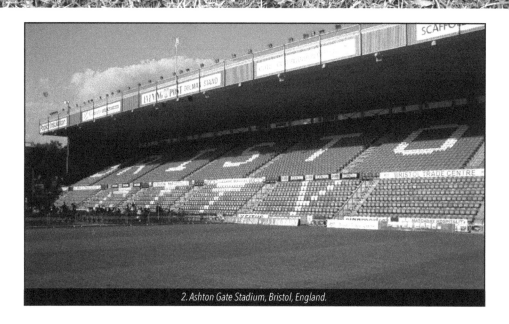

2. Ashton Gate Stadium, Bristol, England.

The 1999 Rugby World Cup was the fourth Rugby Union World Cup and ran from the 1st October to the 6th November 1999. This was the first Rugby World Cup to be held in rugby union's professional era.

THE HOST

The principal host nation was Wales, although the majority of matches were shared with other members of the 'Five Nations' alliance (England, France, Scotland and Ireland) and played outside Wales. France and Scotland hosted six pool matches and two quarter finals each. Ireland hosted six pool matches and one quarter final. England hosted six pool matches, one quarter final and both semi finals, while Wales hosted the opening ceremony, six pool matches, a quarter final, the 3rd/4th playoff and the final match in Cardiff. The overall attendance for the new 20 team tournament was 1.75 million fans.

THE TEAMS

Being the home nation **Wales** were awarded an automatic qualification berth afforded to the tournament hosts. Only three other automatic qualification places were available for the 1999 tournament. The remaining 16 positions were contested by a record 67 teams.

Seeded Teams

The three other seeded tournament places available for the 1999 Rugby World Cup went to the top three teams from the previous World Cup. This meant that **South Africa** (1995 champions), **New Zealand** (1995 runners-up) and third placed **France** all received automatic entry into this tournament.

Qualifying Teams

All other nations vying for a place in the tournament had to qualify for the remaining 16 places through a series of qualification matches.

Namibia won the single African Zone place over Kenya, Zimbabwe, Ivory Coast, Tunisia, Morocco, Zambia, Botswana and a team called the Arabian Gulf. **Argentina, Canada** and the **United States** won the three American Zone places over teams from Trinidad & Tobago, Brazil, Guyana, Bermuda, Bahamas, Barbados, Chile, Uruguay and Paraguay.

The European Zone had six places up for grabs and was contested across three qualifying pools by 30 nations. **Ireland** and **Romania** qualified from pool 1 over teams from Georgia, Croatia, Russia, Denmark, Latvia, Moldova, Norway and Bulgaria. **England** and **Italy** qualified from pool 2 over teams from the Netherlands, Ukraine, Poland, Belgium, Serbia & Montenegro, Switzerland, Israel and Austria. **Scotland** and **Spain** qualified from pool 3 over teams from Portugal, Germany, Czech Republic, Andorra, Sweden, Hungary, Lithuania and Luxembourg.

3. Welsh rugby fans.

4. Parc Lescure, Bordeaux, France.

Japan won the single Asian Zone spot over teams from Taiwan, Malaysia, Sri Lanka, South Korea, Hong Kong, Chinese Taipei, Thailand and Singapore. And **Australia, Fiji** and **Samoa** won the three Oceania Zone places over teams from the Cook Islands, Papua New Guinea, Tahiti and Tonga.

Repechage Teams

In the 1999 Rugby World Cup qualifiers, there were two new repechage positions available to qualify for the final tournament. Seven teams qualified for the repechage, three representing Europe and one each from Africa, Asia, the Americas and Oceania. After a series of 10 matches both **Uruguay** and **Tonga** won their places in the 1999 Rugby World Cup.

THE POOL STAGE

A total of 41 matches across 35 days (30 pool stage and 11 knock-out) were played throughout the tournament. With the expansion of the Rugby World Cup from 16 to 20 teams an unusual and complex competition format was used. The teams were split into five pools of four teams, with each team playing each other in the group.

Pool A was played in Scotland; Pool B was played in England; Pool C was played in France; Pool D was played in the host nation Wales; and Pool E was played in Ireland with matches played in both the Republic of Ireland and Northern Ireland.

Teams gained three points for a win, two for a draw, and one for playing. The five pool winners qualified automatically for the quarter finals. But the 20 team format necessitated a quarter final play-off round involving the five pool runners-up and the best third-placed team, to decide who would join the pool winners in the last eight.

The arrangement meant that two pool winners would have to play each other in the quarter finals. From the quarter final stage it became a simple knockout tournament along the same lines as had been conducted in previous World Cups. The quarter final winners qualified for the semi finals with winners progressing to the final. The semi final losers played off for 3rd place.

'The cavernous Millennium Stadium during Wales' clash with Fiji', by David Roberts (1 Oct 2015). Available at https://commons.wikimedia.org/wiki/File:Millennium_Stadium_RWC2015.jpg under the Creative Commons Attribution 2.0 Generic license.

POOL A - TEAMS

A	SCOTLAND	SPAIN	SOUTH AFRICA	URUGUAY
Coaches:	*Jim Telfer*	*Alfonso Feijoo*	*Nick Mallett*	*Daniel Herrera*
Players:	Gordon Bulloch	Jordi Camps	Bobby Skinstad	Diego Aguirre
	Paul Burnell	José Ignacio Zapatero	Anton Leonard	Sebastián Aguirre
	George Graham	Víctor Torres	Rassie Erasmus	Juan Alzueta
	Stuart Grimes	Luis Javier Martinez	Andre Venter	Martín Cerviño
	David Hilton	Fernando De La Calle	Andre Vos	Pablo Costábile
	Martin Leslie	Diego Zarzosa	Ruben Kruger	Francisco de los Santos
	Cameron Mather	José Miguel Villaú	Krynauw Otto	Nicolás Grillé
	Scott Murray	Steve Tuineau Iloa	Fritz van Heerden	Juan Menchaca
	Budge Pountney	Sergio Souto	Mark Andrews	Martín Mendaro
	Andy Reed	Alberto Malo (c)	Albert van den Berg	Diego Ormaechea (c)
	Stuart Reid	Carlos Souto	Os du Randt	Agustín Ponce de León
	Robert Russell	Oscar Astarloa	Ollie le Roux	Fernando Sosa Díaz
	Gordon Simpson	José Díaz	Adrian Garvey	Guillermo Storace
	Tom Smith	Agustín Malet	Cobus Visagie	Pedro Vecino
	Doddie Weir	Alfonso Mata	Naka Drotske	Juan Carlos Bado
	Peter Walton	Aratz Gallastegui	Chris Rossouw	Eduardo Berruti
	Duncan Hodge	Jaime Alonso	Percy Montgomery	Nicolas Brignoni
	Gary Armstrong (c)	Andrei Kovalenco	Breyton Paulse	Alfonso Cardoso
	Bryan Redpath	Aitor Etxeberría	Pieter Rossouw	Leonardo de Oliveira
	Iain Fairley	Alvar Enciso	Stefan Terblanche	Martín Ferrés
	Glenn Metcalfe	Fernando Díez	Deon Kayser	Guillermo Laffite
	Chris Paterson	Raphaël Bastide	Brendan Venter	Mario Lamé
	Cameron Murray	Alberto Socias	Pieter Muller	Diego Lamelas
	Kenny Logan	Sebastien Loubsens	Robbie Fleck	Pablo Lemoine
	Shaun Longstaff	Oriol Ripol	Wayne Julies	Juan Martín Marqués
	Alan Tait	Antonio Socias	Kaya Molatana	Martín Panizza
	John Leslie	José Ignacio Inchausti	Henry Honiball	Fernando Paullier
	James McLaren	Angel Frechilla	Jannie de Beer	Rodrigo Sánchez
	Jamie Mayer	Ferran Velazco Querol	Joost van der Westhuizen	Federico Sciarra
	Gregor Townsend	Francisco Puertas Soto	Werner Swanepoel	José Viana

5. Netherdale Stadium, Galashiels, Scotland.

Pool A Matches

The nations in Pool A consisted of **Scotland, Spain, South Africa** and **Uruguay**. Both Spain and Uruguay made their World Cup debut in 1999 and were competitive considering their relative rugby histories. Uruguay even recorded their first up World Cup win over Spain (27~15).

Spain finished bottom, but the main competitors in this group were as formidable as they come, with reigning World Cup champions South Africa defeating the 1999 'Five Nations' champions, Scotland (26~29) for the pool supremacy.

POOL A

A.1 Uruguay d. Spain (27~15)
2 October 1999, Netherdale, Galashiels.
Referee: Chris White (England).
Uruguay. Try: Ormaechea; Pen try; Cardoso, Menchaca; Con: Aguirre, Sciarra; Pen: Aguirre.
Spain. Pen: Kovalenco (5).

A.2 South Africa d. Scotland (46~29)
3 October 1999, Murrayfield, Edinburgh.
Referee: Colin Hawke (New Zealand).
South Africa. Try: Le Roux, Kayser, Van der Westhuizen, Fleck, A. Venter, B. Venter; Con: De Beer (5); Pen: De Beer (2).
Scotland. Try: M. Leslie, Tait; Con: Logan (2); Pen: Logan (4); Drop: Townsend.

A.3 Scotland d. Uruguay (43~12)
8 October 1999, Murrayfield, Edinburgh.
Referee: Stuart Dickinson (Australia).
Scotland. Try: Russell, Armstrong, Metcalfe, M. Leslie, Simpson, Townsend; Con: Logan (5); Pen: Logan.
Uruguay. Pen: Aguirre (3), Sciarra.

A.4 South Africa d. Spain (47~3)
10 October 1999, Murrayfield, Edinburgh.
Referee: Paul Honiss (New Zealand).
South Africa. Try: Vos (2), Leonard, Pen try, Muller, Skinstad, Swanepoel; Con: De Beer (6).
Spain. Pen: Velazco Querol.

A.5 South Africa d. Uruguay (39~3)
15 October 1999, Hampden Park, Glasgow.
Referee: Peter Marshall (Australia).
South Africa. Try: Van den Berg (2), Van der Westhuizen, Kayser, Fleck; Con: De Beer (4); Pen: De Beer (2).
Uruguay. Pen: Aguirre.

A.6 Scotland d. Spain (48~0)
16 October 1999, Murrayfield, Edinburgh.
Referee: Clayton Thomas (Wales).
Scotland. Try: Mather (2), McLaren, Longstaff, Hodge, C. Murray, Pen try; Con: Hodge (5); Pen: Hodge.
Spain. Nil.

Results	P	W	D	L	PF	PA	Pts
South Africa	3	3	0	0	132	35	9
Scotland	3	2	0	1	120	58	7
Uruguay	3	1	0	2	42	97	5
Spain	3	0	0	3	18	122	3

6. Lawrence Dallaglio, England (taken 2006).

7. McAlpine Stadium, Huddersfield, England.

POOL B - TEAMS

B	ENGLAND	ITALY	NEW ZEALAND	TONGA
Coaches:	Clive Woodward	Massimo Mascioletti	John Hart	Polutele Tu'ihalamaka
Players:	Gareth Archer	Matt Pini	Craig Dowd	David Edwards
	Neil Back	Nicola Mazzucato	Anton Oliver	Ta'u Fainga'anuku
	Richard Cockerill	Fabio Roselli	Greg Feek	Kuli Faletau
	Martin Corry	Nick Zisti	Robin Brooke	Puku Faletau
	Lawrence Dallaglio	Paolo Vaccari	Norm Maxwell	Isi Fatani
	Darren Garforth	Luca Martin	Andrew Blowers	Benhur Kivalu
	Phil Greening	Cristian Stoica	Josh Kronfeld	Sonatane Koloi
	Richard Hill	Sandro Ceppolino	Taine Randell (c)	Falamani Mafi
	Martin Johnson (c)	Diego Domínguez	Justin Marshall	Latiume Maka
	Jason Leonard	Francesco Mazzariol	Andrew Mehrtens	Tamieni Penisini
	Neil McCarthy	Alessandro Troncon	Jonah Lomu	Ngalu Ta'u
	Danny Grewcock	Giampiero Mazzi	Alama Ieremia	Tevita Taumoepeau
	Tim Rodber	Carlo Caione	Christian Cullen	Mat Te Pou
	Graham Rowntree	Mauro Bergamasco	Tana Umaga	Va'a Toloke
	Victor Ubogu	Massimo Giovanelli (c)	Jeff Wilson (vc)	Katilione Tu'ipulotu
	Phil Vickery	Andrea De Rossi	Daryl Gibson	Fe'ao Vunipola
	Joe Worsley	Stefano Saviozzi	Tony Brown	Semisi Faka'osifolau
	Nick Beal	Andrea Lo Cicero	Byron Kelleher	Salesi Finau (c)
	Kyran Bracken	Alejandro Moreno	Mark Hammett	Sililo Marten
	Mike Catt	Orazio Arancio	Carl Hoeft	Epeli Taione
	Matt Dawson	Laurent Travini	Ian Jones	Isi Tapueluelu
	Phil de Glanville	Carlo Checchinato	Dylan Mika	Taunaholo Taufahema
	Paul Grayson	Walter Cristofoletto	Rhys Duggan	Siua Taumalolo
	Will Greenwood	Mark Giacheri	Glen Osborne	Semi Taupeaafe
	Jeremy Guscott	Franco Properzi	Pita Alatini	Fepikou Tatafu
	Austin Healey	Andrea Castellani	Carlos Spencer	Tevita Tiueti
	Dan Luger	Giampiero de Carli	Kees Meeuws	Sateki Tu'ipulotu
	Matt Perry	Federico Pucciariello	Reuben Thorne	Sione Mone Tu'ipulotu
	David Rees	Alessandro Moscardi	Royce Willis	Elisi Vunipola
	Jonny Wilkinson	Andrea Moretti	Scott Robertson	Brian Wooley

POOL B

B.1 England d. Italy (67~7)

2 October 1999, Twickenham, London.
Attendance: 73,470; Referee: Andre Watson (South Africa).
England. *Try: Wilkinson, Hill, Luger, Back, De Glanville, Corry, Dawson, Perry, Con: Wilkinson (6), Pen: Wilkinson (5).*
Italy. *Try: Dominguez; Con: Dominguez.*

B.2 New Zealand d. Tonga (45~9)

3 October 1999, Ashton Gate, Bristol.
Attendance: 22,000; Referee: Derek Bevan (Wales).
New Zealand. *Try: Lomu (2), Kelleher, Maxwell, Kronfeld; Con: Mehrtens (4); Pen: Mehrtens (4).*
Tonga. *Pen: Taumalolo (3).*

B.3 New Zealand d. England (30~16)

9 October 1999, Twickenham, London.
Attendance: 72,000; Referee: Peter Marshall (Australia).
New Zealand. *Try: Kelleher, Wilson, Lomu; Con: Mehrtens (3); Pen: Mehrtens (3).*
England. *Try: De Glanville; Con: Wilkinson; Pen: Wilkinson (3).*

B.4 Tonga d. Italy (28~25)

10 October 1999, Welford Road, Leicester.
Referee: David McHugh (Ireland).
Tonga. *Try: Taufahema, Fatani, Tuipulotu; Con: Tuipulotu (2); Pen: Tuipulotu (2); Drop: Tuipulotu.*
Italy. *Try: Moscardi; Con: Dominguez; Pen: Dominguez (6).*

B.5 New Zealand d. Italy (101~3)

14 October 1999, McAlpine Stadium, Huddersfield.
Attendance: 24,000; Referee: Jim Fleming (Scotland).
New Zealand. *Try: Wilson (3), Osborne (2), Lomu (2), Randell, Brown, Cullen, Hammett, Gibson, Robertson, Mika; Con: Brown (11); Pen: Brown (3).*
Italy. *Pen: Dominguez.*

B.6 England d. Tonga (101~10)

15 October 1999, Twickenham, London.
Attendance: 72,485; Referee: Wayne Erickson (Australia).
England. *Try: Guscott (2), Greening (2), Luger (2), Healey (2), Greenwood (2), Dawson, Perry, Hill; Con: Grayson (12); Pen: Grayson (4).*
Tonga. *Try: Tiueti; Con: Tuipulotu; Pen: Tuipulotu.*

Results	P	W	D	L	PF	PA	Pts
New Zealand	3	3	0	0	176	28	9
England	3	2	0	1	184	47	7
Tonga	3	1	0	2	47	171	5
Italy	3	0	0	3	35	196	3

Pool B Matches

The nations in Pool B consisted of **England, Italy, New Zealand** and **Tonga**. Both the Italian and Tongan teams were outclassed in this pool. Try as they might these sides had no answer to the sheer talent of New Zealand or England, although Tonga played well to defeat Italy (28~25) in their pool match.

Although both the All Blacks and England managed to reach triple figures in some matches, it was New Zealand that took top spot by defeating England (30~16).

8. The more than vocal English rugby fans.

POOL C - TEAMS

C	CANADA	FIJI	FRANCE	NAMIBIA
Coaches:	Patrick Parfrey	Brad Johnstone	Jean-Claude Skrela	Rudy Joubert
Players:	Ryan Banks	Daniel Rouse	Christian Califano	Sybrand de Beer
	Dan Baugh	Greg Smith	Pieter de Villiers	Mathys van Rooyen
	Richard Bice	Joeli Veitayaki	Cédric Soulette	Jaco Olivier
	Scott Bryan	Emori Katalau	Franck Tournaire	Schalk van der Merwe
	Mark Cardinal	Simon Raiwalui	Marc Dal Maso	Quinn Hough (c)
	Al Charron (vc)	Ifereimi Tawake	Raphaël Ibañez (c)	Sean Furter
	Jeremy Cordle	Setareki Tawake	David Auradou	Herman Lintvelt
	Pat Dunkley	Ilivasi Tabua	Abdelatif Benazzi	Heino Senekal
	John Graf	Jacob Rauluni	Olivier Brouzet	Eben Izaaks
	John Hutchinson	Nicky Little	Fabien Pelous	Pieter Steyn
	Mike James	Fero Lasagavibau	Arnaud Costes	Johannes Theron
	David Lougheed	Waisake Sotutu	Marc Lièvremont	Gerhard Opperman
	Julian Loveday	Viliame Satala	Olivier Magne	Mario Jacobs
	Duane Major	Marika Vunibaka	Lionel Mallier	Eben Smith
	Brian McCarthy	Alfred Uluinayau	Christophe Juillet	Andries Blaauw
	Kyle Nichols	Manasa Bari	Thomas Lièvremont	Hugo Horn
	Joe Pagano	Waisale Serevi	Stéphane Castaignède	Frans Fisch
	David Penney	Mosese Rauluni	Fabien Galthié (r)	Lean van Dyk
	Gareth Rees (c)	Epeli Naituivau	Pierre Mignoni (w)	Deon Mouton
	Rob Robson	Isaia Rasila	Thomas Castaignède	Glovin van Wyk
	Bob Ross	Apenisa Naevo	Christophe Lamaison	Dirk Farmer
	Mike Schmid	Alifereti Mocelutu	Cédric Desbrosse	Arthur Samuelson
	Courtney Smith	Imanueli Tikomaimakogai	Richard Dourthe	Rudie J. van Vuuren
	Rod Snow	Meli Nakauta	Stéphane Glas	Lukas Holtzhausen
	Winston Stanley	Tabai Matson	Philippe Bernat-Salles	Cliff Loubsher
	Scott Stewart	Lawerence Little	Christophe Dominici	Francois van Rensburg
	John Tait	Niko Qoro	Jimmy Marlu	Johan Zaayman
	Jon Thiel	Koli Sewabu	Émile Ntamack	Ronaldo Pedro
	Chris Whittaker	Inoke Male	Ugo Mola	Riaan Jantjies
	Morgan Williams	Alifereti Doviverata	Olivier Sarramea	Sarel J. van Rensburg

9. Stade de Toulouse, Toulouse, France.

POOL C

C.1 Fiji d. Namibia (67~18)

1 October 1999, Stade de la Méditerranée, Béziers.
Referee: David McHugh (Ireland).
Fiji. Try: Lasagavibau (2), Naivaluwaqa, Raulini, Satala, Vuivau, Smith, Tikomaimakogai, Katalau; Con: Serevi (8); Pen: Serevi (2)
Namibia. Try: Jacobs, Senekal; Con: Van Dyk; Pen: Van Dyk (2).

C.2 France d. Canada (33~20)

2 October 1999, Stade de la Méditerranée, Béziers.
Referee: Brian Campsall (England).
France. Try: Ntamack, Glas, Castaignède, Magne; Con: Dourthe (2); Pen: Dourthe (3).
Canada. Try: Williams (2); Con: Ross, Rees; Pen: Ross,Rees.

C.3 France d. Namibia (47~13)

8 October 1999, Parc Lescure, Bordeaux.
Referee: Chris White (England).
France. Try: Mola (3), Ntamack, Mignoni, Bernat-Salles; Con: Dourthe (4); Pen: Dourthe (3).
Namibia. Try: Samuelson; Con: Van Dyk; Pen: Van Dyk (2).

C.4 Fiji d. Canada (38~22)

9 October 1999, Parc Lescure, Bordeaux.
Referee: Ed Morrison (England).
Fiji. Try: Satala (2), Vunibaka, Lasagavibau; Con: Little (3); Pen: Little (3); Drop: Little.
Canada. Try: James; Con: Rees; Pen: Rees (4); Drop: Rees.

C.5 Canada d. Namibia (72~11)

14 October 1999, Stade de Toulouse.
Referee: Andrew Cole (Australia).
Canada. Try: Stanley (2), Snow (2), Nichols (2), Charron, Ross, Williams; Con: Rees (9); Pen: Rees (3).
Namibia. Try: Hough; Pen: Van Dyk (2).

C.6 France d. Fiji (28~19)

16 October 1999, Stade de Toulouse.
Referee: Paddy O'Brien (New Zealand).
France. Try: Juillet, Dominici, Pen try; Con: Dourthe (2); Pen: Dourthe (2), Lamaison.
Fiji. Try: Uluinayau; Con: Little; Pen: Little (4).

Results	P	W	D	L	PF	PA	Pts
France	3	3	0	0	108	52	9
Fiji	3	2	0	1	124	68	7
Canada	3	1	0	2	114	82	5
Namibia	3	0	0	3	42	186	3

10. Wax model of Jonah Lomu, New Zealand.

Pool C Matches

The nations in Pool C consisted of **Canada, Fiji, France** and **Namibia**. The Namibians made their World Cup debut, but were outclassed by the other three teams in this pool. Canada showed great attacking strength in all their matches, scoring a total of 114 points (38 point average per game).

After missing the 1995 tournament Fiji returned to the World Cup with a vengeance recording wins over both Canada and Namibia, but lost narrowly to France (19~28), which decided the group placings.

11. Racecource Ground, Wrexham, Wales.

POOL D - TEAMS

D	ARGENTINA	JAPAN	SAMOA	WALES
Coaches:	Alex Wyllie	Seiji Hirao	Bryan Williams	Graham Henry
	Héctor Mendéz			
Players:	Fernando Díaz Alberdi	Shin Hasegawa	Mike Umaga	Peter Rogers
	Roberto Diego Grau	Toshikazu Nakamichi	Silao Leaega	Andy Lewis
	Omar Hasan	Masahiro Kunda	Tanner Vili	Dai Young
	Mauricio Reggiardo	Masaaki Sakata	Brian Lima	Ben Evans
	Martín Scelzo	Naoto Nakamura	Afato Sooalo	Garin Jenkins
	Mario Ledesma	Kohei Oguchi	Va'aiga Tuigamala	Jonathan Humphreys
	Agustín Canalda	Robert Gordon	Filipo Toala	Chris Wyatt
	Pedro Sporleder	Naoya Okubo	To'o Vaega	Craig Quinnell
	Alejandro Allub	Yoshihiko Sakuraba	George Leaupepe	Mike Voyle
	Ignacio Fernández Lobbe	Hiroyuki Tanuma	Terry Fanolua	Andy Moore
	Raúl Pérez	Greg Smith	Stephen Bachop	Gareth Llewellyn
	Santiago Phelan	Yasunori Watanabe	Earl Va'a	Colin Charvis
	Rolando Martin	Hajime Kiso	Steven Soialo	Geraint Lewis
	Lucas Ostiglia	Ryuji Ishi	Jon Clarke	Scott Quinnell
	Miguel Ruiz	Jamie Joseph	Pat Lam	Brett Sinkinson
	Gonzalo Longo	Takeomi Ito	Junior Paramore	Martyn Williams
	Nicolás Fernández Miranda	Graeme Bachop	Sene Taala	Shane Howarth
	Agustín Pichot	Wataru Murata	Kalolo Toleafoa	Neil Boobyer
	Gonzalo Quesada	Keiji Hirose	Craig Glendinning	Gareth Thomas
	José Cilley	Kensuke Iwabuchi	Semo Sititi	Dafydd James
	Felipe Contepomi	Andrew McCormick (c)	Isaac Feaunati	Nick Walne
	Lisandro Arbizu	Yukio Motoki	Lio Falaniko	Allan Bateman
	José Orengo	Akira Yoshida	Lama Tone	Scott Gibbs
	Eduardo Simone	Atsushi Koga	Opeta Palepoi	Mark Taylor
	Diego Albanese	Terunori Masuho	Kepi Faivaai	Leigh Davies
	Octavio Bartolucci	Daisuke Ohata	Robbie Ale	Jason Jones-Hughes
	Ignacio Corleto	Patiliai Tuidraki	Brendan Reidy	Neil Jenkins
	Manuel Contepomi	Ryohei Miki	Mike Mika	Stephen Jones
	Gonzalo Camardón	Tsutomu Matsuda	Trevor Leota	Rob Howley
	Juan Fernández Miranda	Takafumi Hirao	Onehunga Matauiau	Dai Llewellyn

12. Australian fans getting wound up.

Pool D Matches

The nations in Pool D consisted of **Argentina, Japan, Samoa** and **Wales**. Japan were a grade below Wales, Samoa and Argentina, but it was fascinating to watch the three more evenly matched teams battle for pool placings. Wales defeated Argentina, who defeated Samoa, who defeated Wales!

Helped along by their home crowd the Welsh took out the group on points with Samoa coming in second. But Argentina also qualified for the quarter final playoff round, being the best third placed team.

POOL D

D.1 Wales d. Argentina (23~18)

1 October 1999, Millennium Stadium, Cardiff.
Referee: Paddy O'Brien (New Zealand).
Wales. Try: Charvis, Taylor; Con: Jenkins (2); Pen: Jenkins (3).
Argentina. Pen: Quesada (6).

D.2 Samoa d. Japan (43~9)

3 October 1999, Racecourse Ground, Wrexham.
Referee: Andrew Cole (Australia).
Samoa. Try: Lima (2), So'oialo (2), Leaegailesolo; Con:
Leaegailesolo (3); Pen: Leaegailesolo (4).
Japan. Pen: Hirose (3).

D.3 Wales d. Japan (64~15)

9 October 1999, Millennium Stadium, Cardiff.
Referee: Joël Dume (France).
Wales. Try: Taylor (2), Howley, Gibbs, Llewellyn, Thomas,
Bateman, Howarth, Pen try; Con: Jenkins (8); Pen: Jenkins.
Japan. Try: Tuidraki, Ohata; Con: Hirose; Pen: Hirose.

D.4 Argentina d. Samoa (32~16)

10 October 1999, Stradey Park, Llanelli.
Referee: Wayne Erickson (Australia).
Argentina. Try: Allub; Pen: Quesada (8); Drop: Quesada.
Samoa. Try: Paramore; Con: Leaegailesolo; Pen:
Leaegailesolo (3).

D.5 Samoa d. Wales (38~31)

14 October 1999, Millennium Stadium, Cardiff.
Referee: Ed Morrison (England).
Samoa. Try: Bachop (2), Falaniko, Lam, Leaegailesolo; Con:
Leaegailesolo (5); Pen: Leaegailesolo.
Wales. Try: Thomas, Pen try (2); Con: Jenkins (2); Pen: Jenkins (4).

D.6 Argentina d. Japan (33~12)

16 October 1999, Millennium Stadium, Cardiff.
Referee: Stuart Dickinson (Australia).
Argentina. Try: Albanese, Pichot; Con: Contepomi; Pen:
Quesada (7).
Japan. Pen: Hirose (4).

Results	P	W	D	L	PF	PA	Pts
Wales	3	2	0	1	118	71	7
Samoa	3	2	0	1	97	72	7
Argentina	3	2	0	1	83	51	7
Japan	3	0	0	3	36	140	3

POOL E - TEAMS

E	AUSTRALIA	IRELAND	ROMANIA	USA
Coaches:	Rod MacQueen	Warren Gatland	Mircea Paraschiv	Jack Clark
Players:	Andrew Blades	Conor O'Shea	Constantin Tudor (c)	Vaea Anitoni
	Matt Burke	Girvan Dempsey	Dragos Niculae	Andre Blom
	Dan Crowley	Justin Bishop	Constantin Stan	Jesse Coulson
	Matt Cockbain	James Topping	Laurentiu Rotaru	Kevin Dalzell
	Mark Connors	Matt Mostyn	Nicolae Dima	Juan Grobler
	John Eales (c)	Kevin Maggs	Florin Marioara	Brian Hightower
	Michael Foley	Brian O'Driscoll	Răzvan Mavrodin	David Niu
	Owen Finegan	Jonathan Bell	Petru Bălan	Alatini Saulala
	George Gregan (vc)	Mike Mullins	Stefan Demci	Mark Scharrenberg
	Nathan Grey	David Humphreys	Ovidiu Tonita	Rich Schurfeld
	David Giffin	Eric Elwood	Adrian Petrache	Kurt Shuman
	Richard Harry	Tom Tierney	Catalin Draguceanu	Dave Stroble
	Daniel Herbert	Brian O'Meara	Tiberiu Brînză	Tomasi Takau
	Tim Horan	Paul Wallace	Adrian Petrache	Sinapati Uiagalelei
	Rod Kafer	Peter Clohessy	Daniel Chiriac	Mark Williams
	Phil Kearns	Reggie Corrigan	Florin Corodeanu	Tom Billups
	Toutai Kefu	Justin Fitzpatrick	Marius Tincu	Joe Clayton
	Stephen Larkham	Angus McKeen	Erdinci Septar	Luke Gross
	Chris Latham	Keith Wood	Petre Mitu	Dave Hodges
	Jason Little	Ross Nesdale	Marius Iacob	Kirk Khasigian
	Patricio Noriega	Paddy Johns	Lucian Sîrbu	Marc L'Huillier
	Jeremy Paul	Jeremy Davidson	Lucien Vusec	Ray Lehner
	Brett Robinson	Malcolm O'Kelly	Mihai Ciolacu	Rob Lumkong
	Joe Roff	Bob Casey	Tonut Tofan	Dan Lyle (c)
	Scott Staniforth	Dion O'Cuinneagain	Romeo Gontineac	Fifita Mo'unga
	Tiaan Strauss	Eric Miller	Gabriel Brezoianu	Shaun Paga
	Ben Tune	David Corkery	Christian Lupu	Alec Parker
	Chris Whitaker	Trevor Brennan	Radu Fugigi	Eric Reed
	David Wilson	Andy Ward	Gheorghe Solomie	George Sucher
	Jim Williams	Kieron Dawson	Cristian Sauan	Richard Tardits
			Cristian Hildan	
			Mihai Vioreanu	

13. Thormond Park Stadium, Limerick, Ireland.

POOL E

E.1 Ireland d. United States (53~8)

2 October 1999, Lansdowne Road, Dublin.
Attendance: 30,000; Referee: Joël Dume (France).
Ireland. Try: Wood (4), Elwood (2), O'Driscoll, Bishop; Con: Humphreys (5); Pen: Humphreys.
United States. Try: Dalzell; Pen: Dalzell.

E.2 Australia d. Romania (57~9)

3 October 1999, Ravenhill, Belfast.
Attendance: 12,500; Referee: Paul Honiss (New Zealand).
Australia. Try: Kefu (3), Roff (2), Kafer, Burke, Little, Horan; Con: Burke (5), Eales.
Romania. Pen: Mitu (3).

E.3 Romania d. United States (27~25)

9 October 1999, Lansdowne Road, Dublin.
Attendance: 3,000; Referee: Jim Fleming (Scotland).
Romania. Try: Petrache (2), Solomie (2); Con: Mitu (2); Pen: Mitu.
United States. Try: Shuman, Hightower, Lyle; Con: Dalzell (2); Pen: Dalzell (2).

E.4 Australia d. Ireland (23~3)

10 October 1999, Lansdowne Road, Dublin.
Referee: Clayton Thomas (Wales).
Australia. Try: Tune, Horan; Con: Burke (2); Pen: Burke (2), Eales.
Ireland. Pen: Humphreys

E.5 Australia d. United States (55~19)

14 October 1999, Thomond Park, Limerick.
Attendance: 13,000; Referee: Andre Watson (South Africa).
Australia. Try: Staniforth (2), Latham, Whitaker, Foley, Burke, Larkham, Strauss; Con: Burke (5); Roff; Pen: Burke.
United States. Try: Grobler; Con: Dalzell; Pen: Dalzell (4).

E.6 Ireland d. Romania (44~14)

15 October 1999, Lansdowne Road, Dublin.
Attendance: 33,000; Referee: Brian Campsall (England).
Ireland. Try: O'Shea (2), Ward, Tierney, O'Cuinneagain; Con: Elwood (5); Pen: Elwood (2); Drop: O'Driscoll.
Romania. Try: Sauan; Pen: Mitu (3).

Results	P	W	D	L	PF	PA	Pts
Australia	3	3	0	0	135	31	9
Ireland	3	2	0	1	100	45	7
Romania	3	1	0	2	50	126	5
USA	3	0	0	3	52	135	3

Pool E Matches

The nations in Pool E consisted of **Australia, Ireland, Romania** and the **United States**. Arriving fresh from winning the 'Bledisloe Cup' for the second year in a row against New Zealand, Australia were firming as Cup favourites and they recorded relatively easy wins over all of their pool opponents.

Buoyed by the support of their home crowds, Ireland finished second in the pool through easy wins against both Romania and the USA.

14. George Gregan, Australia (taken 2013).

15. Stade Felix Bollaert, Lens, France.

THE PLAYOFFS

Quarter Final Playoffs

The five group runners-up and the best third-placed team from the group stage, which was Argentina, contested the quarter final play-offs in three one-off matches to decide the remaining three places in the quarter-finals.

England played an intelligent game to defeat the unpredictable and in form Fijians (45~24), grabbing a quarter final berth against

QF PLAYOFFS

PO1 England d. Fiji (45~24)

20 October 1999, Twickenham, London.
Referee: Clayton Thomas (Wales).
England. *Try: Luger, Back, Beal, Greening; Con: Dawson, Wilkinson; Pen: Wilkinson (7).*
Fiji. *Try: Satala, Nakauta, Tikomaimakogai; Con: Little (3); Pen: Serevi.*

PO2 Scotland d. Samoa (35~20)

20 October 1999, Murrayfield, Edinburgh.
Referee: David McHugh (Ireland).
Scotland. *Try: C. Murray, M. Leslie, Pen try; Con: Logan; Pen: Logan (5); Drop: Townsend.*
Samoa. *Try: Lima, Sititi; Con: Leaegailesolo (2); Pen: Leaegailesolo (2).*

PO3 Argentina d. Ireland (28~24)

20 October 1999, Stade Félix Bollaert, Lens.
Attendance: 41,320; Referee: Stuart Dickinson (Australia).
Argentina. *Try: Albanese; Con: Quesada; Pen: Quesada (7).*
Ireland. *Pen: Humphreys (7); Drop: Humphreys.*

South Africa. Scotland fought hard to defeat Samoa (35~20), earning a quarter final slot against New Zealand. But Argentina caused a major stir by defeating and eliminating Ireland (28~24), which kept their Cup hopes alive with a quarter final berth against France.

Quarter Finals

The crossover format of the four quarter finals saw Australia defeat Wales (24~9) with a three try to nil performance to firm as tournament favourites. Then, in what became

QUARTER FINALS

QF1 Australia d. Wales (24~9)

23 October 1999, Millennium Stadium, Cardiff.
Attendance: 74,499; Referee: Colin Hawke (New Zealand).
Australia. Try: Gregan (2), Tune; Con: Burke (3); Pen: Burke.
Wales. Pen: Jenkins (3).

QF 2 South Africa d. England (44~21)

24 October 1999, Stade de France, Saint-Denis.
Referee: Jim Fleming (Scotland).
South Africa. Try: Van der Westhuizen, P. Rossouw; Con: De Beer (2); Pen: De Beer (5); Drop: De Beer (5).
England. Pen: Grayson (6), Wilkinson.

QF3 New Zealand d. Scotland (30~18)

24 October 1999, Murrayfield, Edinburgh.
Attendance: 67,529; Referee: Ed Morrison (England).
New Zealand. Try: Umaga (2), Wilson, Lomu; Con: Mehrtens (2); Pen: Mehrtens (2).
Scotland. Try: C. Murray, Pountney; Con: Logan; Pen: Logan; Drop: Townsend.

QF4 France d. Argentina (47~26)

24 October 1999, Lansdowne Road, Dublin.
Referee: Derek Bevan (Wales).
France. Try: Garbajosa (2), Bernat-Salles (2), Ntamack; Con: Lamaison (5); Pen: Lamaison (4).
Argentina. Try: Pichot, Arbizu; Con: Quesada (2); Pen: Quesada (3), Contepomi.

16. Murrayfield Stadium, Edinburgh, Scotland.

17. Twickenham Stadium, London, England.

mostly a kickers game with 18 goals being scored, the South Africans disposed of England (44~21). Jannie De Beer scored 34 points with five drop goals in this match.

The Scots did all they could to resist a powerful New Zealand team in front of their home crowd at Murrayfield, but the All Blacks personnel was just too talented (30~18). France overcame the Puma's (47~26) to gain their semi final berth, but Argentina's fine performance in this tournament was roundly applauded.

Semi Finals

In the semi finals France was the only team left to defend the honour of the northern hemisphere nations.

The semi finals, which were both played at Twickenham Stadium in London, produced two of the closest matches of the tournament.

In the first semi final, Australia led at the half time break and went ahead twice more only to be equaled by the Springboks. After the regular

SEMI FINALS

Semi Final 1

Australia d. South Africa (27~21 xt)

30 October 1999, Twickenham, London.
Referee: Derek Bevan (Wales).
Australia. Pen: Burke (8); Drop: Larkham.
South Africa. Pen: De Beer (6); Drop: De Beer.

Semi Final 2

France d. New Zealand (43~31)

31 October 1999, Twickenham, London.
Referee: Jim Fleming (Scotland).
France. Try: Lamaison, Dominici, Dourthe, Bernat-Salles; Con: Lamaison (4); Pen: Lamaison (3); Drop: Lamaison (2).
New Zealand. Try: Lomu (2), Wilson; Con: Mehrtens (2); Pen: Mehrtens (4).

match ended with scores locked at 18 points each, the Australians eventually defeated South Africa (27~21) in extra-time, with no tries scored in the game.

The second semi-final between favourites New Zealand and underdogs France was an all-time classic encounter. New Zealand surged ahead from the kick off with Jonah Lomu scoring twice. But France overturned a 10-24 deficit by scoring three second half tries to defeat the All Blacks (43~31) and reach their second World Cup final.

3rd Place Playoff

The playoff for third place was surprisingly contested between South Africa and New Zealand and played at Millenium Stadium in Cardiff, in front of 50,000 spectators on the 4th November 1999.

Although New Zealand drew first blood, South Africa led from the 12th minute on

FINALS

FINAL
Australia d. France (35~12)

6 November 1999, Millennium Stadium, Cardiff.
Attendance: 72,500; Referee: André Watson (South Africa).
Australia. *Try: Tune, Finegan; Con: Burke (2); Pen: Burke (7).*
France. *Pen: Lamaison (4).*

3rd/4th Playoff
South Africa d. New Zealand (22~18)

4 November 1999, Millennium Stadium, Cardiff.
Attendance: 50,000; Referee: Peter Marshall (Australia).
South Africa. *Try: Paulse; Con: Honiball; Pen: Honiball (3);*
Drop: Montgomery (2).
New Zealand. *Pen: Mehrtens (6).*

and scored the only try of the match. Despite the All Blacks catching up to be just one point adrift (18~19) at the 71st minute, the Springboks scored again and held on for the bronze medal (22~18).

THE FINALS

France and Australia met at the Millennium Stadium on 6th November 1999. The game began evenly with two penalties goals apiece midway through the first half. But Australia gradually applied

18. Millenium Stadium, Cardiff, Wales.

the pressure and were never headed from that point on. The Wallabies scored two tries to none with a superb kicking game by Matthew Burke, who booted nine goals in the match. Australia overcame France (35~12) to win the tournament and take possession of the Webb Ellis Cup.

In winning the tournament, Australia became the first nation to do so twice and also the only team ever to win after having to qualify for the tournament. The Rugby World Cup was personally presented by Her Majesty Queen Elizabeth II to the successful Australian captain, John Eales.

CREDITS

TEXT

This article uses material from the Wikipedia article https://en.wikipedia.org/wiki/1999_Rugby_World_Cup which is released under the http://creativecommons.org/licenses/by-sa/3.0/ Creative Commons Attribution-Share-Alike License 3.0.

IMAGES

1. 'Glanmor's Gap, Millennium Stadium, Cardiff, Wales' by al green (29 Nov 2008). Available at https://commons.wikimedia.org/wiki/File:Glanmor%27s_Gap,_Millennium_Stadium,_Cardiff.jpg under the Creative Commons Attribution 2.0 Generic license.

2. 'Ashton Gate Stadium during the daytime' by SGGH (18 Jul 2010). Available at https://commons.wikimedia.org/wiki/File:Ashton_Gate_Stadium_(daytime).jpg Creative Commons Attribution-Share Alike 3.0 Unported license.

3. 'Rugby Fans from Wales on the Streets Of Dublin' by informatique (8 Maar 2008). Available at https://commons.wikimedia.org/wiki/File:RUGBY_FANS_FROM_WALES.jpg under the Creative Commons Attribution-Share Alike 2.0 Generic license.

4. 'Parc Lescure, Bordeaux' by TaraO (8 Apr 2006). Available at https://commons.wikimedia.org/wiki/File:Panorama_Chaban-Delmas.jpg under the Creative Commons Attribution-Share Alike 3.0 Unported license.

5. 'Netherdale, home of Gala Rugby Football Club' by Wallter Baxter (1 Jan 2007). Available at https://upload.wikimedia.org/wikipedia/commons/a/a1/Netherdale_-_geograph-302251.jpg under the Creative Commons Attribution-Share Alike 2.0 Generic license.

6. 'England Rugby Union Player Lawrence Dallaglio' by zoonabar (8 Oct 2006). Available at https://commons.wikimedia.org/wiki/File:Lawrence_Dallaglio_2006.jpg under the Creative Commons Attribution 2.0 Generic license.

7. 'Players warming up at half-time during the Huddersfield Town versus Bradford City fixture in the Football League Cup at the Galpharm Stadium on 12 August 2008' by Peanut4 (12 Aug 2008). Available at https://commons.wikimedia.org/wiki/File:Huddersfield_002.jpg under the Creative Commons Attribution-Share Alike 3.0 Unported license.

8. 'England rugby fans' by digiarnie (15 Nov 2008). Available at https://commons.wikimedia.org/wiki/File:English_Fans.jpg under the Creative Commons Attribution 2.0 Generic license.

9. 'Stade de Toulouse' by Caroline Lena Becker (28 May 2012). Available at https://commons.wikimedia.org/wiki/File:Aerial_Toulouse_01.JPG under the Creative Commons Attribution 3.0 Unported license.

10. 'Jonah Lomu, New Zealand rugby union player, from Madame Tussauds wax museum in London' by http://www.flickr.com/photos/alfahad91/ (21 June 2007). Available at https://commons.wikimedia.org/wiki/File:Jonah_Lomu_Madame_Tussaud_london.jpg under the Creative Commons Attribution-Share Alike 2.0 Generic license. Full terms at http://creativecommons.org/licenses/by/2.0.

11. 'Racecourse Ground, Wrexham' by Markbarnes (5 May 2007). Available at https://commons.wikimedia.org/wiki/File:Wrexham_FC.jpg under the Creative Commons Attribution-Share Alike 3.0 Unported license.

12. 'Australian supporters' by Tracy Rockwell (Sep 2000).

13. 'Thomond Park, Limerick... home of Munster' by James Corbett (1 Nov 2008). Available at https://commons.wikimedia.org/wiki/File:Thomond_Park.jpg under the Creative Commons Attribution-Share Alike 2.0 Generic license.

14. 'George Gregan' by Eva Rinaldi (14 May 2013). Available at https://commons.wikimedia.org/wiki/File:George_Gregan.jpg under the Creative Commons Attribution-Share Alike 2.0 Generic license.

15. 'Bollaert Stadium, Lens, France, Rugby World Cup England v USA' by Liondartois (8 Sep 2007). Available at https://commons.wikimedia.org/wiki/File:Stade_Bollaert_(Coupe_du_Monde_de_Rugby_2007).jpg under the Creative Commons Attribution-Share Alike 3.0 Unported license.

16. 'Murrayfield hosting a Scotland rugby match, this was taken at half time in the Rugby World Cup 2007' by Alistairjh (Nov 2008). Available at https://commons.wikimedia.org/wiki/File:MurrayfieldRugbyWorldCup.JPG under the Creative Commons Attribution 3.0 Unported license.

17. 'Twickenham rugby stadium, from the North Stand' by Gareth Owen (24 Dec 2005). Available at https://commons.wikimedia.org/wiki/File:Twickenham_rfu.jpg This work has been released into the public domain by its author, Gareth Owen at the English Wikipedia project. This applies worldwide.

18. 'Millennium Stadium, Cardiff, Wales' by al_green (14 Feb 2008). Available at https://upload.wikimedia.org/wikipedia/commons/6/68/Millennium_Stadium_panoramic_view.jpg under the Creative Commons Attribution-Share Alike 2.0 Generic license.

Full terms at http://creativecommons.org/licenses/by/2.0.

2003
V RUGBY WORLD CUP
Australia

1. Englands victory parade, London.

V Rugby World Cup

10th October to 22nd November, 2003

2. In lead-up tests France drew 20~20 with New Zealand at the Stade de France in Paris, on the 16th November 2002.

The 2003 Rugby World Cup was the fifth Rugby Union World Cup and ran from the 10th October to the 22nd November 2003.

THE HOST

Australia won the right to host the 2003 World Cup without the involvement of New Zealand after a contractual dispute over ground signage rights between the New Zealand Rugby Football Union and Rugby World Cup Limited. Australia and New Zealand had been expected to co-host the event with New Zealand expected to host 23 of the 48 matches. But New Zealand's insistence on amending the provisions relating to stadium advertising was unacceptable to the IRB. The tournament was spread across all States of Australia with New South Wales providing four venues, Queensland two, and Victoria, Western Australia, South Australia, Tasmania and the ACT each providing one venue. The attendance totaled 1,837,547, an average of 38,282 spectators per match!

THE TEAMS

Following the complex format used in the 1999 Rugby World Cup a simpler competition format was introduced. With 40 matches being played in the pool stage and another eight matches in the knock-out stage, the 2003 Rugby World Cup was the largest tournament to be played to date.

Seeded Teams

All quarter finalists from the 1999 tournament qualified for the 2003 Rugby World Cup. This meant that **France, New Zealand, South Africa, Wales, Scotland, England** and **Argentina** all automatically qualified for the event, and were joined by **Australia** as the host nation.

Qualifying Teams

All other nations vying for a place in the tournament had to qualify for the remaining 12 places through a series of qualification matches, which were contested by a record 81 teams.

Namibia won the single African Zone place over teams from Kenya, Zimbabwe, Ivory Coast, Tunisia, Morocco,

3. South Africa defeats Georgia 46~19 in their Pool C match during the 2003 Rugby World Cup.

105

4. Aussie Stadium, Sydney AU.

Zambia, Cameroon, Uganda, Botswana, Madagascar and Swaziland. **Canada** and **Uruguay** won the two American Zone places over teams from Trinidad & Tobago, Brazil, Venezuela, Peru, Colombia, Guyana, Bermuda, St Lucia, Cayman Islands, Jamaica, Bahamas, Barbados, Chile, the United States and Paraguay.

The European Zone had four places up for grabs, which was contested across five separate rounds by 32 nations. **Ireland, Romania, Georgia** and **Italy** all eventually qualified over teams from Croatia, Russia, Denmark, Latvia, Moldova, Norway, Bulgaria, the Netherlands, Ukraine, Poland, Belgium, Yugoslavia, Switzerland, Israel, Austria, Bosnia & Herzegovina, Portugal, Germany, Czech Republic, Slovenia, Andorra, Sweden, Hungary, Spain, Monaco, Malta, Lithuania and Luxembourg.

Russia defeated Spain on aggregate over two matches (58~41) to determine who could contest the repechage round. However, it was determined that Russia had used ineligible South African players, and were ejected from the competition with Spain advancing to the repechage.

Japan won the single Asian Zone spot over teams from Malaysia, China, Sri Lanka, Kazakhstan, South Korea, Hong Kong, Chinese Taipei, Thailand, Singapore and the Arabian Gulf. **Fiji** and **Samoa** won the two Oceania Zone places over teams from the Cook Islands, Vanuatu, Niue, Solomon Islands, Papua New Guinea, Tahiti and Tonga.

Repechage Teams

There were two repechage positions available in the 2003 Rugby World Cup. The **United States** and **Tonga** eventually qualified through the repechage rounds over teams from Spain, Tunisia and South Korea.

THE POOL STAGE

A total of 48 matches scheduled across 44 days (40 pool stage and 8 knock-out) were played throughout the tournament. With the 20 teams being divided into four pools of five nations, the top two teams in each pool progressed to the knock-out quarter-final stage.

For the first time, a bonus point (BP) system was implemented in pool play. This system was identical to that long used in Southern Hemisphere tournaments, and was soon adopted in most European competitions, though not for the 'Six Nations'.

Teams received four points for a win, two points for a draw and zero points for a loss before any possible bonus points were awarded. Teams could also gain one bonus point for scoring four or more tries, regardless of the final score, and could also gain one bonus point for a loss by seven points or fewer.

In lead up matches, France and New Zealand played a 20~20 draw at the Stade de France in Paris on 16th November 2002.

POOL A - TEAMS

A	ARGENTINA	AUSTRALIA	IRELAND	NAMIBIA	ROMANIA
Coaches:	Marcelo Loffreda	Eddie Jones	Eddie O'Sullivan	David Waterston	Bernard Charreyre
Players:	Ignacio Corleto	Matt Burke	Tyrone Howe	Deon Grunschloss	Danut Dumbrava
	Manuel Contepomi	Chris Latham	Girvan Dempsey	Jurie Booysen	Romeo Gontineac
	Martin Gaitan	Matt Giteau	Paddy Wallace	Vincent Dreyer	Valentin Maftei
	José Orengo	Nathan Grey	Kevin Maggs	Du Preez Grobler	Gabriel Brezoianu
	Diego Albanese	Stirling Mortlock	Brian O'Driscoll	Corne Powell	Vasile Ghioc
	José María Nuñez Piossek	Mat Rogers	Anthony Horgan	Deon Mouton	Cristian Sauan
	Hernan Senillosa	Morgan Turinui	Shane Horgan	Melrick Africa	Ion Teodorescu
	Felipe Contepomi	Joe Roff	John Kelly	Morne Schreuder	Mihai Vioreanu
	Juan Fernandez Miranda	Wendell Sailor	David Humphreys	Rudi van Vuuren	Bogdan Voicu
	Juan Hernández	Lote Tuqiri	Ronan O'Gara	Emile Wessels	Ionut Tofan
	Gonzalo Quesada	Elton Flatley	Neil Doak	Hakkies Husselman	Iulian Andrei
	Nicolas Fernandez	Stephen Larkham	Guy Easterby	Regardt Kruger	Cristian Podea
	Agustín Pichot	George Gregan	Peter Stringer	Ronaldo Pedro	Lucian Sirbu
	Roberto Grau	Chris Whitaker	Simon Best	Neil Swanepoel	Silviu Florea
	Omar Hasan	Al Baxter	Reggie Corrigan	Andries Blaauw	Paulica Ion
	Mauricio Reggiardo	Ben Darwin	John Hayes	Neil du Toit	Cezar Popescu
	Rodrigo Roncero	Peter Fa'alau	Marcus Horan	Johan Jenkins	Marcel Socaciu
	Martin Scelzo	Bill Young	David Wallace	Kees Lensing	Petrişor Toderasc
	Mario Ledesma	Brendan Cannon	Shane Byrne	Phillipus Isaacs	Petru Balan
	Federico Mendez	Jeremy Paul	Frankie Sheahan	Johannes Meyer	Răzvan Mavrodin
	Patricio Albacete	David Giffin	Keith Wood	Cor Van Tonder	Marius Pantelimon
	Rimas Alvarez	Justin Harrison	Gary Longwell	Archie Graham	Cristian Petre
	I. Fernandez Lobbe	Nathan Sharpe	Donncha O'Callaghan	Eben Isaacs	Augustin Petrechei
	Pedro Sporleder	Daniel Vickerman	Paul O'Connell	Heino Senekal	Sorin Socol
	Pablo Bouza	Matt Cockbain	Malcolm O'Kelly	Shaun van Rooi	George Chiriac
	Martin Durand	David Croft	Victor Costello	Wolfie Duvenhage	Marius Niculai
	Rolando Martin	George Smith	Simon Easterby	Herman Lintvelt	Florin Tatu
	Lucas Ostiglia	Phil Waugh	Keith Gleeson	Schalk van der Merwe	Ovidiu Tonita
	Santiago Phelan	David Lyons	Anthony Foley	Sean Furter	Bogdan Tudor
	Gonzalo Longo	John Roe	Eric Miller	Jurgens van Lill	Marian Tudori

5. Stephen Larkham, Australia.

6. Marcus Horan, Ireland.

Pool A Matches

The nations in Pool A consisted of **Argentina, Australia, Ireland, Namibia** and **Romania**. The tournament began with the host nation Australia defeating Argentina (24~8) at Telstra Stadium in Sydney. But both the Romanian and Namibian teams were outclassed in this company.

So the attention focused on whether Ireland or Argentina would progress to the quarter finals. Ireland played magnificently to lose by just the single point to Australia (16~17), and Argentina in turn lost to Ireland also by just one point (15~16), which would otherwise have carried them into the quarter finals in Ireland's place.

Results	P	W	D	L	PF	PA	BP	Pts
Australia	4	4	0	0	273	32	2	18
Ireland	4	3	0	1	141	56	3	15
Argentina	4	2	0	2	140	57	3	11
Romania	4	1	0	3	65	192	1	5
Namibia	4	0	0	4	28	310	0	0

A.1 Australia d. Argentina (24~8)

10 October 2003, Telstra Stadium, Sydney.
Attendance: 81,350; Referee: Paul Honiss (New Zealand).
Australia. Try: Sailor, Roff; Con: Flatley; Pen: Flatley (4).
Argentina. Try: Corleto; Pen: M. Contepomi.

A.2 Ireland d. Romania (45~17)

11 October 2003, Central Coast Stadium, Gosford.
Attendance: 19,123; Referee: Jonathan Kaplan (South Africa).
Ireland. Try: S. Horgan, Wood, Hickie (2), Costello; Con:
Humphreys (3), O'Gara; Pen: Humphreys (4).
Romania. Try: Pen try, Maftei; Con: Tofan, Vioreanu; Pen: Tofan.

A.3 Argentina d. Namibia (67~14)

14 October 2003, Central Coast Stadium, Gosford.
Attendance: 17,887; Referee: Nigel Whitehouse (Wales).
Argentina. Tries: Méndez, Bouza (2), J. Fernández Miranda, Pen
try (2), Gaitán (3); Con: Quesada (7); Pen:
Quesada.
Namibia. Tries: Grobier, Husselman; Con: Wessels (2).

A.4 Australia d. Romania (90~8)

18 October 2003, Suncorp Stadium, Brisbane.
Attendance: 48,778; Referee: Pablo De Luca (Argentina).
Australia. Tries: Flatley, Rogers (3), Burke (2), Larkham (2),
Mortlock, Roff, Giteau, Tuqin, Smith; Con: Flatley (11); Pen:
Flatley.
Romania. Tries: Toderasc; Pen: Tofan.

A.5 Ireland d. Namibia (64~7)

19 October 2003, Aussie Stadium, Sydney.
Attendance: 35,382; Referee: Andrew Cole (Australia).
Ireland. Tries: Quinlan (2), Dempsey, Hickie, Horan, Miller (2), G.
Easterby, S. Horgan, Kelly; Con: O'Gara (7).
Namibia. Tries: Powell; Con: Wessels.

A.6 Argentina d. Romania (50~3)

22 October 2003, Aussie Stadium, Sydney.
Attendance: 33,673; Referee: Chris White (England).
Argentina. Tries: Gaitán, Hernández (2), M. Contepomi, N.
Fernández Miranda, Bouza (2); Con: J. Fernández Miranda (4),
Quesada (2); Pen: J. Fernández Miranda.
Romania. Pen: Ionut Tofan.

A.7 Australia d. Namibia (142~0)

25 October 2003, Adelaide Oval.
Attendance: 28,196; Referee: Joël Jutge (France).
Australia. Tries: Latham (5), Lyons, Mortlock, Tuqiri (3), Pen try,
Rogers (2), Paul, Giteau (3), Grey, Turinui (2), Burke, Roe; Con:
Rogers (16).
Namibia. Nil.
(This remains the biggest winning margin in Rugby World Cup history.)

A.8 Ireland d. Argentina (16~15)

26 October 2003, Adelaide Oval.
Attendance: 30,203; Referee: André Watson (South Africa).
Ireland. Tries: Quinlan; Con: Humphreys; Pen: Humphreys,
O'Gara (2).
Argentina. Pen: Quesada (3); Drop: Quesada, Corleto.

A.9 Romania d. Namibia (37~7)

30 October 2003, York Park, Launceston.
Attendance: 15,457; Referee: Peter Marshall (Australia).
Romania. Tries: Petrichei, Sirbu, Chiriac, Teodorescu, Sauan; Con:
Tofan (3); Pen: Tofan (2).
Namibia. Tries: Isaacs; Con: Wessels.

A.10 Australia d. Ireland (17~16)

1 November 2003, Telstra Dome, Melbourne.
Attendance: 54,206; Referee: Paddy O'Brien (New Zealand)
Australia. Tries: Smith; Pen: Flatley (3); Drop: Gregan.
Ireland. Tries: O'Driscoll; Con: O'Gara; Pen: O'Gara (2); Drop:
O'Driscoll.

7. Suncorp Stadium, Brisbane AU.

POOL B - TEAMS

B	FIJI	FRANCE	JAPAN	SCOTLAND	USA
Coaches:	Mac McCallion	Bernard Laporte	Shogo Mukai	Ian McGeechan	Tom Billups
Players:	Isikeli Nacewa	Jean-Jacques Crenca	Tsutomu Matsuda	Cameron Mather	John Buchholz
	Seru Rabeni	Raphaël Ibañez	Takashi Yoshida	Glenn Metcalfe	Paul Emerick
	Epeli Ruivadra	Sylvain Marconnet	George Konia	Andy Craig	Link Wilfley
	Aisea Tuilevu	Fabien Pelous	Yukio Motoki	Andrew Henderson	Kain Cross
	Alfred Uluinayau	Jérôme Thion	Hideki Namba	Ben Hinshelwood	Philip Eloff
	Rupeni Caucaunibuca	Serge Betsen	Ruben Parkinson	James McLaren	Jason Keyter
	Vilimoni Delasau	Olivier Magne	Junichi Hojo	Simon Danielli	Salesi Sika
	Norman Ligairi	Imanol Harinordoquy	Toru Kurihara	Kenny Logan	David Fee
	Saimoni Rokini	Fabien Galthié	Daisuke Ohata	Chris Paterson	Mose Timoteo
	Marika Vunibaka	Frédéric Michalak	Hirotoki Onozawa	Nikki Walker	Riaan van Zyl
	Nicky Little	Christophe Dominici	Keiji Hirose	Gordon Ross	Mike Hercus
	Moses Rauluni	Yannick Jauzion	Andrew Miller	Gregor Townsend	Matt Sherman
	Jacob Rauluni	Tony Marsh	Yuji Sonoda	Graeme Beveridge	Kevin Dalzell
	Richard Nyholt	Aurélien Rougerie	Takashi Tsuji	Michael Blair	Kimball Kjar
	Isaia Rasila	Dimitri Yachvili	Shin Hasegawa	Bryan Redpath	Daniel Dorsey
	Nacanieli Seru	Yannick Bru	Masahiko Toyoyama	Bruce Douglas	Richard Liddington
	Joeli Veitayaki	Olivier Brouzet	Masahito Yamamoto	Allan Jacobsen	Mike MacDonald
	Bill Gadolo	Olivier Milloud	Ryō Yamamura	Gordon McIlwham	John Tarpoff
	Greg Smith	Gérald Merceron	Masao Amino	Tom Smith	Jacob Waasdorp
	Emori Katalau	Damien Traille	Masaaki Sakata	Gordon Bulloch	Kirk Khasigian
	Kele Leawere	Brian Liebenberg	Takahiro Hayano	Dougie Hall	Matthew Wyatt
	Api Naevo	David Auradou	Hajime Kiso	Rob Russell	Luke Gross
	Alifereti Doviverata	Clément Poitrenaud	Koichi Kubo	Stuart Grimes	Gerhard Klerck
	Sisa Koyamaibole	Sébastien Chabal	Adam Parker	Nathan Hines	Alec Parker
	Ifereimi Rawaqa	Xavier Garbajosa	Ryota Asano	Scott Murray	Todd Clever
	Kitione Salawa	Jean-Baptiste Poux	Takuro Miuchi	Martin Leslie	Oloseti Fifita
	Setareki Tawake	Christian Labit	Naoya Okubo	Jason White	Jurie Gouws
	Vula Maimuri	Nicolas Brusque	Yasunori Watanabe	Ross Beattie	Dave Hodges
	Koli Sewabu	Patrick Tabacco	Takeomi Ito	Jon Petrie	Kort Schubert
	Samisoni Rabaka	Pépito Elhorga	Yuya Saito	Simon Taylor	Dan Lyle
	Alivereti Mocelutu				

Results	P	W	D	L	PF	PA	BP	Pts
France	4	4	0	0	204	70	4	20
Scotland	4	3	0	1	102	97	2	14
Fiji	4	2	0	2	98	114	2	10
USA	4	1	0	3	86	125	2	6
Japan	4	0	0	4	79	163	0	0

Pool B Matches

The nations in pool B consisted of **Fiji, France, Japan, Scotland** and the **United States**. The Japanese in their fifth World Cup were definitely learning with each progressive tournament, but finished bottom of the Pool B, while the United States lost by just a point to Fiji (18~19).

Fiji had an opportunity to progress when they narrowly lost to Scotland in their final pool game (20~22), but the Scots held on to grab a quarter final berth against Australia. The French however, played an unrestrained style of rugby to convincingly win pool B, and progress to the elimination quarterfinal against Ireland.

B.1 France d. Fiji (61~18)
11 October 2003, Suncorp Stadium, Brisbane
Attendance: 46,795; Referee: Alain Rolland (Ireland).
France. *Tries: Dominici (2), Harinordoquy, Jauzion (3), Ibañez; Con: Michalak (4); Pen: Michalak (6).*
Fiji. *Tries: Naevo, Caucaunibuca; Con: Little; Pen: Little (2).*

B.2 Scotland d. Japan (32~11)
11 October 2003, Dairy Farmers Stadium, Townsville.
Attendance: 19,170; Referee: Stuart Dickinson (Australia).
Scotland. *Tries: Paterson (2), Grimes, Taylor, Danielli; Con: Paterson, Townsend; Pen: Paterson.*
Japan. *Tries: Onozawa; Pen: Hirose (2).*

B.3 Fiji d. United States (19~18)
15 October 2003, Suncorp Stadium, Brisbane.
Attendance: 30,990; Referee: Joël Jutge (France).
Fiji. *Tries: Naevo; Con: Little; Pen: Little (4).*
United States. *Tries: van Zyl, Schubert; Con: Hercus; Pen: Hercus (2).*

B.4 France d. Japan (51~29)
18 October 2003, Dairy Farmers Stadium, Townsville.
Attendance: 21,309; Referee: Alan Lewis (Ireland).
France. *Tries: Michalak, Rougerie (2), Pelous, Dominici, Crenca; Con: Michalak (5), Merceron; Pen: Michalak (3).*
Japan. *Tries: Konia, Ohata; Con: Kurihara (2); Pen: Kurihara (5).*

B.5 Scotland d. United States (39~15)
20 October 2003, Suncorp Stadium, Brisbane.
Attendance: 46,796; Referee: Jonathan Kaplan (South Africa).
Scotland. *Tries: Danielli (2), Kerr, Townsend, Paterson; Con: Paterson (4); Pen: Paterson (2).*
United States. *Pen: Hercus (5).*

B.6 Fiji d. Japan (41~13)
23 October 2003, Dairy Farmers Stadium, Townsville.
Attendance: 17,269; Referee: Nigel Whitehouse (Wales)
Fiji. *Tries: Tuilevu (2), Ligairi (2), Vunibaka; Con: Little (2); Pen: Little (4).*
Japan. *Tries: Miller; Con: Miller; Pen: Miller; Drop: Miller.*
(Andy Miller's drop goal at 52m, remains the longest in Rugby World Cup history.)

B.7 France d. Scotland (51~9)
25 October 2003, Telstra Stadium, Sydney.
Attendance: 78,974; Referee: David McHugh (Ireland).
France. *Tries: Betsen, Harinordoquy, Michalak, Galthié, Brusque; Con: Michalak (3), Merceron; Pen: Michalak (4); Drop: Michalak, Brusque.*
Scotland. *Pen: Paterson (3).*

B.8 United States d. Japan (39~26)
27 October 2003, Central Coast Stadium, Gosford.
Attendance: 19,653; Referee: Steve Walsh (New Zealand).
United States. *Tries: Hercus, Eloff, Schubert, van Zyl, Khasigian; Con: Hercus (4); Pen: Hercus (2)*
Japan. *Tries: Kurihara, Ohata; Con: Kurihara (2); Pen: Kurihara (4).*

B.9 France d. United States (41~14)
31 October 2003, WIN Stadium, Wollongong.
Attendance: 17,833; Referee: Paul Honiss (New Zealand).
France. *Tries: Liebenberg (3), Poux, Bru; Con: Merceron (2); Pen: Merceron (3); Drop: Yachvili.*
United States. *Tries: Hercus, Schubert; Con: Hercus (2).*

B.10 Scotland d. Fiji (22~20)
1 November 2003, Aussie Stadium, Sydney
Attendance: 37,137; Referee: Tony Spreadbury (England)
Scotland. *Tries: Smith; Con: Paterson; Pen: Paterson (5).*
Fiji. *Tries: Caucaunibuca (2); Con: Little (2); Pen: Little (2).*

POOL C - TEAMS

C	ENGLAND	GEORGIA	SAMOA	STH AFRICA	URUGUAY
Coaches:	Clive Woodward	Claude Saurel	John Boe	Rudolph Straeuli	Diego Ormaechea
Players:	Josh Lewsey	Bessik Khamashuridze	Fa'atonu Fili	Thinus Delport	Juan Menchaca
	Jason Robinson	Otar Eloshvili	Terry Fanolua	Werner Greeff	Joaquin Pastore
	Stuart Abbott	Irakli Giorgadze	Peter Poulos	Ricardo Loubscher	Diego Aguirre
	Will Greenwood	Vasil Katsadze	Dale Rasmussen	Jaco van der Westhuyzen	Joaquin De Freitas
	Mike Tindall	Tedo Zibzibadze	Romi Ropati	De Wet Barry	Martin Mendaro
	Ben Cohen	Archil Kavtarashvili	Lome Fa'atau	Jaque Fourie	Diego Reyes
	Dan Luger	Badri Khekhelashvili	Ron Fanuatanu	Jorrie Muller	Carlos Baldassari
	Mike Catt	Gocha Khonelidze	Dominic Feaunati	Breyton Paulse	Alfonso Cardoso
	Paul Grayson	Irakli Machkhaneli	Brian Lima	Stefan Terblanche	Emiliano Ibarra
	Jonny Wilkinson	Malkhaz Urjukashvili	Sailosi Tagicakibau	Ashwin Willemse	Jose Viana
	Kyran Bracken	Paliko Jimsheladze	Earl Va'a	Derick Hougaard	Sebastián Aguirre
	Matt Dawson	Irakli Modebadze	Tanner Vili	Louis Koen	Bernardo Amarillo
	Andy Gomarsall	Irakli Abuseridze	John Senio	Neil de Kock	Emiliano Caffera
	Jason Leonard	Merab Kvirikashvili	Steven So'oialo	Joost van der Westhuizen	Juan Campomar
	Danny Grewcock	David Dadunashvili	Denning Tyrell	Richard Bands	Eduardo Berruti
	Simon Shaw (r)	A. Margvelashvili	Kas Lealamanua	Christo Bezuidenhout	Diego Lamelas
	Phil Vickery	Soso Nikolaenko	Simon Lemalu	Faan Rautenbach	Pablo Lemoine
	Julian White	Goderdzi Shvelidze	Jeremy Tomuli	Dale Santon	Juan Machado
	Trevor Woodman	Akvsenti Giorgadze	Tamato Leupolu	Lawrence Sephaka	Rodrigo Sánchez
	Mark Regan	Avtandil Kopaliani	Jonathan Meredith	Danie Coetzee	Guillermo Storace
	Steve Thompson	Victor Didebulidze	Mahonri Schwalger	John Smit	Juan Andres Perez
	Dorian West	Sergo Gujaraidze	Leo Lafaiali'I	Selborne Boome	Juan Álvarez
	Martin Johnson (c)	Zurab Mtchedlishvili	Opeta Palepoi	Bakkies Botha	Juan Alzueta
	Ben Kay	Vano Nadiradze	Kitiona Viliamu	Victor Matfield	Juan Carlos Bado
	Neil Back	David Bolgashvili	Michael von Dincklage	Schalk Burger	Rodrigo Capo Ortega
	Martin Corry	George Chkhaidze	Maurie Fa'asavalu	Corne Krige	Nicolas Brignoni
	Richard Hill	Gia Labadze	Patrick Segi	Danie Rossouw	Ignacio Conti
	Lewis Moody	George Tsiklauri	Semo Sititi	Hendro Scholtz	Nicolas Grille
	Lawrence Dallaglio	Gregoire Yachvili	Des Tuiavi'I	Joe van Niekerk	Marcelo Gutierrez
	Joe Worsley	Ilia Zedginidze	Siaosi Vaili	Juan Smith	Hernan Ponte

8. Jason Robinson, England.

9. Percy Montgomery, South Africa.

C.1 South Africa d. Uruguay (72~6)

11 October 2003, Subiaco Oval, Perth.
Attendance: 16,906; Referee: Paddy O'Brien (New Zealand).
South Africa. *Tries: van der Westhuizen (3), van Niekerk, Botha (2), Delport, Fourie, Bands, Rossouw, Scholtz, Greef; Con: Koen (5), Hougaard.*
Uruguay. *Pen: Aguirre (2).*

C.2 England d. Georgia (84~6)

12 October 2003, Subiaco Oval, Perth
Attendance: 25,501; Referee: Pablo De Luca (Argentina).
England. *Tries: Tindall, Dawson, Thompson, Back, Dallaglio, Greenwood (2), Regan, Cohen (2), Robinson, Luger; Con: Wilkinson (5), Grayson (4); Pen: Wilkinson (2).*
Georgia. *Pen: Urjukashvili, Jimsheladze.*

C.3 Samoa d. Uruguay (60~13)

15 October 2003, Subiaco Oval, Perth.
Attendance: 22,020; Referee: David McHugh (Ireland).
Samoa. *Tries: Fa'asavalu (2), Lima (2), Tagicakibau, Fa'atau, Lemalu, Vili, Feaunati, Palepoi; Con: Va'a (3), Vili (2).*
Uruguay. *Tries: Capó, Lemoine; Pen: Aguirre.*

C.4 England d. South Africa (25~6)

18 October 2003, Subiaco Oval, Perth
Attendance: 38,834; Referee: Peter Marshall (Australia).
England. *Tries: Greenwood; Con: Wilkinson; Pen: Wilkinson (4); Drop: Wilkinson (2).*
South Africa. *Pen: Koen (2).*

C.5 Samoa d. Georgia (46~9)

19 October 2003, Subiaco Oval, Perth.
Attendance: 21,507; Referee: Alain Rolland (Ireland).
Samoa. *Tries: Tagicakibau, Vaa'a, Sititi, So'oialo, Feaunati, Lima; Con: Va'a (5); Pen: Va'a (2).*
Georgia. *Pen: Jimsheladze (2); Drop: Jimsheladze.*

C.6 South Africa d. Georgia (46~19)

24 October 2003, Aussie Stadium, Sydney.
Attendance: 34,308; Referee: Stuart Dickinson (Australia).
South Africa. *Tries: Rossouw (2), Hougaard, van Niekerk, Fourie, Botha, Burger; Con: Hougaard (4); Pen: Hougaard.*
Georgia. *Tries: Dadunashvili; Con: Jimsheladze; Pen: Jimsheladze (3), Kvirikashvili.*

C.7 England d. Samoa (35~22)

26 October 2003, Telstra Dome, Melbourne.
Attendance: 50,647; Referee: Jonathan Kaplan (South Africa).
England. *Tries: Back, Pen try, Balshaw, Vickery; Con: Wilkinson (3); Pen: Wilkinson (2); Drop: Wilkinson.*
Samoa. *Tries: Sititi; Con: Va'a; Pen: Va'a (5).*

C.8 Uruguay d. Georgia (24~12)

28 October 2003, Aussie Stadium, Sydney.
Attendance: 28,576; Referee: Kelvin Deaker (New Zealand).
Uruguay. *Tries: Cardoso, Lamelas, Brignoni; Con: Aguirre (2), Menchaca; Pen: Juan Menchaca.*
Georgia. *Pen: Urjukashvili, Kvirikashvili (3).*

C.9 South Africa d. Samoa (60~10)

1 November 2003, Suncorp Stadium, Brisbane.
Attendance: 48,496; Referee: Chris White (England).
South Africa. *Tries: van Niekerk, Muller, Hougaard, Smith, Willemse, Fourie, van der Westhuyzen, de Kock; Con: Hougaard (5), Koen (2); Pen: Hougaard; Drop: Hougaard.*
Samoa. *Tries: Palepoi; Con: Va'a; Pen: Va'a.*

C.10 England d. Uruguay (111~13)

2 November 2003, Suncorp Stadium, Brisbane.
Attendance: 46,233; Referee: Nigel Whitehouse (Wales).
England. *Tries: Moody, Lewsey (5), Balshaw (2), Catt (2), Gomarsall (2), Luger, Abbott, Robinson (2), Greenwood; Con: Grayson (11), Catt (2).*
Uruguay. *Tries: Lemoine; Con: Menchaca; Pen: Menchaca (2).*

Pool C Matches

The nations in Pool C consisted of **England, Georgia, Samoa, South Africa** and **Uruguay**. Georgia and Uruguay struggled in this group, and South Africa suffered an embarrassing defeat to England (6~25), but still managed to progress to the quarterfinals.

Samoa gave England a fright with an adventurous approach that allowed them to take an early lead. However, England's superior fitness ensure their victory (35~22). This match was marked by controversy, as England fielded 16 players at one point during the game, coinciding with a last-gasp try-saving tackle, which may have won the game for the Samoans.

Results	P	W	D	L	PF	PA	BP	Pts
England	4	4	0	0	255	47	3	19
South Africa	4	3	0	1	184	60	3	15
Samoa	4	2	0	2	138	117	2	10
Uruguay	4	1	0	3	56	255	0	4
Georgia	4	0	0	4	46	200	0	0

113

10. Joe Rokocoko on the rampage for the New Zealand All Blacks.

POOL D - TEAMS

D	CANADA	ITALY	NEW ZEALAND	TONGA	WALES
Coaches:	David Clark	John Kirwan	John Mitchell	Jim Love	Steve Hansen
Players:	Quentin Fyffe	Mirco Bergamasco	Ben Blair	Pierre Hola	Kevin Morgan
	James Pritchard	Gert Peens	Leon MacDonald	Sukanaivalu Hufanga	Rhys Williams
	John Cannon	Matteo Barbini	Mils Muliaina	Gus Leger	Iestyn Harris
	Marco di Girolamo	Manuel Dallan	Daniel Carter	Johnny Ngauamo	Sonny Parker
	Matt King	Andrea Masi	Ma'a Nonu	John Payne	Mark Taylor
	Nikyta Witkowski	Cristian Stoica	Tana Umaga	Tevita Tu'ifua	Garan Evans
	Sean Fauth	Gonzalo Canale	Doug Howlett	Pila Fifita	Mark Jones
	Dave Lougheed	Denis Dallan	Caleb Ralph	Sione Fonua	Tom Shanklin
	Winston Stanley	Nicola Mazzucato	Joe Rokocoko	Sila Va'enuku	Gareth Thomas
	Jared Barker	Francesco Mazzariol	Aaron Mauger	Anthony Alatini	Stephen Jones
	Bob Ross	Rima Wakarua	Carlos Spencer	Sateki Tu'ipulotu	Ceri Sweeney
	Ryan Smith	Matteo Mazzantini	Steve Devine	Lisiate Ulufonua	Gareth Cooper
	Ed Fairhurst	Alessandro Troncon	Byron Kelleher	Sililo Martens	Dwayne Peel
	Morgan Williams	Martin Castrogiovanni	Justin Marshall	David Palu	Shane Williams
	Garth Cooke	Andrea Lo Cicero	Dave Hewett	Heamani Lavaka	Paul James
	Rod Snow	Ramiro Martinez	Carl Hoeft	Tonga Lea'aetoa	Gethin Jenkins
	Jon Thiel	Salvatore Perugini	Kees Meeuws	Kisi Pulu	Adam Jones
	Kevin Tkachuk	Carlo Festuccia	Greg Somerville	Kafalosi Tonga	Iestyn Thomas
	Aaron Abrams	Fabio Ongaro	Corey Flynn	Viliami Ma'asi	Huw Bennett
	Mark Lawson	Cristian Bezzi	Mark Hammett	Ephram Taukafa	Mefin Davies
	Jamie Cudmore	Marco Bortolami	Keven Mealamu	Milton Ngauamo	Robin McBryde
	Mike James	Carlo Checchinato	Chris Jack	Viliami Vaki	Brent Cockbain
	Ed Knaggs	Santiago Dellape	Brad Thorn	Stanley Afeaki	Gareth Llewellyn
	Jeff Reid	Andrea Benatti	Ali Williams	Inoke Afeaki	Robert Sidoli
	Colin Yukes	Mauro Bergamasco	Daniel Braid	Edward Langi	Chris Wyatt
	Jim Douglas	Andrea De Rossi	Marty Holah	Nisifolo Naufahu	Colin Charvis
	Adam van Staveren	Scott Palmer	Richie McCaw	Sione Tu'Amoheloa	Dafydd Jones
	Ryan Banks	Aaron Persico	Reuben Thorne	Ipolito Fenukitau	Jonathan Thomas
	Al Charron	Sergio Parisse	Jerry Collins	Benhur Kivalu	Martyn Williams
	Josh Jackson	Matthew Phillips	Rodney So'oialo	Usaia Latu	Alix Popham

D.1 New Zealand d. Italy (70~7)

11 October 2003, Telstra Dome, Melbourne
Attendance: 41,715; Referee: Andrew Cole (Australia).
New Zealand. Tries: B. Thorn, R. Thorne, Howlett (2), Spencer (2), Rokocoko (2), Marshall, Carter, MacDonald; Con: Carter (6); Pen: Spencer.
Italy. Tries: Phillips; Con: Peens.

D.2 Wales d. Canada (41~10)

12 October 2003, Telstra Dome, Melbourne.
Attendance: 24,874; Referee: Chris White (England).
Wales. Tries: Parker, Cooper, M. Jones, Charvis, Thomas; Con: Harris (5); Pen: Harris (2).
Canada. Tries: Tkachuk; Con: Pritchard; Drop: Ross.

D.3 Italy d. Tonga (36~12)

15 October 2003, Canberra Stadium.
Attendance: 18,967; Referee: Steve Walsh (New Zealand).
Italy. Tries: M. Dallan, D. Dallan (2); Con: Wakarua (3); Pen: Wakarua (5).
Tonga. Tries: Payne, Tu'ifua; Con: Tu'ipulotu.

D.4 New Zealand d. Canada (68~6)

17 October 2003, Telstra Dome, Melbourne.
Attendance: 38,899; Referee: Tony Spreadbury (England).
New Zealand. Tries: Ralph (2), So'oialo (2), Muliaina (4), Meeuws, Nonu; Con: Carter (9).
Canada. Pen: Barker (2).

D.5 Wales d. Tonga (27~20)

19 October 2003, Canberra Stadium.
Attendance: 19,806; Referee: Paul Honiss (New Zealand).
Wales. Tries: Cooper, M. Williams; Con: S. Jones; Pen: S. Jones (4); Drop: M. Williams.
Tonga. Tries: Hola, Kivalu, Lavaka; Con: Hola; Pen: Hola.

D.6 Italy d. Canada (19~14)

21 October 2003, Canberra Stadium.
Attendance: 20,515; Referee: Paddy O'Brien (New Zealand).
Italy. Tries: Parisse; Con: Wakarua; Pen: Wakarua (4).
Canada. Tries: Fyffe; Pen: Barker (3).

D.7 New Zealand d. Tonga (91~7)

24 October 2003, Suncorp Stadium, Brisbane.
Attendance: 47,588; Referee: Pablo De Luca (Argentina).
New Zealand. Tries: Braid, Carter, Flynn, Ralph (2), Spencer, Meeuws, Pen try, Muliaina (2), MacDonald, Howlett (2); Con: MacDonald (12), Spencer.
Tonga. Tries: Hola; Con: Tu'ipulotu.

D.8 Wales d. Italy (27~15)

25 October 2003, Canberra Stadium
Attendance: 22,641; Referee: Andrew Cole (Australia).
Wales. Tries: M. Jones, Parker, D. Jones; Con: Harris (3); Pen: Harris (2).
Italy. Pen: Wakarua (5).

D.9 Canada d. Tonga (24~7)

29 October 2003, WIN Stadium, Wollongong.
Attendance: 15,630; Referee: Alain Rolland (Ireland).
Canada. Tries: Fauth, Abrams; Con: Pritchard; Pen: Ross (4).
Tonga. Tries: Kivalu; Con: Hola.

D.10 New Zealand d. Wales (53~37)

2 November 2003, Telstra Stadium, Sydney.
Attendance: 80,012; Referee: André Watson (South Africa).
New Zealand. Tries: Rokocoko (2), MacDonald, Williams, Howlett (2), Spencer, Mauger; Con: MacDonald (5); Pen: MacDonald.
Wales. Tries: Taylor, Parker, Charvis, S. Williams; Con: S. Jones (4); Pen: S. Jones (3).

Pool D Matches

The nations in Pool D consisted of **Canada, Italy, New Zealand, Tonga** and **Wales**. Both Tonga and Canada failed to repeat previous World Cup glories, although Canada finished with a better points differential. Italy were more than competitive in winning two of their four matches and weren't too far adrift in their loss to Wales (15~27), who in coming through that encounter earned a quarter final berth.

New Zealand were outstanding in their first three pool matches, but Wales pushed the All Blacks to the wire in the final encounter, after adopting an outgoing style of play with a fringe selection (53~37).

Results	P	W	D	L	PF	PA	BP	Pts
New Zealand	4	4	0	0	282	57	4	20
Wales	4	3	0	1	132	98	2	14
Italy	4	2	0	2	77	123	0	8
Canada	4	1	0	3	54	135	1	5
Tonga	4	0	0	4	46	178	1	1

11. The Australian crowd sings 'Waltzing Matilda' before the start of a game.

THE PLAYOFFS

Quarter Finals

The quarter final knock-out stage produced the widely predicted set of semi finalists. In the first two matches, a disappointing South Africa fell to New Zealand (9~29), and Australia had no difficulty in defeating Scotland (33~16).

France destroyed an Irish side in quarter final 3 (43~21), that had gone into the match hopeful of a win, but France scored most of their points early to put the game out of Ireland's reach.

QUARTER FINALS

QF1 New Zealand d. South Africa (29~9)
8 November 2003, Telstra Dome, Melbourne.
Attendance: 40,734; Referee: Tony Spreadbury (England).
New Zealand. Tries: MacDonald, Mealamu, Rokococo; Con: MacDonald; Pen: MacDonald (3); Drop: Mauger.
South Africa. Pen: Hougaard (3).

QF2 Australia d. Scotland (33~16)
8 November 2003, Suncorp Stadium, Brisbane.
Attendance: 45,412; Referee: Steve Walsh (New Zealand).
Australia. Tries: Mortlock, Gregan, Lyons; Con: Flatley (3); Pen: Flatley (4).
Scotland. Tries: Russell; Con: Paterson; Pen: Paterson (2); Drop: Paterson.

QF3 France d. Ireland (43~21)
9 November 2003, Telstra Dome, Melbourne.
Attendance: 33,134; Referee: Jonathan Kaplan (South Africa).
France. Tries: Magne, Dominici, Harinordoquy, Crenca; Con: Michalak (4); Pen: Michalak (5).
Ireland. Tries: Maggs, O'Driscoll (2); Con: Humphreys (3).

QF4 England d. Wales (28~17)
9 November 2003, Suncorp Stadium, Brisbane.
Attendance: 45,252; Referee: Alain Rolland (Ireland).
England. Try: Greenwood; Con: Wilkinson; Pen: Wilkinson (6); Drop: Wilkinson.
Wales. Tries: S. Jones, Charvis, M. Williams; Con: Harris.

England were widely rated as the world's best team, but in quarter final 4 they struggled for their win (28~17) against a Welsh side full of belief after a great showing against New Zealand.

Semi Finals

The first semi-final produced an upset, when Australia defeated the hugely fancied New Zealand (22~10) to become the first defending champions to reach the following championship final. Unfortunately, it was probably the last match for Australian star Ben Darwin, who injured his neck in a scrum. Although Darwin never played rugby again, the actions of Kees Meeuws who immediately stopped exerting pressure when he heard the call "neck, neck, neck", may well have saved his opponent's life and certainly prevented further injury. The match was

SEMI FINALS

Semi Final 1
Australia d. New Zealand (22~10)

15 November 2003, Telstra Stadium, Sydney.
Attendance: 82,444; Referee: Chris White (England).
Australia. Try: Mortlock; Con: Flatley; Pen: Flatley (5).
New Zealand. Try: Thorne; Con: MacDonald; Pen: MacDonald.

Semi Final 2
England d. France (24~7)

16 November 2003, Telstra Stadium, Sydney.
Attendance: 82,346; Referee: Paddy O'Brien (New Zealand).
England. Pen: Wilkinson (5); Drop: Wilkinson (3).
France. Try: Betsen; Con: Michalak.

12. Telstra Stadium, Sydney AU.

decided by a Stirling Mortlock interception try, after a loose pass from highly rated All Blacks fly-half Carlos Spencer.

The second semi-final saw France face England. The boot of Johnny Wilkinson was the difference between the two sides, with England coming out victors (24~7).

3rd Place Playoff

Two days before the Australia and England final, the playoff for third place was contested between New Zealand and France at Telstra Stadium in Sydney. After their respective semi final losses, both teams had to raise their spirits and refocus on the task ahead.

By the half-time break the All Blacks had jumped out to a 14~0 lead, but France reduced that to seven just after the restart. But there was no stopping New Zealand who then applied the pressure to score three converted tries in a seven minute period with another in the 72nd minute, which won them the bronze medal and closed the gate on France (40~13).

THE FINAL

The final between Australia and England was played at Sydney's Telstra Stadium in front of a crowd of 82,957 fans. Australia opened the scoring after they decided to run a penalty instead of kicking for touch. Lote Tuqiri beat England's right wing, Jason Robinson, to a high cross-field kick and went over for the first

13. England celebrates after winning the 2003 Rugby World Cup final in Sydney.

try, but Elton Flatley was not able to add the conversion. The rest of the half was a tight affair, with England edging in front by applying pressure and Johnny Wilkinson's boot put them up to a 9~5 lead after Australian indiscipline gave away several penalties, but were unable to capitalise on their territory. Towards the end of the first half, England stretched their lead further. Lawrence Dallaglio made a break and popped the ball inside to Johnny Wilkinson, who drew the defense before putting Robinson away in the corner for a try. The conversion was missed, but England went in at half time leading by 14~5.

In the second half Australia tightened their discipline, and solid play forced mistakes from England. The game swung from end to end, with both sides having try-scoring opportunities, but neither able to take an advantage. Australia managed to get points on the board and Elton Flatley scored two penalties to nudge the difference to 14~11 to England. In the 79th minute, Australia were putting pressure on England in their half, and

FINALS

FINAL
England d. Australia (20~17 xt)

22 November 2003, Telstra Stadium, Sydney.
Attendance: 82,957; Referee: André Watson (South Africa).
England. *Try: Robinson, Pen: Wilkinson (4); Drop: Wilkinson.*
Australia. *Try: Tuqiri, Pen: Flatley (4).*

3rd/4th Playoff
New Zealand d. France (40~13)

20 November 2003, Telstra Stadium, Sydney.
Attendance: 62,712; Referee: Chris White (England).
New Zealand. *Tries: Jack, Howlett, Rokocoko, Thorn, Muliaina, Holah; Con: MacDonald; Carter (4).*
France. *Try: Elhorga, Con: Yachvili; Pen: Yachvili; Drop: Yachvili.*

Australia were awarded a penalty right before full-time, with the potential to tie the score. Flatley converted the penalty to push the score to 14~14 and take the game into an additional 20 minutes of extra time.

England opened the scoring in extra time with another Wilkinson penalty, but with two and a half minutes of extra time remaining Australia were awarded another penalty, which Flatley kicked successfully (17~17). Then with just 20 seconds left before sudden death, Wilkinson booted a drop goal to silence the Australian crowd, win the match and take England's first world rugby championship.

CREDITS

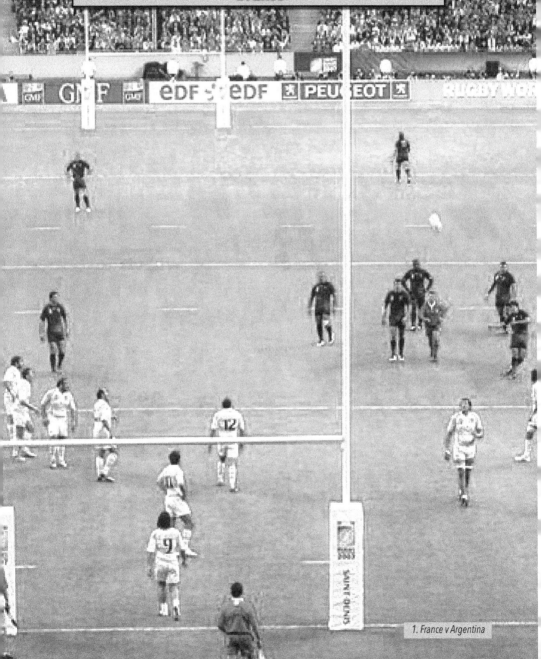

2007
VI RUGBY WORLD CUP
France

1. France v Argentina

VI Rugby World Cup

7th September to 20th October, 2007

2. The Opening Ceremony of the 2007 Rugby World Cup.

The 2007 Rugby World Cup was the sixth Rugby World Cup, a quadrennial international rugby union competition first inaugurated in 1987.

THE HOST

Twenty nations competed for the Webb Ellis Cup in the tournament, which was hosted by France from 7th September to 20th October. France had won the hosting rights in 2003, beating a bid from England. The competition consisted of 48 matches played over 44 days, with some 42 matches being played in ten cities throughout France. The French cities to host games were Bordeaux, Lens, Lyon, Marseille, Montpellier, Nantes, St. Etienne, Toulouse and Paris, and it was also announced that the final would be at the Stade de France in Saint-Denis. There were another four matches played in Cardiff, Wales, and two more matches in Edinburgh, Scotland. The attendance at the 6th Rugby World Cup totaled 2,263,223 fans through the gates, or an average of 47,150 spectators per match!

THE TEAMS

The eight quarter-finalists from 2003 were granted automatic qualification, while 12 other nations were required to gain entry through the regional qualifying competitions that began in 2004. Ten of the 20 positions available in the tournament were filled by regional qualifiers, with an additional two being filled by repechage qualification.

Seeded Teams

All quarter finalists from the 2003 tournament qualified for the 2007 Rugby World Cup. This meant that **England, Australia, New Zealand, South Africa, Wales, Ireland** and **Scotland** all automatically qualified for the event, and were joined by **France** as the host nation.

Qualifying Teams

All other nations vying for a place in the tournament had to qualify for the remaining 12 places through a series of qualification matches, which were contested by a record 85 teams.

Namibia won the single African Zone place over teams from Kenya, Zimbabwe, Ivory Coast, Tunisia, Morocco, Zambia, Cameroon, Senegal, Nigeria, Uganda, Botswana, Madagascar and Swaziland.

3. The Rugby World Cup ball hangs in la tour Eiffel.

4. Canada prepare for battle at the 2007 Rugby World Cup.

Argentina, Canada and the **United States** won the three American Zone places over teams from Trinidad & Tobago, Brazil, Venezuela, Peru, Colombia, Guyana, Bermuda, St Lucia, Cayman Islands, Jamaica, Bahamas, Barbados, Chile, Uruguay and Paraguay.

The European Zone had three places up for grabs, which was contested across six separate rounds by 31 nations. **Romania, Georgia** and **Italy** all eventually qualified over teams from Croatia, Russia, Denmark, Latvia, Moldova, Norway, Finland, Bulgaria, the Netherlands, Ukraine, Poland, Belgium, Switzerland, Israel, Austria, Bosnia & Herzegovina, Serbia & Montenegro, Portugal, Germany, Czech Republic, Slovenia, Andorra, Sweden, Hungary, Spain, Malta, Lithuania and Luxembourg.

Japan won the single Asian Zone spot over teams from Malaysia, India, Guam, China, Sri Lanka, Kazakhstan, South Korea, Hong Kong, Chinese Taipei, Thailand, Singapore and the Arabian Gulf.

Fiji and **Samoa** won the two hotly contested Oceania Zone places over teams from the Cook Islands, Vanuatu, Niue, Solomon Islands, Papua New Guinea, Tahiti and the talented Tongans.

Repechage Teams

The repechage was a great initiative, essentially giving a few unlucky teams a second chance. There were two repechage positions available in the 2007 Rugby World Cup. **Portugal** and **Tonga** eventually qualified through the repechage rounds over teams from Morocco, Uruguay and South Korea.

THE POOL STAGE

A total of 48 matches scheduled across 44 days (40 pool stage and 8 knock-out) were played throughout the tournament. With the 20 teams being divided into four pools of five nations, the top two teams in each pool progressed to the knock-out quarter final stage.

Classification within each pool was based on a scoring system where four match points were awarded for a win; two for a draw; and zero for a loss. Bonus points, contributing to a team's cumulative match-point score, were awarded for a team that scores four or more tries (regardless of the match result), and a team that loses by seven points (a converted try) or fewer.

At the end of the pool stage, teams were ranked from first to fifth based on cumulative match points, with the top two nations proceeding to the quarter finals.

The 'Boutique Officielle' for the 2007 Rugby World Cup in Paris.

POOL A - TEAMS

A	ENGLAND	SAMOA	STH AFRICA	TONGA	USA
Coaches:	Brian Ashton	Michael Jones	Jake White	Quddus Fielea	Peter Thorburn
Players:	George Chuter	Tani Fuga	Gary Botha	Aleki Lutui	Blake Burdette
	Lee Mears	Mahonri Schwalger	Bismarck du Plessis	Ephraim Taukafa	Owen Lentz
	Mark Regan	Silao Vaisola Sefo	John Smit (c)	Taufa'ao Filise	Mike MacDonald
	Perry Freshwater	Census Johnston	BJ Botha	Sateki Mata'u	Matekitonga Moeakiola
	Andrew Sheridan	Kas Lealamanua	Jannie du Plessis	Kisi Pulu	Chris Osentowski
	Matt Stevens	Na'ama Leleimalefaga	Os du Randt	Toma Toke	Jonathan Vitale
	Phil Vickery (c)	Fosi Pala'amo	Gurthro Steenkamp	Soane Tonga'uiha	Luke Gross
	Steve Borthwick	Muliufi Salanoa	CJ van der Linde	Inoke Afeaki	Mike Mangan
	Ben Kay	Justin Va'a	Bakkies Botha	Lisiate Fa'aoso	Hayden Mexted
	Simon Shaw	Leo Lafaiali'i	Victor Matfield	Paino Hehea	Alec Parker
	Martin Corry (vc)	Joe Tekori	Johann Muller	Emosi Kauhenga	John van der Giessen
	Lewis Moody	Kane Thompson	Albert van den Berg	Nili Latu (c)	Mark Aylor
	Tom Rees	Daniel Leo	Schalk Burger	Maama Molitika	Inaki Basauri
	Joe Worsley	Justin Purdie	Juan Smith	Hale T-Pole	Todd Clever
	Lawrence Dallaglio	Semo Sititi (c)	Wikus van Heerden	Viliami Vaki	Louis Stanfill
	Nick Easter	Ulia Ulia	Danie Rossouw	Lotu Filipine	Henry Bloomfield
	Andy Gomarsall	Henry Tuilagi	Bobby Skinstad	Finau Maka	Fifita Mounga
	Shaun Perry	Alfie To'oala	Fourie du Preez	Soane Havea	Dan Payne
	Peter Richards	Junior Poluleuligaga	Ricky Januarie	Enele Taufa	Chad Erskine
	Olly Barkley	Steven So'oialo	Ruan Pienaar	Sione Tu'ipulotu	Mike Petri
	Jonny Wilkinson	Lolo Lui	Butch James	Pierre Hola	Mike Hercus (c)
	Toby Flood	Eliota Fuimaono-Sapolu	André Pretorius	Suka Hufanga	Valenese Malifa
	Mike Catt	Brian Lima	Jean de Villiers	Epi Taione	Philip Eloff
	Andy Farrell	Seilala Mapusua	Jaque Fourie	Hudson Tonga'uiha	Paul Emerick
	Dan Hipkiss	Jerry Meafou	Wayne Julies	Isileli Tupou	Vahafolau Esikia
	Jamie Noon	Elvis Seveali'i	Wynand Olivier	Aisea Havili	Albert Tuipulotu
	Mathew Tait	Anitele'a Tuilagi	Francois Steyn	Ualosi Kailea	Takudzwa Ngwenya
	Mark Cueto	Gavin Williams	Bryan Habana	Seti Kiole	Thretton Palamo
	Josh Lewsey	Lome Fa'atau	Akona Ndungane	Tevita Tu'ifua	Salesi Sika
	Paul Sackey	David Lemi	JP Pietersen	Joseph Vaka	Francois Viljoen
	Nick Abendanon	Sailosi Tagicakibau	Ashwin Willemse	Vunga Lilo	Chris Wyles
	Jason Robinson	Alesana Tuilagi	Percy Montgomery		
		Loki Crichton			

5. Samoa perform their traditional island war cry, the 'Manu Siva Tau.'

Pool A Matches

The nations in Pool A consisted of **England, Samoa, South Africa, Tonga** and the **United States**. The number one and two teams in this group, South Africa and England played according to prediction and both defeated the other three nations. England however, was given a thrashing by the South African Springboks (0~36) in a very lop-sided match during their top of the table clash.

Results	P	W	D	L	PF	PA	BP	Pts
South Africa	4	4	0	0	189	47	3	19
England	4	3	0	1	108	88	2	14
Tonga	4	2	0	2	89	96	1	9
Samoa	4	1	0	3	69	143	1	5
USA	4	0	0	4	61	142	1	1

The United States lost all games, but were competitive for the most part, except against the South Africans. Tonga won the battle for third placing in this pool with their narrow wins over Samoa (19~15) and the United States (25~15).

A.1 England d. United States (28~10)
8 September 2007, Stade Félix Bollaert, Lens.
Attendance: 36,755; Referee: Jonathan Kaplan (South Africa).
England. *Tries: Robinson, Barkley, Rees; Con: Barkley (2/3); Pen: Barkley (3/3).*
United States. *Tries: Moeakiola; Con: Hercus; Pen: Hercus.*

A.2 South Africa d. Samoa (59~7)
9 September 2007, Parc des Princes, Paris.
Attendance: 46,575; Referee: Paul Honiss (New Zealand).
South Africa. *Tries: Habana (4), Montgomery (2), Fourie, JP Pietersen; Con: Montgomery (5/8); Pen: Montgomery (3/3).*
Samoa. *Try: Williams, Con: Williams.*

A.3 Tonga d. United States (25~15)
12 September 2007, Stade de la Mosson, Montpellier.
Attendance: 25,000; Referee: Stuart Dickinson (Australia).
Tonga. *Tries: Maka, Vaka, Vaki; Con: Hola (2/3); Pen: Hola (2/2).*
United States. *Tries: MacDonald, Stanfill; Con: Hercus (1/2); Pen: Hercus (1/2).*

A.4 South Africa d. England (36~0)
14 September 2007, Stade de France, Saint-Denis.
Attendance: 77,523; Referee: Joël Jutge (France).
South Africa. *Tries: Smith, Pietersen (2); Con: Montgomery (3/3); Pen: Steyn (1/1), Montgomery (4/4).*
England. *Nil.*

A.5 Tonga d. Samoa (19~15)
16 September 2007, Stade de la Mosson, Montpellier.
Attendance: 24,128; Referee: Jonathan Kaplan (South Africa).
Tonga. *Try: Taione; Con: Hola; Pen: Hola (4/5).*
Samoa. *Pen: Williams (5/6).*

A.6 South Africa d. Tonga (30~25)
22 September 2007, Stade Félix Bollaert, Lens.
Attendance: 40,069; Referee: Wayne Barnes (England).
South Africa. *Tries: Pienaar (2), Smith, Skinstad; Con: Pretorius, Montgomery (1/3); Pen: Steyn, Montgomery.*
Tonga. *Tries: Pulu, Hufanga, Vaki; Con: Hola (2/3); Pen: Hola (2/3).*

A.7 England d. Samoa (44~22)
22 September 2007, Stade de la Beaujoire, Nantes.
Attendance: 37,022; Referee: Alan Lewis (Ireland).
England. *Tries: Corry (2), Sackey (2); Con: Wilkinson (3/4); Pen: Wilkinson (4/6); Drop: Wilkinson (2/3).*
Samoa. *Try: Polu; Con: Crichton (1/1); Pen: Crichton (5/5).*

A.8 Samoa d. United States (25~21)
26 September 2007, Stade Geoffroy-Guichard, Saint-Étienne.
Attendance: 34,124; Referee: Wayne Barnes (England).
Samoa. *Tries: Fa'atau, Tuilagi, Thompson; Con: Crichton (2/3); Pen: Crichton (2/2).*
United States. *Tries: Ngwenya, Stanfill; Con: Hercus (1/2); Pen: Hercus (3/4).*

A.9 England d. Tonga (36~20)
28 September 2007, Parc des Princes, Paris.
Attendance: 45,085; Referee: Alain Rolland (Ireland).
England. *Tries: Sackey (2), Tait, Farrell; Con: Wilkinson (2/4); Pen: Wilkinson (2/3); Drop: Wilkinson (2/2).*
Tonga. *Tries: Hufanga, Pole; Con: Hola (2/2); Pen: Hola (2/2).*

A.10 South Africa d. United States (64~15)
30 September 2007, Stade de la Mosson, Montpellier.
Attendance: 28,750; Referee: Tony Spreadbury (England)
South Africa. *Tries: Burger, Steyn, Habana (2), van der Linde, du Preez, Fourie (2), Smith; Con: Montgomery (6/7), James (2/2); Pen: Montgomery (1/1).*
United States. *Tries: Ngwenya, Wyles; Con: Hercus (1/2); Pen: Hercus (1/1).*

6. Wales v Japan at Millenium Stadium, Cardiff, Wales.

POOL B - TEAMS

B	AUSTRALIA	CANADA	FIJI	JAPAN	WALES
Coaches:	John Connolly	Ric Suggitt	Ilivasi Tabua	John Kirwan	Gareth Jenkins
Players:	Adam Freier	Aaron Carpenter	Bill Gadolo	Ryo Yamamura	Huw Bennett
	Sean Hardman	Pat Riordan	Sunia Koto	Masahito Yamamoto	Matthew Rees
	Stephen Moore	Scott Franklin	Vereniki Sauturaga	Tomokazu Soma	T. Rhys Thomas
	Al Baxter	Dan Pletch	Graham Dewes	Tatsukichi Nishiura	Chris Horsman
	Matt Dunning	Mike Pletch	Henry Qiodravu	Yuji Matsubara	Gethin Jenkins
	Greg Holmes	Rod Snow	Jone Railomo	Yusuke Aoki	Adam Jones
	Guy Shepherdson	Jon Thiel	Alefoso Yalayalatabua	Hitoshi Ono	Duncan Jones
	Mark Chisholm	Mike Burak	Isoa Domolailai	Takanori Kumagae	Ian Evans
	Hugh McMeniman	Mike James	Kele Leawere	Luatangi Vatuvei	Ian Gough
	Nathan Sharpe	Josh Jackson	Wame Lewaravu	Luke Thompson	Will James
	Daniel Vickerman	Luke Tait	Ifereimi Rawaqa	Yasunori Watanabe	Alun Wyn Jones
	Rocky Elsom	David Biddle	Semisi Naevo	Hajime Kiso	Colin Charvis
	George Smith (vc)	Jamie Cudmore	Akapusi Qera	Hare Makiri	Martyn Williams
	Phil Waugh	Adam Kleeberger	Aca Ratuva	Philip O'Reilly	Jonathan Thomas
	Wycliff Palu	Colin Yukes	Netani Talei	Takamichi Sasaki	Michael Owen
	Stephen Hoiles	Sean-Michael Stephen	Sisa Koyamaibole	Takuro Miuchi (c)	Alix Popham
	Sam Cordingley	Mike Webb	Jone Qovu	Yuki Yatomi	Gareth Cooper
	George Gregan (vc)	Ed Fairhurst	Jone Daunivucu	Tomoki Yoshida	Dwayne Peel (vc)
	Berrick Barnes	Matt Weingart	Mosese Rauluni (c)	Kim Chul Won	Mike Phillips
	Stephen Larkham	Morgan Williams (c)	Nicky Little	Eiji Ando	Stephen Jones (vc)
	Morgan Turinui	Nathan Hirayama	Waisea Luveniyali	Kousei Ono	Ceri Sweeney
	Matt Giteau	Ander Monro	Seremaia Bai (vc)	Shotaro Onishi	James Hook
	Stirling Mortlock (c)	Ryan Smith	Maleli Kunavore	Nataniela Oto	Sonny Parker
	Scott Staniforth	Craig Culpan	Gabiriele Lovobalavu	Yuta Imamura	Jamie Robinson
	Adam Ashley-Cooper	Derek Daypuck	Seru Rabeni	Koji Taira	Tom Shanklin
	Cameron Shepherd	David Spicer	Sireli Bobo	Bryce Robins	Dafydd James
	Lote Tuqiri	Nick Trenkel	Vilimoni Delasau	Hirotoki Onozawa	Mark Jones
	Drew Mitchell	Justin Mensah-Coker	Isoa Neivua	Kosuke Endo	Shane Williams
	Julian Huxley	James Pritchard	Norman Ligairi	Tomoki Kitagawa	Kevin Morgan
	Chris Latham	DTH van der Merwe	Kameli Ratuvou	Christian Loamanu	Gareth Thomas (c)
		Mike Pyke		Go Aruga	

Results	P	W	D	L	PF	PA	BP	Pts
Australia	4	4	0	0	215	41	4	20
Fiji	4	3	0	1	114	136	3	15
Wales	4	2	0	2	168	105	4	12
Japan	4	0	1	3	64	210	1	3
Canada	4	0	1	3	51	120	0	2

Pool B Matches

The nations in Pool B consisted of **Australia, Canada, Fiji, Japan** and **Wales**. The Australians streaked ahead and lead this group from the start, despite having some difficulty in their match against Wales (32~20). Japan and Canada found the going tough, but drew their pool encounter (12~12).

The real excitement in this pool was watching who would qualify for the quarter finals between Fiji and Wales. Wales had a much better points differential (63 to -22), but the final pool match contested between these two teams resulted in a boil-over victory for Fiji (38~34), who eliminated Wales to claim a quarterfinal berth.

B.1 Australia d. Japan (91~3)

8 September 2007, Stade de Gerland, Lyon.
Attendance: 40,043; Referee: Alan Lewis (Ireland).
Australia. Tries: Sharpe, Elsom (3), Ashley-Coope, Latham (2), Barnes (2), Mitchell (2), Smith, Freier; Con: Mortlock (7/10); Giteau (3/3); Pen: Mortlock (2/2).
Japan. Pen: K. Ono.

B.2 Wales d. Canada (42~17)

9 September 2007, Stade de la Beaujoire, Nantes.
Attendance: 37,500; Referee: Alain Rolland (Ireland).
Wales. Try: Parker, A. W. Jones, S. Williams (2), Charvis; Con: S. Jones (4/5); Pen: Hook (3/4).
Canada. Tries: Cudmore, Culpan, Williams; Con: Pritchard (1/3).

B.3 Fiji d. Japan (35~31)

12 September 2007, Stadium de Toulouse, Toulouse.
Attendance: 34,500; Referee: Marius Jonker (South Africa).
Fiji. Tries: Qera (2), Rabeni, Leawere; Con: Little (3/4); Pen: Little (3/3).
Japan. Tries: Thompson (2), Soma; Con: Onishi (2/3); Pen: Onishi (4/4).

B.4 Australia d. Wales (32~20)

15 September 2007, Millennium Stadium, Cardiff.
Attendance: 71,022; Referee: Steve Walsh (New Zealand).
Australia. Tries: Giteau, Mortlock, Latham (2); Con: Mortlock (2/2), Giteau (1/2); Pen: Mortlock (1/2); Drop: Barnes (1/1).
Wales. Tries: J. Thomas, S. Williams; Con: Hook (2/2); Pen: S. Jones (1/3), Hook (1/2).

B.5 Fiji d. Canada (29~16)

16 September 2007, Millennium Stadium, Cardiff.
Attendance: 45,000; Referee: Tony Spreadbury (England).
Fiji. Tries: Leawere, Ratuvou (2), Delasau; Con: Little (3/4); Pen: Little (1/3).
Canada. Tries: Smith; Con: Pritchard (1/1); Pen: Pritchard (3/4).

B.6 Wales d. Japan (72~18)

20 September 2007, Millennium Stadium, Cardiff.
Attendance: 35,245; Referee: Joël Jutge (France).
Wales. Tries: A. W. Jones, Hook, T. R. Thomas, Morgan, Phillips, S. Williams (2), D. James, Cooper, M. Williams (2); Con: S. Jones (5/7), Sweeney (2/4); Pen: S. Jones.
Japan. Tries: Endo, Onozawa; Con: Robins; Pen: Onishi (2/2).

B.7 Australia d. Fiji (55~12)

23 September 2007, Stade de la Mosson, Montpellier.
Attendance: 32,231; Referee: Nigel Owens (Wales).
Australia. Tries: Giteau (2), Mitchell (3), Ashley-Cooper, Hoiles; Con: Giteau (4/6); Pen: Giteau (3/3); Drop: Barnes.
Fiji. Tries: Neivua, Ratuva; Con: Bai (1/1).

B.8 Canada dr. Japan (12~12)

25 September 2007, Stade Chaban-Delmas, Bordeaux.
Attendance: 33,810; Referee: Jonathan Kaplan (South Africa).
Canada. Tries: Riordan, van der Merwe; Con: Pritchard (1/1).
Japan. Tries: Endo, Taira; Con: Onishi (1/2).

B.9 Australia d. Canada (37~6)

29 September 2007, Stade Chaban-Delmas, Bordeaux.
Attendance: 35,200; Referee: Chris White (England).
Australia. Tries: Baxter, Freier, Smith, Mitchell (2), Latham; Con: Shepherd (2/3); Pen: Huxley.
Canada. Pen: Pritchard (2/2).

B.10 Fiji d. Wales (38~34)

29 September 2007, Stade de la Beaujoire, Nantes.
Attendance: 37,080; Referee: Stuart Dickinson (Australia).
Fiji. Tries: Qera, Delasau, Leawere, Dewes; Con: Little (3/4); Pen: Little (4/5).
Wales. Try: Popham, S. Williams, G. Thomas, M. Jones, M. Williams; Con: Hook, S. Jones (2/4); Pen: S. Jones (1/2).

POOL C - TEAMS

C	ITALY	NEW ZEALAND	PORTUGAL	ROMANIA	SCOTLAND
Coaches:	Pierre Berbizier	Graham Henry	Tomaz Morais	Daniel Santamans	Frank Hadden
Players:	Carlo Festuccia	Carl Hayman	Rui Cordeiro	Petru Bălan	Ross Ford
	Leonardo Ghiraldini	Greg Somerville	Ruben Spachuck	Bogdan Bălan	Scott Lawson
	Fabio Ongaro	Neemia Tialata	Duarte Figueiredo	Silviu Florea	Fergus Thomson
	Matías Agüero	Tony Woodcock	André Silva	Cezar Popescu	Allan Jacobsen
	Martin Castrogiovanni	Andrew Hore	Juan Muré	Petrişor Toderasc	Gavin Kerr
	Andrea Lo Cicero	Keven Mealamu	João Correia	Marius Tincu	Euan Murray
	Salvatore Perugini	Anton Oliver	Joaquim Ferreira (vc)	Răzvan Mavrodin	Craig Smith
	Valerio Bernabò	Chris Jack	Gonçalo Uva	Sorin Socol (c)	James Hamilton
	Marco Bortolami (c)	Keith Robinson	David Penalva	Cristian Petre	Nathan Hines
	Carlo Del Fava	Ali Williams	Marcello d'Orey	Valentin Ursache	Scott MacLeod
	Santiago Dellapè	Jerry Collins (vc)	Salvador Palha	Augustin Petrechei	Scott Murray
	Mauro Bergamasco	Chris Masoe	João Uva	Ovidiu Toniţa (vc)	John Barclay
	Silvio Orlando	Richie McCaw (c)	Paulo Murinello	Florin Corodeanu	Kelly Brown
	Josh Sole	Reuben Thorne	Diogo Coutinho	Alexandru Manta	Allister Hogg
	Alessandro Zanni	Sione Lauaki	Tiago Girão	Alexandru Tudori	Jason White (c)
	Sergio Parisse	Rodney So'oialo	Juan Severino Somoza	Cosmin Raţiu	David Callam
	Manoa Vosawai	Andrew Ellis	Vasco Uva (c)	Valentin Calafateanu	Simon Taylor
	Paul Griffen	Byron Kelleher	Luís Pissarra	Lucian Sirbu	Mike Blair
	Alessandro Troncon (vc)	Brendon Leonard	José Pinto	Ionuţ Dimofte	Chris Cusiter
	Roland de Marigny	Dan Carter	Gonçalo Malheiro	Dănuţ Dumbrava	Rory Lawson
	Ramiro Pez	Nick Evans	Duarte Cardoso Pinto	Romeo Gontineac	Dan Parks
	Mirco Bergamasco	Aaron Mauger	Pedro Cabral	Minya Csaba Gál	Rob Dewey
	Gonzalo Canale	Luke McAlister	Diogo Mateus	Dan Vlad	Marcus di Rollo
	Andrea Masi	Conrad Smith	Diogo Gama	Ionuţ Tofan	Andrew Henderson
	Pablo Canavosio	Isaia Toeava	Miguel Portela	Cătălin Fercu	Simon Webster
	Matteo Pratichetti	Doug Howlett	Frederico Sousa	Ion Teodorescu	Sean Lamont
	Kaine Robertson	Joe Rokocoko	António Aguilar	Gabriel Brezoianu	Nikki Walker
	Marko Stanojevic	Sitiveni Sivivatu	Pedro Carvalho	Cătălin Nicolae	Chris Paterson
	David Bortolussi	Leon MacDonald	Gonçalo Foro	Iulian Dumitraş	Rory Lamont
	Ezio Galon	Mils Muliaina	David Mateus	Florin Vlaicu	Hugo Southwell
			Pedro Leal		

7. The crowd for the Australia v Fiji Pool C match at the Stade de la Mosson, in Montpellier, France.

C.1 New Zealand d. Italy (76~14)
8 September 2007, Stade Vélodrome, Marseille.
Attendance: 58,612; Referee: Wayne Barnes (England).
New Zealand. Tries: McCaw (2), Howlett (3), Muliaina, Sivivatu (2), Jack, Collins (2); Con: Carter (7/9), McAlister (2/2); Pen: Carter.
Italy. Tries: Stanojevic, Mi. Bergamasco; Con: Bortolussi, de Marigny.

C.2 Scotland d. Portugal (56~10)
9 September 2007, Stade Geoffroy-Guichard, Saint-Étienne.
Attendance: 34,162; Referee: Steve Walsh (New Zealand).
Scotland. Tries: R. Lamont (2), S. Lawson, Dewey, Parks, Southwell, Brown, Ford; Con: Parks (5/5), Paterson (3/3).
Portugal. Try: Carvalho, Con: D. Pinto; Pen: D. Pinto.

C.3 Italy d. Romania (24~18)
12 September 2007, Stade Vélodrome, Marseille.
Attendance: 44,241; Referee: Tony Spreadbury (England).
Italy. Tries: Dellap, Pen try; Con: Pez; Pen: Bortolussi (1/2), Ramiro Pez (3/3).
Romania. Tries: Manta, Tincu; Con: Dimofte; Pen: Dimofte (2/2).

C.4 New Zealand d. Portugal (108~13)
15 September 2007, Stade de Gerland, Lyon.
Attendance: 40,729; Referee: Chris White (England).
New Zealand. Tries: Rokocoko (2), Toeava, Williams, Mauger (2), Collins, Masoe, Hore, Leonard, Evans, Ellis, MacDonald, Smith (2), Hayman; Con: Evans (14/16).
Portugal. Try: Cordeiro; Con: D. Pinto; Pen: D. Pinto; Drop: Malheiro (1/2).

C.5 Scotland d. Romania (42~0)
18 September 2007, Murrayfield Stadium, Edinburgh.
Attendance: 31,222; Referee: Nigel Owens (Wales).
Scotland. Tries: Paterson, Hogg (3), R. Lamont (2); Con: Paterson (6/6).
Romania. Nil.

C.6 Italy d. Portugal (31~5)
19 September 2007, Parc des Princes, Paris.
Attendance: 45,476; Referee: Marius Jonker (South Africa).
Italy. Tries: Masi (2), Ma. Bergamasco; Con: Bortolussi (2/3); Pen: Bortolussi (4/4).
Portugal. Try: Penalva.

C.7 New Zealand d. Scotland (40~0)
23 September 2007, Murrayfield Stadium, Edinburgh.
Attendance: 64,558; Referee: Marius Jonker (South Africa).
New Zealand. Tries: McCaw, Howlett (2), Kelleher, Williams, Carter; Con: Carter (2/6); Pen: Carter (2/3).
Scotland. Nil.

C.8 Romania d. Portugal (14~10)
25 September 2007, Stadium de Toulouse, Toulouse.
Attendance: 35,526; Referee: Paul Honiss (New Zealand).
Romania. Tries: Tincu, Corodeanu; Con: Calafeteanu, Dan Dumbrava.
Portugal. Try: Ferreira; Con: D. Pinto; Pen: Malheiro.

C.9 New Zealand d. Romania (85~8)
29 September 2007, Stadium de Toulouse, Toulouse.
Attendance: 35,608; Referee: Joël Jutge (France).
New Zealand. Tries: Sivivatu (2), Masoe, Rokocoko (3), Evans, Mauger, Toeava (2), Hore, Smith, Howlett; Con: McAlister (4/7), Evans (6/6).
Romania. Try: Tincu; Pen: Vlaicu.

C.10 Scotland d. Italy (18~16)
29 September 2007, Stade Geoffroy-Guichard, Saint-Étienne.
Attendance: 34,701; Referee: Jonathan Kaplan (South Africa).
Scotland. Pen: Paterson (6/6).
Italy. Try: Troncon; Con: Bortolussi; Pen: Bortolussi (3/6).

Pool C Matches

The nations in Pool C consisted of **Italy, New Zealand, Portugal, Romania** and **Scotland**. New Zealand were way ahead of the other four teams in this group and proved their dominance with a complete rout of the number two team, Scotland (40~0).

Portugal were making their debut and went very close to defeating Romania in their pool match (10~14). The battle for second place in the pool between Scotland and Italy was extraordinarily close. Italy had soundly defeated Scotland in the 'Six Nations' earlier in the year, but Scotland narrowly won the final pool match (18~16) to grab a quarterfinal place.

Results	P	W	D	L	PF	PA	BP	Pts
New Zealand	4	4	0	0	309	35	4	20
Scotland	4	3	0	1	116	66	2	14
Italy	4	2	0	2	85	117	1	9
Romania	4	1	0	3	40	161	1	5
Portugal	4	0	0	4	38	209	1	1

8. Argentina and France line up at the 2007 Rugby World Cup.

POOL D - TEAMS

D	ARGENTINA	FRANCE	GEORGIA	IRELAND	NAMIBIA
Coaches:	Marcelo Loffreda	Bernard Laporte	Malkhaz Cheishvili	Eddie O'Sullivan	Hakkies Husselman
Players:	Eusebio Guiñazú	Pieter de Villiers	David Khinchaguishvili	Simon Best	Jané du Toit
	Mario Ledesma	Nicolas Mas	Avtandil Kopaliani	John Hayes	Kees Lensing (c)
	Alberto Vernet Basualdo	Olivier Milloud	Mamuka Magrakvelidze	Marcus Horan	Johnny Redelinghuys
	Marcos Ayerza	Jean-Baptiste Poux	Goderdzi Shvelidze	Bryan Young	Marius Visser
	S. González Bonorino	Sébastien Bruno	Davit Zirakashvili	Rory Best	Skipper Badenhorst
	Omar Hasan	Raphaël Ibañez (c)	Akvsenti Giorgadze	Jerry Flannery	Hugo Horn
	Rodrigo Roncero	Dimitri Szarzewski	Levan Datunashvili	Frankie Sheahan	Johannes Meyer
	Martín Scelzo	Sébastien Chabal	Victor Didebulidze	Donncha O'Callaghan	Nico Esterhuyse
	Patricio Albacete	Lionel Nallet	Zurab Mtchedlishvili	Paul O'Connell	Domingo Kamonga
	Rimas Álvarez Kairelis	Fabien Pelous	Mamuka Gorgodze	Malcolm O'Kelly	Uakazuwaka Kazombiaze
	Ig. Fernández Lobbe	Jérôme Thion	Ilia Zedguinidze (c)	Neil Best	Heino Senekal
	Esteban Lozada	Serge Betsen (vc)	George Chkhaidze	Simon Easterby	Jacques Burger
	Martín Alberto Durand	Thierry Dusautoir	Gia Labadze	Stephen Ferris	Tinus du Plessis
	Lucas Ostiglia	Rémy Martin	Ilia Maissuradze	Alan Quinlan	Herman Lintvelt
	JM Fernández Lobbe	Yannick Nyanga	Zviad Maissuradze	David Wallace	Michael MacKenzie
	Martín Schusterman	Julien Bonnaire	Rati Urushadze	Denis Leamy	Jacques Nieuwenhuis
	Juan M Leguizamón	Imanol Harinordoquy	Besso Udessiani	Isaac Boss	Eugene Jantjies
	Gonzalo Longo	Jean-Bap. Élissalde (vc)	Irakli Abuseridze (vc)	Eoin Reddan	Jurie van Tonder
	N. Fernández Miranda	Pierre Mignoni	Meko Kvirikashvili	Peter Stringer	Morné Schreuder
	Agustín Pichot (c)	Lionel Beauxis	Bidzina Samkharadze	Ronan O'Gara	Lu-Wayne Botes
	Juan Martín Hernández	Frédéric Michalak	Otar Barkalaia	Paddy Wallace	Du Preez Grobler
	Federico Todeschini	David Skrela	Paliko Jimsheladze	Gordon D'Arcy	Bratley Langenhoven
	Felipe Contepomi (vc)	Yannick Jauzion	Revaz Gigauri	Gavin Duffy	Piet van Zyl
	Manuel Contepomi	David Marty	Irakli Giorgadze	Brian O'Driscoll (c)	Emile Wessels
	Hernán Senillosa (r)	Damien Traille	Davit Kacharava	Brian Carney	Melrick Africa
	Gonzalo Tiesi	Vincent Clerc	Malkhaz Urjukashvili	Denis Hickie	John Drotsky
	Horacio Agulla	Christophe Dominici	Giorgi Elizbarashvili	Shane Horgan	Deon Mouton
	Lucas Borges	Cédric Heymans	Otar Eloshvili	Andrew Trimble	Ryan Witbooi
	Federico M Aramburú	Aurélien Rougerie	Besik Khamashuridze	Girvan Dempsey	Heini Bock
	Ignacio Corleto	Clément Poitrenaud	Irakli Machkhaneli	Geordan Murphy	Tertius Losper
	Federico Serra Miras		George Shkinini		

D.1 Argentina d. France (17~12)

7 September 2007, Stade de France, Saint-Denis.
Attendance: 79,312; Referee: Tony Spreadbury (England).
Argentina. Try: Corleto; Pen: F. Contepomi (4/6).
France. Pen: Skrela (4/5).

D.2 Ireland d. Namibia (32~17)

9 September 2007, Stade Chaban-Delmas, Bordeaux.
Attendance: 33,694; Referee: Joël Jutge (France).
Ireland. Tries: O'Driscoll, Trimble, Easterby, Pen try, Flannery;
Con: O'Gara (2/5); Pen: O'Gara.
Namibia. Tries: Nieuwenhuis, Van Zyl; Con: Wessels (2/2); Pen:
Wessels (1/2).

D.3 Argentina d. Georgia (33~3)

11 September 2007, Stade de Gerland, Lyon.
Attendance: 40,240; Referee: Nigel Owens (Wales).
Argentina. Tries: Borges, Albacete, Martin Aramburu, Con: F.
Contepomi (1/3), Hernández; Pen: F. Contepomi (3/3).
Georgia. Pen: Kvirikashvili (1/2).

D.4 Ireland d. Georgia (14~10)

15 September 2007, Stade Chaban-Delmas, Bordeaux.
Attendance: 33,807; Referee: Wayne Barnes (England).
Ireland. Tries: R. Best, Dempsey; Con: O'Gara (2/2).
Georgia. Try: Shkinin; Con: Kvirikashvili; Pen: Kvirikashvili (1/2).

D.5 France d. Namibia (87~10)

16 September 2007, Stadium de Toulouse, Toulouse.
Attendance: 35,339; Referee: Alain Rolland (Ireland).
France. Tries: Heyman, Marty, Dusautoir, Nallet (2), Clerc (3),
Bonnaire, Chabal (2), Elissalde, Ibañez; Con: Elissalde (11/13).
Namibia. Try: Langenhoven; Con: Losper; Drop: Wessels.

D.6 France d. Ireland (25~3)

21 September 2007, Stade de France, Saint-Denis.
Attendance: 80,267; Referee: Chris White (England).
France. Tries: Clerc (2); Pen: Élissalde (5/6).
Ireland. Drop: O'Gara

D.7 Argentina d. Namibia (63~3)

22 September 2007, Stade Vélodrome, Marseille.
Attendance: 55,067; Referee: Stuart Dickinson (Australia).
Argentina. Tries: Roncero, Leguizamón (2), M. Contepomi, F.
Contepomi, Tiesi, Corleto, Pen try, Todeschini; Con: Contepomi
(4/7), Todeschini (2/2); Pen: F. Contepomi (2/2).
Namibia. Pen: Schreuder.

D.8 Georgia d. Namibia (30~0)

26 September 2007, Stade Félix Bollaert, Lens.
Attendance: 32,549; Referee: Steve Walsh (New Zealand).
Georgia. Tries: Giorgadze, Machkhaneli, Kacharava; Con:
Kvirikashvili (3/3); Pen: Kvirikashvili (3/6).
Namibia. Nil.

D.9 France d. Georgia (64~7)

30 September 2007, Stade Vélodrome, Marseille.
Attendance: 58,695; Referee: Alan Lewis (Ireland).
France. Tries: Poitrenau, Nyanga, Beauxis, Dominici (2), Bruno,
Nallet, Martin, Bonnaire; Con: Beauxis (5/9); Pen: Beauxis (3/3).
Georgia. Try: Z. Maisuradze; Con: Urjukashvili.

D.10 Argentina d. Ireland (30~15)

30 September 2007, Parc des Princes, Paris.
Attendance: 45,450; Referee: Paul Honiss (New Zealand).
Argentina. Tries: Borges, Aguila; Con: F. Contepomi (1/2); Pen: F.
Contepomi (3/4); Drop: Hernández (3/5).
Ireland. Tries: O'Driscoll, Murphy; Con: O'Gara (1/2); Pen:
O'Gara.

Pool D Matches

The nations in Pool D consisted of **Argentina, France, Georgia, Ireland** and **Namibia**. The tournament opened with a match between hosts France and Argentina on

Results	P	W	D	L	PF	PA	BP	Pts
Argentina	4	4	0	0	143	33	2	18
France	4	3	0	1	188	37	3	15
Ireland	4	2	0	2	64	82	1	9
Georgia	4	1	0	3	50	111	1	5
Namibia	4	0	0	4	30	212	0	0

7th September at the Stade de France, outside Paris. Los Puma's staged an upset first up win (17~12) and then defeated Ireland (30~15) in their final match to win the pool. In the process, Argentina recorded the best defensive figures of all 20 teams in the pools.

France were pitted against a determined Ireland in a race to finish second in the pool. But Ireland's losses to both France (3~25) and Argentina in their final match (15~30) relegated them to third position.

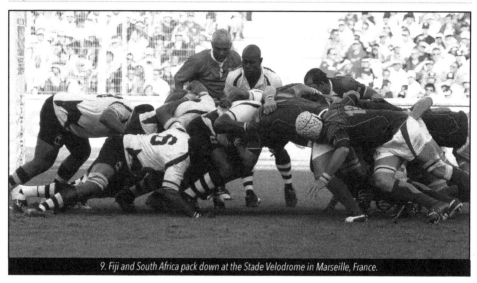

9. Fiji and South Africa pack down at the Stade Velodrome in Marseille, France.

THE PLAYOFFS

Quarter Finals

The quarter final games produced quite a few shock results. In the first two matches, a disappointing Australia fell to England (10~12), and France rebounded from the embarrassment of losing their opening pool match to the Puma's, with a narrow victory over New Zealand (20~18).

South Africa was in fine form to defeat a talented Fiji (37~20) in quarter final 3, which gained them a semi final berth. This left Scotland and Argentina pitted against each other for the last semi final spot. Watched by 76,866 fans at the Stade de France, Argentina defeated the Scots (19~13) to qualify for their first ever World Cup semi-final.

Semi Finals

The first semi-final drew an enormous crowd with over

QUARTER FINALS

QF1 England d. Australia (12~10)

6 October 2007, Stade Vélodrome, Marseille.
Attendance: 59,102; Referee: Alain Rolland (Ireland).
England. Pen: Wilkinson (4/7).
Australia. Try: Tuqiri; Con: Mortlock; Pen: Mortlock (1/4).

QF2 France d. New Zealand (20~18)

6 October 2007, Millennium Stadium, Cardiff.
Attendance: 71,669; Referee: Wayne Barnes (England).
France. Try: Dusautoir, Jauzion; Con: Beauxis, Élissalde; Pen: Beauxis (2/3).
New Zealand. Try: McAlister, So'oialo; Con: Carter; Pen: Carter (2/2).

QF3 South Africa d. Fiji (37~20)

7 October 2007, Stade Vélodrome, Marseille.
Attendance: 55,943; Referee: Alan Lewis (Ireland).
South Africa. Try: Fourie, Smit, Pietersen, Smith, James; Con: Montgomery (3/5); Pen: Steyn, Montgomery (1/2).
Fiji. Try: Delasau, Bobo; Con: Bai (2/2); Pen: Bai (2/2).

QF4 Argentina d. Scotland (19~13)

7 October 2007, Stade de France, Saint-Denis.
Attendance: 76,866; Referee: Joël Jutge (France).
Argentina. Try: Longo Elia; Con: F. Contepomi; Pen: F. Contepomi (3/4); Drop: Hernández (1/4).
Scotland. Try: Cusiter; Con: Paterson; Pen: Parks (1/2), Paterson.

80,000 fans crowding into the Stade de France, in Saint Denis to watch the 2007 'Six Nations' champions, France against England. England scored a try just two minutes into the match, which was to be the difference as both sides produced a further nine points each from kicks. The French fans were terribly disappointed to witness this loss to England (9~14) and see their hopes of a Rugby World Cup dashed.

The second semi final was a 'David and Goliath' encounter between South Africa and Argentina, who had surprised the entire rugby fraternity all throughout the tournament.

SEMI FINALS

Semi Final 1
England d. France (14~9)

13 October 2007, Stade de France, Saint-Denis.
Attendance: 80,283; Referee: Jonathan Kaplan (South Africa).
England. Try: Lewsey; Pen: Wilkinson (2/3); Drop: Wilkinson (1/4).
France. Pen: Beauxis (3/3).

Semi Final 2
South Africa d. Argentina (37~13)

14 October 2007, Stade de France, Saint-Denis.
Attendance: 77,055; Referee: Steve Walsh (Australia).
South Africa. Try: du Preez, Habana (2), Rossouw; Con: Montgomery (4/4); Pen: Montgomery (3/3).
Argentina. Try: M. Contepomi; Con: F. Contepomi; Pen: F. Contepomi (2

But Argentina's 'fairy story' came to an abrupt end as the experienced Springboks cut through to score five tries to one. South Africa secured both the victory over Argentina

10. The French and Argentine forward packs strive for dominance.

11. The South Africans score a try in their 36-0 Pool A thrashing of England.

(37~13) and the right to contest for a second World Cup.

3rd Place Playoff

The playoff for third place was contested between France and Argentina at the Stade de France, in Saint Denis on the outskirts of Paris in front of 45,958 spectators on the 19th October 2007.

The French crowd fully expected their team to defeat Argentina, although the Puma's had a different idea. France kicked a penalty to start off the scoring, but Argentina struck back scoring four unanswered tries before France could reply. Argentina's Felipe Contepomi masterfully led his side to a 34~10 win, with a personal contribution of 19 points from two tries and four goals. In victory, Los Pumas had gained a historic World Cup bronze medal and were hero's right across Argentina.

THE FINAL

The Stade de France in Saint-Denis, outside Paris was also the venue of the final match between England and South Africa on 20th October 2007. England had already been walloped by the Springboks (36~0) in their pool stage encounter, so most pundits dismissed England's prospects.

As it turned out, the match was much closer than

expected. Unfortunately no tries were scored, but the two teams went goal for goal and England fought back just after the half time break to be only three points adrift 6~9, before the Springboks kicked another two penalties. The final result saw South Africa defeat England (15~6) and in the process capture their second Rugby World Cup from just two attempts.

In a new initiative, the top three nations from each pool automatically qualified for the 2011 World Cup. It was thought that this strategy provided an incentive for lesser teams to perform better on the world stage.

FINALS

FINAL
South Africa d. England (15~6)

20 October 2007, Stade de France, Saint-Denis.
Attendance: 80,430; Referee: Alain Rolland (Ireland).
South Africa. Pen: Montgomery (4/4); Steyn (1/2).
England. Pen: Wilkinson (2/2).

3rd/4th Playoff
Argentina d. France (34~10)

19 October 2007, Parc des Princes, Paris.
Attendance: 45,958; Referee: Paul Honiss (New Zealand).
Argentina. Try: F. Contepomi (2), Hasan Jalil, Martín Aramburú, Corleto; Con: F. Contepomi (3/5); Pen: F. Contepomi.
France. Try: Poitrenaud; Con: Beauxis; Pen: Élissalde.

12. Bryan Habana holds South Africa's second World Cup high during a homecoming parade.

CREDITS

2011
VII RUGBY WORLD CUP
New Zealand

1. Richie McCaw, captain of New Zealand.

VII Rugby World Cup
9th September to 23rd October, 2011

2. The Rugby World Cup returned to New Zealand for the 2011 tournament.

The 2011 Rugby World Cup was the seventh Rugby World Cup. The International Rugby Board (IRB) selected New Zealand as the host country in preference to bids from Japan and South Africa.

THE HOST

The IRB Council meeting in Dublin on 17 November 2005 announced that New Zealand had been selected following the IRB inspections of each applicant host nation during June and July of 2005.

In the years between winning the bid and the staging of the event, New Zealand news media and social agencies cast aspersions on the nation's readiness and appropriate use of national funds for sports infrastructure, as has happened with most large, international, quadrennial, multi-location sporting events of recent decades such as the 2010 FIFA World Cup, the 2010 Commonwealth Games and the 2012 Olympic Games.

Ticket sales exceeded NZ$285m, accommodation related spending another NZ$260 million, and NZ$236 million spent on food and drink provided a significant fiscal stimulus, of nearly 1.4% of the quarterly New Zealand GDP. The attendance totaled 1,477,294, which was an average of 30,777 fans per match!

THE TEAMS

After some speculation that the number of participating teams might be reduced to 16, the IRB announced on 30 November 2007 that the 2011 tournament would again feature 20 teams. Of the 20 countries that competed in the previous World Cup in 2007, there was only one change with Russia replacing Portugal. Each nation was allowed a squad of 30 players for the tournament.

Seeded Teams

Twelve teams qualified as a result of finishing in the top three in each pool in the 2007 Rugby World Cup tournament. This meant that **South Africa, England, Tonga, Australia, Fiji, Wales, Scotland, Italy, Argentina, France** and **Ireland** all automatically qualified for the event, and were joined by **New**

3. Ireland celebrates their 'Six Nations' Rugby Championship in 2009.

Zealand as the host nation. The remaining eight berths were determined by regional qualifying tournaments.

Qualifying Teams

All other nations vying for a place in the tournament had to qualify through a series of qualification matches, which were contested by some 79 teams worldwide.

Namibia won the single African Zone place over teams from Kenya, Zimbabwe, Ivory Coast, Tunisia, Morocco, Nigeria, Swaziland, Zambia, Cameroon, Senegal, Uganda, Botswana, and Madagascar. **Canada** and the **United States** won the two America's Zone places over teams from Trinidad & Tobago, Brazil, Venezuela, Peru, Colombia, Guyana, Bermuda, Cayman Islands, Mexico, Jamaica, Bahamas, Barbados, St Vincent & The Grenadines, Chile, Uruguay and Paraguay.

The European Zone had two places up for grabs, which was contested across five separate rounds by 31 nations. **Georgia** and **Russia** eventually qualified over teams from Armenia, Croatia, Denmark, Latvia, Moldova, Norway, Greece, Bulgaria, the Netherlands, Ukraine, Poland, Belgium, Switzerland, Israel, Austria, Serbia, Portugal, Germany, Czech Republic,

'*Match between South Africa and Fiji during 2011, Rugby World Cup in New Zealand' by Craig Boyd (17 Sep 2011). Available at https://en.wikipedia.org/wiki/File:South_Africa_vs_Fiji_2011_RWC_(4).jpg under the Creative Commons Attribution-Share Alike 2.0 Generic license.*

Slovenia, Andorra, Sweden, Hungary, Spain, Romania, Malta, Lithuania, Finland and Luxembourg.

Japan won the single Asian Zone spot over teams from Malaysia, Pakistan, India, Sri Lanka, Kazakhstan, South Korea, Hong Kong, Chinese Taipei, Thailand and the Arabian Gulf. **Samoa** won the single Oceania Zone place over teams from the Cook Islands, Vanuatu, Niue and Papua New Guinea.

Repechage Teams

The repechage was a great initiative, essentially giving a few unlucky teams a second chance. There was only one repechage position available in the 2011 Rugby World Cup. **Romania** eventually qualified through the repechage rounds over teams from Kazakhstan, Tunisia and Uruguay.

THE POOL STAGE

A total of 48 matches scheduled across 44 days (40 pool stage games and 8 knock-out stage games) were played throughout the tournament. With the 20 teams being divided into four pools of five nations, the top two teams in each pool progressed to the knock-out quarter-final stage.

Teams were awarded four points for a win, two points for a draw and none for a defeat. The bonus point system was retained whereby a team scoring four or more tries in one match scored a bonus point, as did a team losing by seven or fewer points.

POOL A - TEAMS

A	CANADA	FRANCE	JAPAN	NEW ZEALAND	TONGA
Coaches:	Kieran Crowley	Marc Lièvremont	John Kirwan	Graham Henry	Isitolo Maka
Players:	Ryan Hamilton	Guilhem Guirado	Yusuke Aoki	Corey Flynn	Aleki Lutui
	Pat Riordan (c)	William Servat	Shota Horie	Andrew Hore	Ilaisa Ma'asi
	Hubert Buydens	Dimitri Szarzewski	Hiroki Yuhara	Keven Mealamu (vc)	Ephraim Taukafa
	Scott Franklin	Fabien Barcella	Nozomu Fujita	John Afoa	Halani Aulika
	Jason Marshall	Luc Ducalcon	Kensuke Hatakeyama	Ben Franks	Taufa'ao Filise
	Andrew Tiedemann	Nicolas Mas	Hisateru Hirashima	Owen Franks	Kisi Pulu
	Frank Walsh	Jean-Baptiste Poux	Naoki Kawamata	Tony Woodcock	Sona Taumalolo
	Jamie Cudmore	Romain Millo-Chluski	Toshizumi Kitagawa	Anthony Boric	Soane Tonga'uiha
	Brian Erichsen	Lionel Nallet	Yuji Kitagawa	Brad Thorn	Paino Hehea
	Tyler Hotson	Pascal Papé	Hitoshi Ono	Sam Whitelock	Tukulua Lokotui
	Nanyak Dala	Julien Pierre	Luke Thompson	Ali Williams	Sione Timani
	Adam Kleeberger	Julien Bonnaire	Takashi Kikutani (c)	Jerome Kaino	Joe Tuineau
	Chauncey O'Toole	Thierry Dusautoir (c)	Michael Leitch	Richie McCaw (c)	Sione Kalamafoni
	Jebb Sinclair	Imanol Harinordoquy	Sione Vatuvei	Adam Thomson	Finau Maka (c)
	Aaron Carpenter	Fulgence Ouedraogo	Itaru Taniguchi	Kieran Read	Sione Vaiomo'unga
	Jeremy Kyne	Raphaël Lakafia	Toetu'u Taufa	Victor Vito	Viliami Ma'afu
	Jamie Mackenzie	Louis Picamoles	Ippei Asada	Jimmy Cowan	Samiu Vahafolau
	Sean White	Morgan Parra	Atsushi Hiwasa	Andy Ellis	Samisoni Fisilau
	Nathan Hirayama	Dimitri Yachvili	Fumiaki Tanaka	Piri Weepu	Taniela Moa
	Ander Monro (vc)	Jean-Marc Doussain	James Arlidge	Aaron Cruden	Thomas Palu
	Mike Scholz	François Trinh-Duc	Murray Williams	Stephen Donald	Kurt Morath
	Ryan Smith	David Skrela	Ryan Nicholas	Richard Kahui	Alipate Fatafehi
	Conor Trainor	Fabrice Estebanez	Bryce Robins	Ma'a Nonu	Suka Hufanga
	DTH van der Merwe	David Marty	Koji Taira	Conrad Smith	Andrew Ma'ilei
	Ciaran Hearn	Maxime Mermoz	Alisi Tupuailai	Sonny Bill Williams	Siale Piutau
	Phil Mackenzie	Aurélien Rougerie	Kosuke Endo	Hosea Gear	William Helu
	Taylor Paris	Vincent Clerc	Hirotoki Onozawa	Zac Guildford	Alaska Taufa
	Matt Evans	Maxime Médard	Takehisa Usuzuki	Cory Jane	Fetu'u Vainikolo
	James Pritchard	Alexis Palisson	Taihei Ueda	Israel Dagg	Viliame Iongi
		Cédric Heymans	Shaun Webb	Isaia Toeava	Vunga Lilo (vc)
		Damien Traille			

4. France defeats Tonga (41~10) in their Pool A match.

Pool A Matches

The nations in Pool A consisted of **Canada, France, Japan, New Zealand** and **Tonga**. The tournament began with the host nation New Zealand defeating Tonga (41~10) at Eden Park in Auckland. The only real threat to the All Blacks came from France, whom they also soundly defeated (37~17).

The attention in this pool focused on whether France or Tonga would progress to the quarter finals, and

Results	P	W	D	L	PF	PA	BP	Pts
New Zealand	4	4	0	0	240	49	4	20
France	4	2	0	2	124	96	3	11
Tonga	4	2	0	2	80	98	1	9
Canada	4	1	1	2	82	168	0	6
Japan	4	0	1	3	69	184	0	2

France didn't do themselves any favours in going down to Tonga (14~19). But Tonga's loss to Canada (20~25), along with three bonus points allowed France to grab second place and just sneak into the quarterfinals.

A.1 New Zealand d. Tonga (41~10)

9 September 2011, Eden Park, Auckland.
Attendance: 60,214; Referee: George Clancy (Ireland).
New Zealand. Try: Dagg (2), Kahui (2), Kaino, Nonu; Con: Carter (3/5), Slade; Pen: Carter.
Tonga. Try: Taumalolo; Con: Morath; Pen: Morath (1/2).

A.2 France d. Japan (47~21)

10 September 2011, North Harbour Stadium, Auckland.
Attendance: 28,569; Referee: Steve Walsh (Australia).
France. Try: Pierre, Trinh-Duc, Clerc, Nallet, Papé, Parra; Con: Yachvili (4/6); Pen: Yachvili (3/3).
Japan. Try: Arlidge (2); Con: Arlidge (1/2); Pen: Arlidge (3/3).

A.3 Canada d. Tonga (25~20)

14 September 2011, Northland Events Centre, Whangarei.
Attendance: 17,174; Referee: Jonathan Kaplan (South Africa).
Canada. Try: Sinclair, Carpenter, Mackenzie; Con: Pritchard (2/3); Pen: Pritchard (2/2).
Tonga. Try: Piutau (2); Con: Morath (2/2); Pen: Morath (2/4).

A.4 New Zealand d. Japan (83~7)

16 September 2011, Waikato Stadium, Hamilton.
Attendance: 30,484; Referee: Nigel Owens (Wales).
New Zealand. Try: Smith, Kahui (2), Kaino, Mealamu, Ellis, Slade, S. Williams (2), Toeava, Hore, Nonu, Thomson; Con: Slade (9/13).
Japan. Try: Onozawa; Con: M. Williams.

A.5 France d. Canada (46~19)

18 September 2011, McLean Park, Napier.
Attendance: 14,230; Referee: Craig Joubert (South Africa).
France. Try: Clerc (3), Traille; Con: Parra (4/4); Pen: Parra (5/6); Drop: Trinh-Duc.
Canada. Try: Smith; Con: Pritchard; Pen: Pritchard (2/4); Drop: Monro (2).

A.6 Tonga d. Japan (31~18)

21 September 2011, Northland Events Centre, Whangarei.
Attendance: 17,364; Referee: Dave Pearson (England).
Tonga. Try: Ma'afu, Lokotui, Vainikolo; Con: Morath (2/3); Pen: Morath (4/4).
Japan. Try: Hatakeyama, Leitch, Tupuailai; Pen: Webb.

A.7 New Zealand d. France (37~17)

24 September 2011, Eden Park, Auckland.
Attendance: 60,856; Referee: Alain Rolland (Ireland)
New Zealand. Try: Thomson, Jane, Dagg (2), S. Williams; Con: Carter (3/5); Pen: Carter; Drop: Carter.
France. Try: Mermoz, Trinh-Duc; Con: Yachvili (2/2). Pen: Yachvili.

A.8 Canada dr. Japan (23~23)

27 September 2011, McLean Park, Napier.
Attendance: 14,335; Referee: Jonathan Kaplan (South Africa).
Canada. Try: Van der Merwe, Mackenzie, Monro; Con: Pritchard (1/1); Pen: Monro (2/3).
Japan. Try: Horie, Endo; Con: Arlidge (2/2); Pen: Arlidge (3/3).

A.9 Tonga d. France (19~14)

1 October 2011, Westpac Stadium, Wellington.
Attendance: 32,763; Referee: Steve Walsh (Australia).
Tonga. Try: Hufanga; Con: Morath; Pen: Morath (4/8).
France. Try: Clerc; Pen: Yachvili (3/3).

A.10 New Zealand d. Canada (79~15)

2 October 2011, Westpac Stadium, Wellington.
Attendance: 37,665; Referee: Romain Poite (France).
New Zealand. Try: Guildford (4), Vito (2), Dagg, Muliaina, Cowan, Kaino (2), S. Williams; Con: Slade (4/8), Weepu (4/4); Pen: Slade.
Canada. Try: Trainor (2); Con: Monro (1/2); Pen: Monro.

5. Argentine fans at the quarter final against New Zealand.

POOL B - TEAMS

B	ARGENTINA	ENGLAND	GEORGIA	ROMANIA	SCOTLAND
Coaches:	Santiago Phelan	Martin Johnson	Richie Dixon	Romeo Gontineac	Andy Robinson
Players:	Agustín Creevy	Dylan Hartley	Jaba Bregvadze	Marius Tincu (c)	Ross Ford
	Mario Ledesma	Lee Mears	Akvsenti Giorgadze	Bogdan Zebega	Dougie Hall
	Marcos Ayerza	Steve Thompson	Vasil Kakovin	Dragoş Dima	Scott Lawson
	Maximiliano Bustos	Dan Cole	Davit Khinchagishvili	Silviu Florea	Geoff Cross
	Juan Figallo	Alex Corbisiero	Davit Kubriashvili	Paulică Ion	Alasdair Dickinson
	Rodrigo Roncero	Matt Stevens	Goderdzi Shvelidze	Mihaita Lazăr	Allan Jacobsen
	Martín Scelzo	David Wilson	Davit Zirakashvili	Nicolae Nere	Moray Low
	Patricio Albacete	Louis Deacon	Levan Datunashvili	Cristian Petre (vc)	Euan Murray
	Manuel Carizza	Courtney Lawes	Vakhtang Maisuradze	Valentin Popirlan	Richie Gray
	Mariano Galarza	Tom Palmer	Giorgi Nemsadze	Cosmin Raţiu	Jim Hamilton
	Tomas Vallejos	Simon Shaw	Ilia Zedginidze	Valentin Ursache	Nathan Hines
	Alejandro Campos	Tom Croft	Givi Berishvili	Stelian Burcea	Alastair Kellock (c)
	Julio Farías Cabello	James Haskell	Giorgi Chkhaidze	Daniel Ianus	John Barclay
	Genaro Fessia	Lewis Moody (c)	Viktor Kolelishvili	Mihai Macovei	Kelly Brown
	JM Leguizamón	Tom Wood	Shalva Sutiashvili	Daniel Carpo	Ross Rennie
	JM Fernández Lobbe (vc)	Nick Easter	Dimitri Basilaia	Ovidiu Toniţa	Alasdair Strokosch
	Leonardo Senatore	Thomas Waldrom	Mamuka Gorgodze	Valentin Calafeteanu	Richie Vernon
	Alfredo Lalanne	Joe Simpson	Irakli Abuseridze (c)	Lucian Sîrbu	Mike Blair
	Nicolás Vergallo	Richard Wigglesworth	Bidzina Samkharadze	Florin Surugiu	Chris Cusiter
	Santiago Fernández	Ben Youngs	Lasha Khmaladze	Ionuţ Dimofte	Rory Lawson
	Nicolás Sánchez	Toby Flood	Merab Kvirikashvili	Dănuţ Dumbravă	Ruaridh Jackson
	Marcelo Bosch	Jonny Wilkinson	Lasha Malaghuradze	Ionel Cazan	Dan Parks
	Felipe Contepomi (c)	Shontayne Hape	Davit Kacharava	Csaba Gál	Joe Ansbro
	Agustin Gosio	Mike Tindall (vc)	Alexander Todua	Constantin Gheara	Nick De Luca
	Horacio Agulla	Manu Tuilagi	Tedo Zibzibadze	Adrian Apostol	Graeme Morrison
	Lucas Borges	Delon Armitage	Irakli Chkhikvadze	Stefan Ciuntu	Simon Danielli
	Gonzalo Camacho	Chris Ashton	Lexo Gugava	Mădălin Lemnaru	Max Evans
	Juan Imhoff	Matt Banahan	Irakli Machkhaneli	Cătălin Nicolae	Sean Lamont
	L González Amorosino	Mark Cueto	Revaz Gigauri	Iulian Dumitraș	Rory Lamont
	Martín Rodríguez	Ben Foden	Malkhaz Urjukashvili	Florin Vlaicu	Chris Paterson

Results	P	W	D	L	PF	PA	BP	Pts
England	4	4	0	0	137	34	2	18
Argentina	4	3	0	1	90	40	2	14
Scotland	4	2	0	2	73	59	3	11
Georgia	4	1	0	3	48	90	0	4
Romania	4	0	0	4	44	169	0	0

Pool B Matches

The nations in Pool B consisted of **Argentina, England, Georgia, Romania** and **Scotland**. Both Georgia and Romania were definitely developing as rugby nations and registered some very good results.

But pool B witnessed a desperate battle between three roughly equal rugby nations in Argentina, England and Scotland. The 'Six Nations' champions, England managed to win all four of their matches, although after very close calls against Argentina (13~9) and Scotland (16~12). Argentina also had a desperate battle to defeat Scotland (13~12), but in being so close were also able to gain a quarterfinal berth.

B.1 Scotland d. Romania (34~24)

10 September 2011, Rugby Park Stadium, Invercargill. Attendance: 12,592; Referee: Dave Pearson (England). **Scotland.** Try: Blair, Ansbro, Danielli (2); Con: Paterson (1/4); Pen: Paterson (4/5). **Romania.** Try: Lazăr, Carpo; Con: Dimofte (1/2); Pen: Dumbravă (2/4), Dimofte (2/2).

B.2 England d. Argentina (13~9)

10 September 2011, Otago Stadium, Dunedin. Attendance: 30,700; Referee: Bryce Lawrence (New Zealand). **England.** Try: Youngs; Con: Wilkinson; Pen: Wilkinson (2/7). **Argentina.** Pen: Contepomi (1/2), Rodríguez (2/7).

B.3 Scotland d. Georgia (15~6)

14 September 2011, Rugby Park Stadium, Invercargill. Attendance: 10,267, Referee: George Clancy (Ireland). **Scotland.** Pen: Parks (4/7); Drop: Parks. **Georgia.** Pen: Kvirikashvili (2/2).

B.4 Argentina d. Romania (43~8)

17 September 2011, Rugby Park Stadium, Invercargill. Attendance: 12,605; Referee: Steve Walsh (Australia). **Argentina.** Try: Fernández, Leguizamón, Figallo, Go, Amorosino, Imhoff, Fessia; Con: Rodríguez (5/6); Pen: Rodríguez (1/3). **Romania.** Try: Cazan; Pen: Dimofte (1/2).

B.5 England d. Georgia (41~10)

18 September 2011, Otago Stadium, Dunedin. Attendance: 20,117; Referee: Jonathan Kaplan (South Africa). **England.** Try: Hape (2), Armitage, Tuilagi, Ashton (2); Con: Flood (4/6); Pen: Flood. **Georgia.** Try: Basilaia; Con: Kvirikashvili; Pen: Kvirikashvili (1/6).

B.6 England d. Romania (67~3)

24 September 2011, Otago Stadium, Dunedin. Attendance: 25,687; Referee: Romain Poite (France). **England.** Try: Cueto (3), Ashton (3), Youngs, Foden, Tuilagi, Croft; Con: Wilkinson (3/5), Flood (4/5); Pen: Wilkinson. **Romania.** Pen: Dumbravă (1/5).

B.7 Argentina d. Scotland (13~12)

25 September 2011, Wellington Regional Stadium, Wellington. Attendance: 26,937; Referee: Wayne Barnes (England). **Argentina.** Try: González Amorosino; Con: Contepomi; Pen: Contepomi (2/5). **Scotland.** Pen: Paterson (1/2), Jackson; Drop: Jackson, Parks (1/2).

B.8 Georgia d. Romania (25~9)

28 September 2011, Arena Manawatu, Palmerston North. Attendance: 13,228; Referee: Dave Pearson (England). **Georgia.** Try: Gorgodze; Con: Kvirikashvili; Pen: Kvirikashvili (5/7), Urjukashvili. **Romania.** Pen: Dumbravă (2/4), Vlaicu.

B.9 England d. Scotland (16~12)

1 October 2011, Eden Park, Auckland. Attendance: 58,213; Referee: Craig Joubert (South Africa). **England.** Try: Ashton; Con: Flood; Pen: Wilkinson (2/5); Drop: Wilkinson (1/2). **Scotland.** Pen: Paterson (2/2), Parks; Drop: Parks (1/3).

B.10 Argentina d. Georgia (25~7)

2 October 2011, Arena Manawatu, Palmerston North. Attendance: 13,754; Referee: Alain Rolland (Ireland). **Argentina.** Try: Imhoff, Contepomi, Gosio; Con: Contepomi (1/2), Bosch; Pen: Contepomi (2/4). **Georgia.** Try: Khmaladze; Con: Urjukashvili.

POOL C - TEAMS

C	AUSTRALIA	IRELAND	ITALY	RUSSIA	USA
Coaches:	Robbie Deans	Declan Kidney	Nick Mallett	Nikolay Nerush	Eddie O'Sullivan
Players:	Saia Fainga'a	Rory Best	Leonardo Ghiraldini (vc)	Vladislav Korshunov (c)	Chris Biller
	Stephen Moore	Sean Cronin	Fabio Ongaro	Yevgeny Matveyev	Brian McClenahan
	Tatafu Polota-Nau	Damien Varley	Franco Sbaraglini	Valeri Tsnobiladze	Phil Thiel
	Ben Alexander	Tony Buckley	Martin Castrogiovanni	Alexander Khrokin	Eric Fry
	Sekope Kepu	Tom Court	Lorenzo Cittadini	Sergey Popov	Mike MacDonald
	Salesi Ma'afu	Cian Healy	Andrea Lo Cicero	Ivan Prishchepenko	Mate Moeakiola
	James Slipper	Mike Ross	Salvatore Perugini	Alexei Travkin	Shawn Pittman
	James Horwill (c)	Leo Cullen	Marco Bortolami	Denis Antonov	Scott LaValla
	Nathan Sharpe	Donncha O'Callaghan	Carlo Del Fava	Adam Byrnes	Hayden Smith
	Rob Simmons	Paul O'Connell (vc)	Quintin Geldenhuys	Andrei Ostrikov	John van der Giessen
	Dan Vickerman	Donnacha Ryan	Corniel van Zyl	Alexander Voytov	Inaki Basauri
	Rocky Elsom	Stephen Ferris	Robert Barbieri	Artem Fatakhov	Todd Clever (c)
	Scott Higginbotham	Shane Jennings	Mauro Bergamasco	Andrey Garbuzov	Pat Danahy
	Matt Hodgson	Sean O'Brien	Paul Derbyshire	Mikhail Sidorov	Louis Stanfill
	David Pocock	Jamie Heaslip	Alessandro Zanni	Viacheslav Grachev (vc)	JJ Gagiano
	Ben McCalman	Denis Leamy	Sergio Parisse (c)	Victor Gresev	Nic Johnson
	Radike Samo	Isaac Boss	Pablo Canavosio	Andrei Bykanov	Mike Petri (vc)
	Luke Burgess	Conor Murray	Edoardo Gori	Alexander Shakirov	Tim Usasz
	Will Genia	Eoin Reddan	Fabio Semenzato	Alexander Yanyushkin	Valenese Malifa
	Nick Phipps	Ronan O'Gara	Riccardo Bocchino	Yuri Kushnarev	Roland Suniula
	Berrick Barnes	Jonathan Sexton	Luciano Orquera	Konstantin Rachkov	Paul Emerick
	Quade Cooper	Gordon D'Arcy	Gonzalo Canale	Mikhail Babaev	Tai Enosa
	Adam Ashley-Cooper	Fergus McFadden	Gonzalo Garcia	Alexey Makovetskiy	Junior Sifa
	Anthony Fainga'a	Brian O'Driscoll (c)	Matteo Pratichetti	Sergey Trishin	Andrew Suniula
	Rob Horne	Paddy Wallace	Alberto Sgarbi	Vasily Artemiev	Colin Hawley
	Pat McCabe	Tommy Bowe	Tommaso Benvenuti	Andrei Kuzin	Takudzwa Ngwenya
	Digby Ioane	Keith Earls	Mirco Bergamasco	Vladimir Ostroushko	James Paterson
	James O'Connor	Andrew Trimble	Giulio Toniolatti	Denis Simplikevich	Kevin Swiryn
	Lachie Turner	Rob Kearney	Andrea Masi	Igor Klyuchnikov	Blaine Scully
	Kurtley Beale	Geordan Murphy	Luke McLean		Chris Wyles

6. The Australians take on the USA in their Pool C encounter.

C.1 Australia d. Italy (32~6)

11 September 2011, North Harbour Stadium, Auckland. Attendance: 25,731; Referee: Alain Rolland (Ireland). **Australia.** Try: Alexander, Ashley-Cooper, O'Connor, Ioane; Con: O'Connor (3/4); Pen: Cooper (2/3). **Italy.** Pen: Mi. Bergamasco (2/3).

C.2 Ireland d. United States (22~10)

11 September 2011, Stadium Taranaki, New Plymouth. Attendance: 20,823; Referee: Craig Joubert (South Africa). **Ireland.** Try: Bowe (2), Best; Con: Sexton, O'Gara (1/2); Pen: Sexton (1/5). **United States.** Try: Emerick; Con: Malifa; Pen: Paterson (1/2).

C.3 United States d. Russia (13~6)

15 September 2011, Stadium Taranaki, New Plymouth. Attendance: 13,931; Referee: Dave Pearson (England). **United States.** Try: Petri; Con: Wyles; Pen: Wyles (2/5). **Russia.** Pen: Kushnarev (1/4), Rachkov.

C.4 Ireland d. Australia (15~6)

17 September 2011, Eden Park, Auckland. Attendance: 58,678; Referee: Bryce Lawrence (New Zealand). **Ireland.** Pen: Sexton (2/5), O'Gara (2/2); Drop: Sexton. **Australia.** Pen: O'Connor (2/4).

C.5 Italy d. Russia (53~17)

20 September 2011, Trafalgar Park, Nelson. Attendance: 12,418; Referee: Wayne Barnes (England). **Italy.** Try: Parisse, Toniolatti (2), Benvenuti (2), Pen try, Gori, McLean, Zanni; Con: Bocchino (4/6). **Russia.** Try: Yanyushkin, Ostroushko, Makovetski; Con: Rachkov (1/3).

C.6 Australia d. United States (67~5)

23 September 2011, Wellington Regional Stadium, Wellington. Attendance: 33,824; Referee: Nigel Owens (Wales). **Australia.** Try: Horne, Elsom, Beale, Fainga'a (2), Mitchell, McCabe, Ashley-Cooper (3), Samo; Con: Cooper (2/5), Barnes (4/5). **United States.** Try: Gagiano.

C.7 Ireland d. Russia (62~12)

25 September 2011, Rotorua International Stadium, Rotorua. Attendance: 25,661; Referee: Craig Joubert (South Africa). **Ireland.** Try: McFadden, O'Brien, Boss, Earls (2), Trimble, Kearney, Jennings, Buckley; Con: O'Gara (6/7), Sexton (1/2); Pen: O'Gara. **Russia.** Try: Artemyev, Simplikevich; Con: Rachkov.

C.8 Italy d. United States (27~10)

27 September 2011, Trafalgar Park, Nelson. Attendance: 14,997; Referee: George Clancy (Ireland). **Italy.** Try: Parisse, Orquera, Castrogiovanni, Pen try; Con: Mi. Bergamasco (2/4); Pen: Mi. Bergamasco. **United States.** Try: Wyles; Con: Wyles; Pen: Wyles.

C.9 Australia d. Russia (68~22)

1 October 2011, Trafalgar Park, Nelson. Attendance: 16,307; Referee: Bryce Lawrence (New Zealand). **Australia.** Try: Barnes (2), Mitchell (2), McCalman, Pocock (2), Moore, Ashley-Cooper, Ma'afu; Con: O'Connor (9/10). **Russia.** Try: Ostroushko, Simplikevich, Rachkov; Con: Rachkov (2/2); Drop: Rachkov.

C.10 Ireland d. Italy (36~6)

2 October 2011, Otago Stadium, Dunedin. Attendance: 28,027; Referee: Jonathan Kaplan (South Africa). **Ireland.** Try: O'Driscoll, Earls (2); Con: O'Gara (2/2), Sexton; Pen: O'Gara (4/5), Sexton. **Italy.** Pen: Mi. Bergamasco (2/3).

Pool C Matches

The nations in Pool C consisted of **Australia, Ireland, Italy, Russia** and the **United States**. In pool C Russia struggled, but the United States fared better with a solid game against Ireland (10~22), and the Italians exhibited some occasional moments of brilliance.

The focus in pool C was on the Australians, who easily accounted for Italy, Russia and the USA. But the Wallabies ran into a very determined Ireland in their second pool match. The Irish defense remained solid throughout the entire match, and their kickers won the day (15~6), which had further implications for the quarterfinal match ups.

Results	P	W	D	L	PF	PA	BP	Pts
Ireland	4	4	0	0	135	34	1	17
Australia	4	3	0	1	173	48	3	15
Italy	4	2	0	2	92	95	2	10
United States	4	1	0	3	38	122	0	4
Russia	4	0	0	4	57	196	1	1

7. Samoa pushed Wales to the limit in their Pool D match.

POOL D - TEAMS

D	FIJI	NAMIBIA	SAMOA	STH AFRICA	WALES
Coaches:	Sam Domoni	Johan Diergaardt	Titimaea Tafua	Peter de Villiers	Warren Gatland
Players:	Sunia Koto	Hugo Horn	Ole Avei	Bismarck du Plessis	Huw Bennett
	Talemaitoga Tuapati	Bertus O'Callaghan	Ti'i Paulo	Chiliboy Ralepelle	Lloyd Burns
	Viliame Veikoso	Jané du Toit	Mahonri Schwalger (c)	John Smit (c)	Ken Owens
	Waisea Daveta	Raoul Larson	Census Johnston	Jannie du Plessis	Ryan Bevington
	Campese Ma'afu	Johnny Redelinghuys	Logovi'i Mulipola	Tendai Mtawarira	Paul James
	Deacon Manu (c)	Marius Visser	Anthony Perenise	Gurthrö Steenkamp	Gethin Jenkins
	Setefano Somoca	Nico Esterhuyse	Sakaria Taulafo	CJ van der Linde	Adam Jones
	Sekonaia Kalou	Henk Franken	Daniel Leo	Bakkies Botha	Craig Mitchell
	Wame Lewaravu	Uakazuwaka Kazombiaze	Filipo Levi	Victor Matfield (vc)	Luke Charteris
	Leone Nakarawa	Heinz Koll	Joe Tekori	Johann Muller	Bradley Davies
	Rupeni Nasiga	Jacques Burger (c)	Kane Thompson	Danie Rossouw	Alun Wyn Jones
	Akapusi Qera (vc)	Tinus du Plessis	Maurie Fa'asavalu	Willem Alberts	Ryan Jones
	Malakai Ravulo	Rohan Kitshoff	Manaia Salavea	Heinrich Brüssow	Dan Lydiate
	Netani Talei	Renaud van Neel	Ofisa Treviranus	Schalk Burger	Sam Warburton (c)
	Dominiko Waqaniburotu	Jacques Nieuwenhuis (vc)	Taiasina Tuifu'a	Francois Louw	Taulupe Faletau
	Sisa Koyamaibole	Pieter-Jan van Lill	George Stowers	Pierre Spies	Andy Powell
	Sakiusa Matadigo	Ryan de la Harpe	Kahn Fotuali'i	Fourie du Preez	Tavis Knoyle
	Vitori Buatava	Eugene Jantjies	Junior Poluleuligaga	Francois Hougaard	Mike Phillips
	Nemia Kenatale	Theuns Kotzé	Jeremy Su'a	Ruan Pienaar	Lloyd Williams
	Nicky Little	Tertius Losper	Tasesa Lavea	Butch James	James Hook
	Waisea Luveniyali	Darryl de la Harpe	Tusi Pisi	Morné Steyn	Stephen Jones
	Seremaia Bai	David Philander	Eliota Fuimaono-Sapolu	Juan de Jongh	Rhys Priestland
	Ravai Fatiaki	Danie van Wyk	Johnny Leota	Jean de Villiers	Jonathan Davies
	Gabiriele Lovobalavu	Piet van Zyl	Seilala Mapusua	Jaque Fourie	Jamie Roberts
	Albert VuliVuli	Heini Bock	George Pisi	Gio Aplon	Scott Williams
	Vereniki Goneva	Conrad Marais	David Lemi	Bryan Habana	Aled Brew
	Napolioni Nalaga	McGrath van Wyk	Sailosi Tagicakibau	Odwa Ndungane	George North
	Michael Tagicakibau	Llelwellyn Winkler	Alesana Tuilagi	JP Pietersen	Shane Williams
	Iliesa Keresoni	Chrysander Botha	James So'oialo	Patrick Lambie	Lee Byrne
	Kini Murimurivalu	Danie Dames	Paul Williams	Zane Kirchner	Leigh Halfpenny

D.1 Fiji d. Namibia (49~25)

*10 September 2011, Rotorua International Stadium, Rotorua.
Attendance: 10,100; Referee: Nigel Owens (Wales).*
Fiji. *Try: Goneva (4), Nakarawa, Nalaga; Con: Bai (5/6); Pen: Bai (3/3).*
Namibia. *Try: Koll, Botha; Pen: Kotzé (2/3); Drop: Kotzé (3/3).*

D.2 South Africa d. Wales (17~16)

*11 September 2011, Wellington Regional Stadium, Wellington.
Attendance: 33,331; Referee: Wayne Barnes (England).*
South Africa. *Try: F. Steyn, Hougaard; Con: M. Steyn (2/2); Pen: M. Steyn.*
Wales. *Try: Faletau; Con: Hook; Pen: Hook (3/5).*

D.3 Samoa d. Namibia (49~12)

*14 September 2011, Rotorua International Stadium, Rotorua.
Attendance: 12,752; Referee: Romain Poite (France).*
Samoa. *Try: Fotuali'i, Tuilagi (3), Williams, Pen try; Con: T. Pisi (2/2), Williams (2/3); Pen: T. Pisi (2/2), William.*
Namibia. *Try: Van Wyk, Kotzé; Con: Kotzé (1/2).*

D.4 South Africa d. Fiji (49~3)

*17 September 2011, Wellington Regional Stadium, Wellington.
Attendance: 33,262; Referee: Romain Poite (France).*
South Africa. *Try: Steenkamp, Fourie, F. Steyn, M. Steyn, Mtawarira, Rossouw; Con: M. Steyn (5/6); Pen: M. Steyn (2/4); F. Steyn.*
Fiji. *Pen: Bai.*

D.5 Wales d. Samoa (17~10)

*18 September 2011, Waikato Stadium, Hamilton.
Attendance: 30,804; Referee: Alain Rolland (Ireland).*
Wales. *Try: Williams; Pen: Hook (2/3), Priestland (2/2).*
Samoa. *Try: Perenise; Con: Williams; Pen: Williams (1/3).*

D.6 South Africa d. Namibia (87~0)

*22 September 2011, North Harbour Stadium, Auckland.
Attendance: 26,839; Referee: George Clancy (Ireland).*
South Africa. *Try: Aplon (2), Habana, Pen try, Fourie, F. Steyn, M. Steyn, De Jongh (2), Hougaard (2), Rossou; Con: M. Steyn (6/6), Pienaar (6/6); Pen: M. Steyn.* **Namibia.** *Nil.*

D.7 Samoa d. Fiji (27~7)

*25 September 2011, Eden Park, Auckland.
Attendance: 60,327; Referee: Bryce Lawrence (New Zealand).*
Samoa. *Try: Fotuali'i, Stowers; Con: Williams; Pen: Pisi (4/6); Drop: Pisi (1/2).*
Fiji. *Try: Talei; Con: Luveniyali.*

D.8 Wales d. Namibia (81~7)

*26 September 2011, Stadium Taranaki, New Plymouth.
Attendance: 13,710; Referee: Steve Walsh (Australia).*
Wales. *Try: S. Williams (3), Brew, Faletau, Jenkins, North (2), J. Davies, L. Williams, Byrne, A.W. Jones; Con: S. Jones (6/7), Priestland (3/5); Pen: S. Jones.*
Namibia. *Try: Koll; Con: Kotzé.*

D.9 South Africa d. Samoa (13~5)

*30 September 2011, North Harbour Stadium, Auckland.
Attendance: 29,734; Referee: Nigel Owens (Wales).*
South Africa. *Try: Habana; Con: M. Steyn; Pen: F. Steyn (1/3), M. Steyn (1/2).*
Samoa. *Try: Stowers.*

D.10 Wales d. Fiji (66~0)

*2 October 2011, Waikato Stadium, Hamilton.
Attendance: 28,476; Referee: Wayne Barnes (England).*
Wales. *Try: Roberts (2), Scott Williams, North, Warburton, Burns, Halfpenny, L. Williams, J. Davies; Con: Priestland (5/5); S. Jones (4/4); Pen: Priestland.* **Fiji.** *Nil.*

Pool D Matches

The nations in Pool D consisted of **Fiji, Namibia, Samoa, South Africa** and **Wales**. After struggling to narrowly defeat Wales (17~16) in their opening match, South Africa only allowed eight more points against them from the other three teams, which included Samoa. This was an amazing defensive achievement even for a tier one team!

After their victory against Samoa (17~10), the Welsh sailed into the number two spot in the pool and qualified for the quarter finals. Namibia struggled in this group and Fiji couldn't find any form. Samoa played very well, but lost their two most important games against Wales and the Springboks.

Results	P	W	D	L	PF	PA	BP	Pts
South Africa	4	4	0	0	166	24	2	18
Wales	4	3	0	1	180	34	3	15
Samoa	4	2	0	2	91	49	2	10
Fiji	4	1	0	3	59	167	1	5
Namibia	4	0	0	4	44	266	0	0

8. The All Blacks ended Argentina's hopes in their quarter final bout at Eden Park, Auckland.

THE PLAYOFFS

Quarter Finals

The quarter final matches saw mostly upsets with three pool runners-up defeating three pool winners! In the first two matches, Wales overcame an in form Ireland (22~10), and France finally hit back to inflict defeat over England (19~12).

Australia also played well to narrowly defeat South Africa (11~9) in quarter final number three and book a semi final spot. In the last quarter final Argentina played great rugby, but couldn't match the speed and power of New Zealand (33~10).

QUARTER FINALS

QF1 Wales d. Ireland (22~10)

8 October 2011, Regional Stadium, Wellington.
Attendance: 35,787; Referee: Craig Joubert (South Africa).
Wales. Try: Williams, Phillips, J. Davies; Con: Priestland (2/3);
Pen: Halfpenny.
Ireland. Try: Earls; Con: O'Gara; Pen: O'Gara.

QF2 France d. England (19~12)

8 October 2011, Eden Park, Auckland.
Attendance: 49,105; Referee: Steve Walsh (Australia).
France. Try: Clerc, Médard; Pen: Yachvili (2/3); Drop: Trinh-Duc.
England. Try: Foden, Cueto; Con: Wilkinson (1/2).

QF3 Australia d. South Africa (11~9)

9 October 2011, Regional Stadium, Wellington.
Attendance: 34,914; Referee: Bryce Lawrence (New Zealand).
Australia. Try: Horwill; Pen: O'Connor (2/2).
South Africa. Pen: M. Steyn (2/4); Drop: M. Steyn.

QF4 New Zealand d. Argentina (33~10)

9 October 2011, Eden Park, Auckland.
Attendance: 57,192; Referee: Nigel Owens (Wales).
New Zealand. Try: Read, Thom; Con: Cruden; Pen: Weepu (7/7).
Argentina. Try: Farías Cabello; Con: Contepomi; Pen: Bosch.

Semi Finals

The first semi-final of the 2011 Rugby World Cup was an absolute cracker, in front of 58,630 fans at Eden Park in Auckland. France had walloped Wales (28~9) scoring four tries to nil, in their most recent encounter in the 'Six Nations' championship in March 2011, so the Welsh were determined not to repeat the experience. Wales drew first blood, then France scored three successive penalties before Mike Phillips scored a try for Wales. The missed conversion could have won the match for Wales, but it wasn't to be and France progressed to the final after a very close shave (9~8).

SEMI FINALS

Semi Final 1
France d. Wales (9~8)

15 October 2011, Eden Park, Auckland.
Attendance: 58,630; Referee: Alain Rolland (Ireland).
France. Pen: Parra (3/3).
Wales. Try: Phillips; Pen: Hook (1/3).

Semi Final 2
New Zealand d. Australia (20~6)

16 October 2011, Eden Park, Auckland.
Attendance: 60,087; Referee: Craig Joubert (South Africa).
New Zealand. Try: Nonu; Pen: Weepu (4/7); Drop: Cruden.
Australia. Pen: O'Connor; Drop: Cooper.

In the second semi final, with 60,087 black-clad fans in attendance New Zealand put on a display of control to lead the Aussies 14~6 at the half and then increased that lead by six to defeat Australia (20~6). The win ominously lined the

9. New Zealand were unstoppable on their way to the final, and defeated the Wallabies (20~6).

10. All Blacks Brad Thorn and Ma'a Nonu are supported by Conrad Smith (13) in the final against France.

All Blacks up for another shot at the World Cup at their hallowed Eden Park ground.

3rd Place Playoff

The playoff for third place was contested between Australia and Wales at Eden Park, in Auckland in front of 53,014 spectators on the 21st October 2011.

In the very first Rugby World Cup in 1987, these two teams had faced off for the same prize with the Welsh taking bronze on that occasion. But the Australians were much more forward focused in this encounter.

The Wallabies scored the first try in the 12th minute and led 7~3 at the half. After another try each, and with the match almost wrapped up at 21~13, the Welsh scored a second try in injury time, but missed the conversion. The game ended in an Australian victory (21~18).

THE FINAL

New Zealand were considered the favourites as they went into the final unbeaten and the French had lost two pool games, including one to New Zealand. The French team had also experienced a player revolt against their coach Marc Lievremont, confirmed after the tournament by veteran back-rower lmanol Harinordoquy.

France won the toss for choice

of playing colours ahead of the final at Eden Park but agreed to play in white shirts (their change colours) as a mark of respect for New Zealand and the organisation of the tournament.

After the national anthems, the New Zealand players performed their traditional 'haka' as the French team stared back and then advanced towards them in a V-shaped formation before fanning out into a straight line.

In a match of 'grim physical attrition', New Zealand scored first. From a line-out in the French 22m, Tony Woodcock received the ball and broke through a hole in the French defense to score his first try of the World Cup. Piri Weepu, who had already missed a penalty kick, failed with his conversion effort. Weepu missed another attempt in the 25th minute. Nine minutes later, New Zealand's Aaron Cruden, the team's third choice fly-half, only playing due to injuries to Dan Carter and Colin Slade, hyper-extended his knee and was replaced by

FINALS

FINAL
New Zealand d. France (8~7)

23 October 2011, Eden Park, Auckland.
Attendance: 61,079; Referee: Craig Joubert (South Africa).
New Zealand. Try: Woodcock; Pen: Donald.
France. Try: Dusautoir; Con: Trinh-Duc.

3rd/4th Playoff
Australia d. Wales (21~18)

21 October 2011, Eden Park, Auckland.
Attendance: 53,014; Referee: Wayne Barnes (England).
Australia. Try: Barnes, McCalman; Con: O'Connor (1/2); Pen:
O'Connor (2/4); Drop: Barnes.
Wales. Try: Shane Williams, Halfpenny; Con: S. Jones; Pen:
Hook (1/2), S. Jones.

11. New Zealand celebrate their second Rugby World Cup victory in front of their adoring Eden Park supporters.

Two of New Zealand's heroes celebrate their victory (from left): Sonny Bill Williams and Brad Thorn.

Stephen Donald. The French were forced to defend stoically for much of the first half, due to New Zealand playing a frantic running game.

The French came back into the game in the second half, although it did not begin well for them. Dimitri Yachvili missed the team's first penalty

12. Brad Thorn holds aloft the Rugby World Cup flanked by captain Richie McCaw and coach Graham Henry.

attempt after two minutes, and Stephen Donald pushed New Zealand further into the lead by successfully kicking a penalty two minutes later. The French reacted straight away when Trinh-Due made a run towards the line and after several attempts, Dusautoir scored a try, which Trinh-Due converted to see France trail by a single point, 8~7. Trinh-Due attempted a penalty kick from 48 metres in the 65th minute, but missed the goal, and thereafter there were few chances for either side.

French captain Thierry Dusautoir was named man of the match. Another historic milestone occurred when Jean-Marc Doussain came on as a late substitute for France, to become the first player ever to make a test debut and receive a national cap in a Rugby World Cup Final!

The result marked the third time that the tournament was won by the country that hosted the event (following New Zealand in 1987 and South Africa in 1995).

CREDITS

Text

This article uses material from the Wikipedia article https://en.wikipedia.org/wiki/2011_Rugby_World_Cup which is released under the http://creativecommons.org/licenses/by-sa/3.0/ Creative Commons Attribution-Share-Alike License 3.0.

Images

1. 'New Zealand All Blacks' captain Richie McCaw holding the Webb Ellis Cup after defeating France in the final of the 2011 Rugby World Cup Final' by Jeanfrancois Beausejour (23 October, 2011). Available at https://upload.wikimedia.org/wikipedia/commons/f/fa/Richie_McCaw_and_the_Webb_Ellis_cup_after_the_Rugby_World_Cup_final_2011.jpg under the Creative Commons Attribution 2.0 Generic license.

2. 'Eden Park, Auckland, New Zealand. Taken April 2005 from Mount Eden, Auckland' by Gadfium (26 May 2011). Available at https://commons.wikimedia.org/wiki/File:Eden_Park_cropped.jpg This work has been released into the public domain by its author, gadfium.

3. 'Ireland winning the 2009 Six Nations Championship, Millennium Stadium, Cardiff, Wales' by ArunMarsh (21 Mar 2009). Available at https://commons.wikimedia.org/wiki/File:2009_Six_Nations_Champions_-_Ireland.jpg under the Creative Commons Attribution 2.0 Generic license.

4. 'Match between France and Tonga during 2011 Rugby World Cup in New Zealand by Stewart Baird (1 Oct 2011). Available at https://commons.wikimedia.org/wiki/File:France_vs_Tonga_2011_RWC_(1).jpg under the Creative Commons Attribution 2.0 Generic license.

5. 'COUPE DU MONDE DE RUGBY 2011 NOUVELLE ZELANDE ARGENTINE' by jean-francois beausejour (9 Oct 2011). Available at https://commons.wikimedia.org/wiki/File:Rugby_world_cup_2011_NEW_ZEALAND_AR GENTINA_(7309679538).jpg under the Creative Commons Attribution 2.0 Generic license.

6. 'Match between Australia and USA during 2011 Rugby World Cup in New Zealand' by Craig Boyd (23 Sep 2011). Available at https://commons.wikimedia.org/wiki/File:Australia_vs_USA_2011_RWC_(1).jpg under the Creative Commons Attribution-Share Alike 2.0 Generic license.

7. '2011 Rugby World Cup Wales vs Samoa' by Jolon Penna (18 Sep 2011). Available at https://en.wikipedia.org/wiki/File:2011_Rugby_World_Cup_Wales_vs_Samoa_(6168183 024).jpg under the Creative Commons Attribution-Share Alike 2.0 Generic license.

8. 'Rugby World Cup 2011- New Zealand v Argentina' by by Jean-Francois Beausejour (9 Oct 2011). Available at https://upload.wikimedia.org/wikipedia/commons/0/04/Rugby_world_cup_2011_NEW_Z EALAND_ARGENTINA_%287309673390%29.jpg under the Creative Commons Attribution 2.0 Generic license. Full terms at http://creativecommons.org/licenses/by/2.0.

9. 'blacks australia 020 IMG_2569 internet' by jeanfrancois beausejour (16 Oct 2011). Available at https://commons.wikimedia.org/wiki/File:2011_Rugby_World_Cup_Australia_vs_New_Z ealand_(7296130050).jpg under the Creative Commons Attribution 2.0 Generic license.

10. 'French fly-half François Trinh-Duc (no. 21) attempts to get past an opponent while Ma'a Nonu tackles him from behind and Conrad Smith (no. 13) is watching over' by Jean-Francois Beausejour (23 Oct 2011). Available at https://upload.wikimedia.org/wikipedia/commons/2/26/RWC_2011_final_FRA_-_NZL_Tri nh-Duc_and_C_Smith.jpg under the Creative Commons Attribution 2.0 Generic license. Full terms at http://creativecommons.org/licenses/by/2.0.

11. 'Rugby world cup 2011 new zealand france finale' by jeanfrancois beausejour (23 Oct 2011). Available at https://www.flickr.com/photos/jeanfrancoisbeausejour/7310313524 under the Creative Commons Attribution 2.0 Generic license.

12. '2011 Rugby World Cup New Zealand Celebrating World Cup Victory' by Kylie & Rob (and Helen) (26 Oct 2011). Available at https://commons.wikimedia.org/wiki/File:Rugby_World_Cup_Parade_(6761056485).j pg under the Creative Commons Attribution 2.0 Generic license.

Full terms at http://creativecommons.org/licenses/by/2.0.

2015

VIII RUGBY WORLD CUP

England

1. *The Rugby World Cup returned to England in 2015.*

VIII Rugby World Cup

18th September to 31st October, 2015

2. Japan qualifies for the 2015 Rugby World Cup.

The 2015 Rugby World Cup was the eighth Rugby World Cup, the quadrennial rugby union world championship. The tournament was hosted by England from the 18th September to 31st October.

THE HOST

England was chosen to host the competition in July 2009 over rival bids from Italy, Japan and South Africa.

The competition's organisers, Rugby World Cup Limited, had recommended England to the International Rugby Board (IRB; now known as World Rugby).

On 28 July 2009, the IRB confirmed that England would host the 2015 Rugby World Cup, and Japan would host the 2019 event, having voted 16~10 in favour of approving the recommendation from

Rugby World Cup Ltd (RWCL) that England and Japan should be named hosts.

THE TEAMS

The first round or pool stage, saw the 20 teams divided into four pools of five teams, using the same format that was used in 2003, 2007 and 2011. The pool stage draw was conducted at the Tate Modern on the 3rd December 2012, where teams were drawn from five separate 'pots' and allocated to the four respective pools.

Seeded Teams

Twelve teams qualified as a result of finishing in the top three in each pool at the 2011 Rugby World Cup tournament. This meant that **New Zealand, South Africa, Australia, France, Ireland, Samoa, Argentina, Wales, Italy, Tonga** and **Scotland** all automatically qualified for the event, and were joined by **England** as the host nation.

Qualifying Teams

All other nations vying for a place in the tournament had to qualify for the remaining eight places through a series of qualification matches, which were contested by 84 teams.

Namibia won the single African Zone place over teams

3. Uruguay (blue) defeats Russia for the last remaining 2015 Rugby World Cup place, through the Repechage.

4. 'Newcastle was a host city for the Rugby World Cup 2015.

from Kenya, Zimbabwe, Ivory Coast, Morocco, Mauritius, Nigeria, Zambia, Cameroon, Senegal, Uganda, Botswana and Madagascar. **Canada** and the **United States** won the two America's Zone places over teams from Trinidad & Tobago, Brazil, Venezuela, Colombia, Guyana, Bermuda, Cayman Islands, Jamaica, Mexico, Bahamas, Barbados, Chile, Peru, St Vincent & Grenadines, Uruguay and Paraguay.

The European Zone had two places up for grabs, which was contested across six separate rounds by 31 nations. **Romania** and **Georgia** both eventually qualified over teams from Croatia, Russia, Denmark, Latvia, Moldova, Norway, Bulgaria, the Netherlands, Ukraine, Poland, Belgium, Serbia, Switzerland, Israel, Austria, Bosnia & Herzegovina, Portugal, Finland, Germany, Greece, Czech Republic, Slovenia, Andorra, Sweden, Hungary, Spain, Malta, Lithuania and Luxembourg.

Japan won the single Asian Zone slot over teams from Malaysia, China, Sri Lanka, Kazakhstan, South Korea, Guam, Hong Kong, India, Chinese Taipei, Indonesia, Iran, Pakistan, the Philippines, Thailand, Singapore and the United Arab Emirates. **Fiji** won the single Oceania Zone place over teams from the Cook Islands, the Solomon Islands, Papua New Guinea and Tahiti.

Repechage Teams

The repechage was again a great initiative, essentially giving a few unlucky teams a second chance. But there was only one repechage position available in the 2015 Rugby World Cup. **Uruguay** eventually qualified through the repechage rounds over teams from Russia, Zimbabwe and Hong Kong.

2015 Rugby World Cup Draw				
Band 1	Band 2	Band 3	Band 4	Band 5
New Zealand	England	Wales	Oceania	Africa
South Africa	Ireland	Italy	Europe 1	Europe 2
Australia	Samoa	Tonga	Asia	America's 2
France	Argentina	Scotland	America's 1	Repechage

THE POOL STAGE

A total of 48 matches were scheduled across 44 days (40 pool stage and 8 knock-out) throughout the tournament. The pool stage saw the 20 teams divided into four pools of five teams adopting the same format that was used in 2003, 2007 and 2011. The pool stage draw divided the 12 automatic qualifiers into three bands according to their place in the most recent World Rankings.

Each pool was a single round-robin of ten games, in which each team played one match against each of the other teams in the same pool. Teams were awarded four points for a win, two points for a draw and zero for a defeat. A team scoring four or more tries in one match scored a bonus point, as did a team that lost by seven points or fewer.

The teams that finished in the top two of each pool advanced to the quarter-finals. The top three teams of each pool received automatic qualification into the 2019 Rugby World Cup.

POOL A - TEAMS

A	AUSTRALIA	ENGLAND	FIJI	URUGUAY	WALES
Coaches:	*Michael Cheika*	*Stuart Lancaster*	*John McKee*	*Pablo Lemoine*	*Warren Gatland*
Players:	Stephen Moore (c)	Jamie George	Sunia Koto	Germán Kessler	Scott Baldwin
	Tatafu Polota-Nau	Rob Webber	Talemaitoga Tuapati	Nicolás Klappenbach	Ken Owens
	Greg Holmes	Tom Youngs	Viliame Veikoso	Carlos Arboleya	Tomas Francis
	Sekope Kepu	Kieran Brookes	Lee Roy Atalifo	Alejo Corral	Paul James
	Scott Sio	Dan Cole	Isei Colati	Oscar Durán	Aaron Jarvis
	James Slipper	Joe Marler	Campese Ma'afu	Mario Sagario	Gethin Jenkins
	Toby Smith	Mako Vunipola	Peni Ravai	Mateo Sanguinetti	Samson Lee
	Kane Douglas	David Wilson	Manasa Saulo	Franco Lamanna	Jake Ball
	Dean Mumm	George Kruis	Tevita Cavubati	Mathias Palomeque	Luke Charteris
	Rob Simmons	Joe Launchbury	Leone Nakarawa	Santiago Vilaseca (c)	Bradley Davies
	Will Skelton	Courtney Lawes	Api Ratuniyarawa	Jorge Zerbino	Dominic Day
	Scott Fardy	Geoff Parling	Nemia Soqeta	Agustín Alonso	Alun Wyn Jones
	Michael Hooper (vc)	James Haskell	Akapusi Qera (c)	Fernando Bascou	James King
	Sean McMahon	Chris Robshaw (c)	Malakai Ravulo	Matías Beer	Dan Lydiate
	David Pocock	Tom Wood	Dom Waqaniburotu	Juan de Freitas	Justin Tipuric
	Ben McCalman	Ben Morgan	Peceli Yato	Juan Manuel Gaminara	Sam Warburton (c)
	Wycliff Palu	Billy Vunipola	Sakiusa Matadigo	Diego Magno	Taulupe Faletau
	Will Genia	Danny Care	Netani Talei	Alejandro Nieto	Gareth Davies
	Nick Phipps	Richard Wigglesworth	Nemia Kenatale	Alejo Durán	Rhys Webb
	Quade Cooper	Ben Youngs	Nikola Matawalu	Agustín Ormaechea	Lloyd Williams
	Bernard Foley	Owen Farrell	Henry Seniloli	Felipe Berchesi	Dan Biggar
	Kurtley Beale	George Ford	Josh Matavesi	Manuel Blengio	Rhys Priestland
	Matt Giteau	Brad Barritt	Ben Volavola	Joaquín Prada	Cory Allen
	Tevita Kuridrani	Sam Burgess	Levani Botia	Alberto Román	Jamie Roberts
	Adam Ashley-Cooper (vc)	Jonathan Joseph	Vereniki Goneva	Andrés Vilaseca	Scott Williams
	Matt Toomua	Henry Slade	Gabiriele Lovobalavu	Francisco Bulanti	Hallam Amos
	Rob Horne	Jonny May	Nemani Nadolo	Jerónimo Etcheverry	Alex Cuthbert
	Drew Mitchell	Jack Nowell	Waisea Nayacalevu	Santiago Gibernau	George North
	Henry Speight	Anthony Watson	Asaeli Tikoirotuma	Leandro Leivas	Liam Williams
	Joe Tomane	Mike Brown	Kini Murimurivalu	Gastón Mieres	Leigh Halfpenny
	Israel Folau	Alex Goode	Metuisela Talebula	Rodrigo Silva	Matthew Morgan

5. City of Manchester Stadium, Manchester, England.

Pool A Matches

The nations in Pool A with their respective world rankings consisted of **Australia (2), England (4), Fiji (9), Uruguay (19)** and **Wales (5)**. This group was expected to be the most competitive and was even labeled as the 'group of death'.

England as hosts, commenced their campaign in fine form with a win over Fiji (35~11), which was matched with wins by both Wales and Australia. The crunch game for England was against Wales,

Results	P	W	D	L	PF	PA	BP	Pts
Australia	4	4	0	0	141	35	1	17
Wales	4	3	0	1	111	62	1	13
England	4	2	0	2	133	75	3	11
Fiji	4	1	0	3	84	101	1	5
Uruguay	4	0	0	4	30	226	0	0

which virtually guaranteed second place in the group, but resulted in a boil-over win for the Welsh (28~25). Australia held on to defeat both England and Wales to take top place in the pool, which resulted in the historic elimination of England from the quarter finals.

A.1 England d. Fiji (35~11)

18 September 2015, Twickenham Stadium, London.
Attendance: 80,015; Referee: Jaco Peyper (South Africa).
England: Try: Penalty Try, M Brown (2), V. Vunipola; Con: Ford (1/2), Farrell (2/2); Pen: Ford (2/3), Farrell.
Fiji: Try: Nadolo; Pen: Nadolo (1/3), Volavola (1/2).

A.2 Wales d. Uruguay (54~9)

20 September 2015, Millennium Stadium, Cardiff.
Attendance: 71,887; Referee: Romain Poite (France).
Wales: Try: Lee, Allen (3), Amos, G.Davies (2), Tipuric; Con: Priestland (7/8).
Uruguay: Pen: Berchesi (3/4).

A.3 Australia d. Fiji (28~13)

23 September 2015, Millennium Stadium, Cardiff.
Attendance: 67,253; Referee: Chris Pollock (New Zealand).
Australia: Try: Pocock (2), Kepu; Con: Foley (2/3); Pen: Foley (3/3).
Fiji: Try: Volavola 60; Con: Nadolo; Pen: Nadolo (2/2).

A.4 Wales d. England (28~25)

26 September 2015, Twickenham Stadium, London.
Attendance: 81,129; Referee: Jérôme Garcès (France).
Wales: Try: G. Davies; Con: Biggar; Pen: Biggar (7/7).
England: Try: May; Con: Farrell; Pen: Farrell (5/5); Drop: Farrell.

A.5 Australia d. Uruguay (65~3)

27 September 2015, Villa Park, Birmingham.
Attendance: 39,605; Referee: Pascal Gaüzère (France).
Australia: Try: McMahon (2), Tomane, Mumm, Speight, McCalman (2), Mitchell (2), Toomua, Kuridrani; Con: Cooper (5/11).
Uruguay: Pen: Berchesi.

A.6 Wales d. Fiji (23~13)

1 October 2015, Millennium Stadium, Cardiff.
Attendance: 71,576; Referee: John Lacey (Ireland).
Wales: Try: G. Davies, Baldwin;
Con: Biggar (2/2); Pen: Biggar (3/3).
Fiji: Try: Goneva; Con: Volavola; Pen: Volavola (2/4).

A.7 Australia d. England (33~13)

3 October 2015, Twickenham Stadium, London.
Attendance: 81,010; Referee: Romain Poite (France).
Australia: Try: Foley (2), Giteau; Con: Foley (3/3); Pen: Foley (4/4).
England: Try: Watson; Con: Farrell; Pen: Farrell (2/2).

A.8 Fiji d. Uruguay (47~15)

6 October 2015, Stadium 'mk', Milton Keynes.
Attendance: 30,048; Referee: JP Doyle (England).
Fiji: Try: Penalty try (2), Kenatale, Nakarawa, Cavubati, Murimurivalu, Nadolo; Con: Nadolo (6/7).
Uruguay: Try: Arboleya, Ormaechea; Con: Ormaechea (1/2); Pen: Durán.

A.9 Australia d. Wales (15~6)

10 October 2015, Twickenham Stadium, London.
Attendance: 80,863; Referee: Craig Joubert (South Africa).
Australia: Pen: Foley (5/6).
Wales: Pen: Biggar (2/3).

A.10 England d. Uruguay (60~3)

10 October 2015, City of Manchester Stadium, Manchester.
Attendance: 50,778; Referee: Chris Pollock (New Zealand).
England: Try: Watson (2), Easter (3), Slade, Nowell (3), Penalty try; Con: Farrell (4/6), Ford (1/4).
Uruguay: Pen: Berchesi.

6. Olympic Stadium, London, England.

POOL B - TEAMS

B	JAPAN	SAMOA	SCOTLAND	STH AFRICA	USA
Coaches:	Eddie Jones	Stephen Betham	Vern Cotter	Heyneke Meyer	Mike Tolkin
Players:	Shota Horie	Ole Avei	Fraser Brown	Schalk Brits	Zach Fenoglio
	Takeshi Kizu	Manu Leiataua	Ross Ford	Bismarck du Plessis	Phil Thiel
	Hiroki Yuhara	Motu Matu'u	Stuart McInally	Adriaan Strauss	Chris Baumann
	Kensuke Hatakeyama	Viliamu Afatia	Alasdair Dickinson	Jannie du Plessis	Eric Fry
	Keita Inagaki	Jake Grey	Ryan Grant	Frans Malherbe	Olive Kilifi
	Masataka Mikami	Logovi'i Mulipola	WP Nel	Tendai Mtawarira	Titi Lamositele
	Hiroshi Yamashita	Anthony Perenise	Gordon Reid	Trevor Nyakane	Matekitonga Moeakiola
	Shoji Ito	Sakaria Taulafo	Jon Welsh	Coenie Oosthuizen	Joe Taufete'e
	Shinya Makabe	Fa'atiga Lemalu	Grant Gilchrist	Lood de Jager	Cam Dolan
	Hitoshi Ono	Filo Paulo	Jonny Gray	Pieter-Steph du Toit	Greg Peterson
	Luke Thompson	Joe Tekori	Richie Gray	Eben Etzebeth	Hayden Smith
	Michael Broadhurst	Kane Thompson	Tim Swinson	Victor Matfield	Louis Stanfill
	Justin Ives	Maurie Fa'asavalu	John Hardie	Willem Alberts	Andrew Durutalo
	Michael Leitch (c)	Alafoti Faosiliva	Alasdair Strokosch	Schalk Burger	Matt Trouville
	Hendrik Tui	Jack Lam	Ryan Wilson	Siya Kolisi	Alastair McFarland
	Ryu Holani	Ofisa Treviranus (c)	David Denton	Francois Louw	John Quill
	Amanaki Lelei Mafi	TJ Ioane	Josh Strauss	Duane Vermeulen	Danny Barrett
	Atsushi Hiwasa	Sanele Vavae Tuilagi	Sam Hidalgo-Clyne	Fourie du Preez	Samu Manoa
	Fumiaki Tanaka	Vavao Afemai	Greig Laidlaw (c)	Rudy Paige	Niku Kruger
	Harumichi Tatekawa	Kahn Fotuali'i	Henry Pyrgos	Ruan Pienaar	Mike Petri
	Kosei Ono	Patrick Fa'apale	Finn Russell	Pat Lambie	AJ MacGinty
	Kotaro Matsushima	Tusi Pisi	Duncan Weir	Handré Pollard	Shalom Suniula
	Male Sa'u	Michael Stanley	Mark Bennett	Morné Steyn	Seamus Kelly
	Yu Tamura	Rey Lee-Lo	Peter Horne	Damian de Allende	Folau Niua
	Craig Wing	Johnny Leota	Matt Scott	Jean de Villiers (c)	Thretton Palamo
	Yoshikazu Fujita	Paul Perez	Richie Vernon	Jesse Kriel	Andrew Suniula
	Kenki Fukuoka	George Pisi	Sean Lamont	Bryan Habana	Takudzwa Ngwenya
	Karne Hesketh	Fa'atoina Autagavaia	Sean Maitland	Lwazi Mvovo	Blaine Scully
	Toshiaki Hirose	Ken Pisi	Tommy Seymour	JP Pietersen	Zack Test
	Akihito Yamada	Alesana Tuilagi	Tim Visser	Zane Kirchner	Brett Thompson
	Ayumu Goromaru	Tim Nanai-Williams	Stuart Hogg	Willie le Roux	Chris Wyles (c)

Results	P	W	D	L	PF	PA	BP	Pts
South Africa	4	3	0	1	176	56	4	16
Scotland	4	3	0	1	136	93	2	14
Japan	4	3	0	1	98	100	0	12
Samoa	4	1	0	3	69	124	2	6
United States	4	0	0	4	50	156	0	0

Pool B Matches

The nations in Pool B with their respective world rankings consisted of **Japan (13), Samoa (12), Scotland (10), South Africa (3)** and the **United States (15)**.

This group commenced with the earth-shattering Japanese defeat of South Africa (34~32), under ex-Wallaby coach, Eddie Jones. The result reverberated around the rugby world, heralding a new era for the sport and was voted as the best moment of Rugby World Cup 2015.

South Africa gradually recovered to take first place in the group, but their 'aura' had been severely damaged. Scotland finished second with Japan taking an honorable third place in the pool.

B.1 Japan d. South Africa (34~32)

19 September 2015, Falmer Stadium, Brighton.
Attendance: 29,290; Referee: Jérôme Garcès (France).
Japan: Try: Leitch, Goromaru, Hesketh; Con: Goromaru (2/3); Pen: Goromaru (5/6).
South Africa: Try: Louw, B. Du Plessis, De Jager, Strauss; Con: Lambie (2/3), Pollard; Pen: Lambie, Pollard.

B.2 Samoa d. United States (25~16)

20 September 2015, Falmer Stadium, Brighton.
Attendance: 29,178; Referee: George Clancy (Ireland).
Samoa: Try: Nanai-Williams, Treviranus; Pen: T. Pisi (4/5), Stanley.
USA: Try: Wyles, Baumann; Pen: MacGinty (2/2).

B.3 Scotland d. Japan (45~10)

23 September 2015, Kingsholm, Gloucester
Attendance: 14,354; Referee: John Lacey (Ireland).
Scotland: Try: Hardie, Bennett (2), Seymour, Russell; Con: Laidlaw (4/5); Pen: Laidlaw (4/5).
Japan: Try: Mafi; Con: Goromaru; Pen: Goromaru (1/3).

B.4 South Africa d. Samoa (46~6)

26 September 2015, Villa Park, Birmingham.
Attendance: 39,526; Referee: Wayne Barnes (England).
South Africa: Try: Pietersen (3), Burger, Brits, Habana; Con: Pollard (1/4), Lambie (1/2); Pen: Pollard (4/4).
Samoa: Pen: Stanley (2/5).

B.5 Scotland d. United States (39~16)

27 September 2015, Elland Road, Leeds.
Attendance: 33,521; Referee: Chris Pollock (New Zealand).
Scotland: Try: Visser, Maitland, Nel, Scott, Weir; Con: Russell (1/2), Laidlaw (3/5); Pen: Hogg (1/2), Russell (1/2).
USA: Try: Lamositele; Con: MacGinty; Pen: MacGinty (3/3).

B.6 Japan d. Samoa (26~5)

3 October 2015, Stadium 'mk', Milton Keynes
Attendance: 29,019; Referee: Craig Joubert (South Africa).
Japan: Try: Penalty try, Yamada; Con: Goromaru (2/2); Pen: Goromaru (4/6). **Samoa:** Try: Perez.

B.7 South Africa d. Scotland (34~16)

3 October 2015, St. James' Park, Newcastle.
Attendance: 50,900; Referee: Nigel Owens (Wales).
South Africa: Try: Burger, Pietersen, Habana; Con: Pollard (2/3); Pen: Pollard (4/4); Drop: Pollard.
Scotland: Try: Seymour; Con: Laidlaw; Pen: Laidlaw (2/3), Weir.

B.8 South Africa d. United States (64~0)

7 October 2015, Olympic Stadium, London.
Attendance: 54,658; Referee: Pascal Gaüzère (France).
South Africa: Try: De Allende, Penalty try, Habana (3), Du Plessis, Louw (2), Kriel, Mvovo; Con: Pollard (4/5), Steyn (3/5).
USA - Nil.

B.9 Scotland d. Samoa (36~33)

10 October 2015, St. James' Park, Newcastle.
Attendance: 51,982; Referee: Jaco Peyper (South Africa).
Scotland: Try: Seymour, Hardie, Laidlaw; Con: Laidlaw (3/3); Pen: Laidlaw (5/7).
Samoa: Try: T. Pisi, Leiataua, Lee-Lo, Matu'u; Con: T. Pisi (1/3); Fa'apale; Pen: T. Pisi (3/3).

B.10 Japan d. United States (28~18)

11 October 2015, Kingsholm, Gloucester.
Attendance: 14,517; Referee: Glen Jackson (New Zealand).
Japan: Try: Matsushima, Fujita, Mafi; Con: Goromaru (2/3); Pen: Goromaru (3/3).
USA: Try: Ngwenya, Wyles; Con: MacGinty (1/2); Pen: MacGinty (2/2).

POOL C - TEAMS

C	ARGENTINA	GEORGIA	NAMIBIA	NEW	TONGA
Coaches:	Daniel Hourcade	Milton Haig	Phil Davies	Steve Hansen	Mana Otai
Players:	Agustín Creevy (c)	Jaba Bregvadze	Torsten van Jaarsveld	Dane Coles	Aleki Lutui
	Julián Montoya	Shalva Mamukashvili	L van der Westhuizen	Keven Mealamu	Paul Ngauamo
	Marcos Ayerza	Simon Maisuradze	Aranos Coetzee	Codie Taylor	Elvis Taione
	Juan Pablo Orlandi	Kakha Asieshvili	AJ de Klerk	Wyatt Crockett	Halani Aulika
	Ramiro Herrera	Levan Chilachava	Jaco Engels	Charlie Faumuina	Tevita Mailau
	Lucas Noguera Paz	Davit Kubriashvili	Raoul Larson	Ben Franks	Sila Puafisi
	Nahuel Tetaz Chaparro	Mikheil Nariashvili	Johnny Redelinghuys	Owen Franks	Sona Taumalolo
	Matías Alemanno	Davit Zirakashvili	Casper Viviers	Tony Woodcock	Soane Tonga'uiha
	Mariano Galarza	Giorgi Chkhaidze	Tjiuee Uanivi	Brodie Retallick	Uili Kolo'ofai
	Tomás Lavanini	Levan Datunashvili	Janco Venter	Luke Romano	Tukulua Lokotui
	Guido Petti Pagadizábal	Konstantin Mikautadze	Renaldo Bothma	Sam Whitelock	Steve Mafi
	JM Fernández Lobbe	Giorgi Nemsadze	Jacques Burger (c)	Sam Cane	Joe Tuineau
	JM Leguizamón	Mamuka Gorgodze (c)	Wian Conradie	Jerome Kaino	Sione Kalamafoni
	Pablo Matera	Viktor Kolelishvili	Tinus du Plessis	Richie McCaw (c)	Nili Latu (c)
	Javier Ortega Desio	Shalva Sutiashvili	Rohan Kitshoff	Liam Messam	Jack Ram
	Facundo Isa	Giorgi Tkhilaishvili	Leneve Damens	Kieran Read	Hale T-Pole
	Leonardo Senatore	Lasha Lomidze	PJ van Lill	Victor Vito	Opeti Fonua
	Tomás Cubelli	Giorgi Begadze	Eniell Buitendag	Tawera Kerr-Barlow	Viliami Ma'afu
	Martín Landajo	Vazha Khutsishvili	Eugene Jantjies	TJ Perenara	Samisoni Fisilau
	Santiago González Iglesias	Vasil Lobzhanidze	Damian Stevens	Aaron Smith	Sosefo Ma'ake
	Nicolás Sánchez	Lasha Khmaladze	Theuns Kotzé	Beauden Barrett	Sonatane Takulua
	Marcelo Bosch	Lasha Malaghuradze	Darryl de la Harpe	Dan Carter	Latiume Fosita
	Jerónimo de la Fuente	Davit Kacharava	Johan Deysel	Colin Slade	Kurt Morath
	Juan Martín Hernández	Merab Sharikadze	JC Greyling	Malakai Fekitoa	Sione Piukala
	Matías Moroni	Tamaz Mchedlidze	Danie van Wyk	Ma'a Nonu	Siale Piutau
	Juan Pablo Socino	Giorgi Aptsiauri	Conrad Marais	Conrad Smith	Viliami Tahitu'a
	Horacio Agulla	Muraz Giorgadze	David Philander	Sonny Bill Williams	David Halaifonua
	Santiago Cordero	Giorgi Pruidze	Heinrich Smit	Nehe Milner-Skudder	William Helu
	Juan Imhoff	Alexander Todua	Russell van Wyk	Waisake Naholo	Fetu'u Vainikolo
	L. González Amorosino	Merab Kvirikashvili	Chrysander Botha	Julian Savea	Telusa Veainu
	Joaquín Tuculet	Beka Tsiklauri	Johan Tromp	Ben Smith	Vunga Lilo

7. Wembley Stadium, London, England.

C.1 Georgia d. Tonga (17~10)

19 September 2015, Kingsholm, Gloucester.
Attendance: 14,200; Referee: Nigel Owens (Wales).
Georgia: Try: Gorgodze, Tkhilaishvili; Con: Kvirikashvili (2/2); Pen: Kvirikashvili (1/3).
Tonga: Try: Vainikolo; Con: Morath; Pen: Morath.

C.2 New Zealand d. Argentina (26~16)

20 September 2015, Wembley Stadium, London.
Attendance: 89,019; Referee: Wayne Barnes (England)
New Zealand: Try: A. Smith, Cane; Con: Carter (2/2); Pen: Carter (4/4).
Argentina: Try: Petti Pagadizábal; Con: Sánchez; Pen: Sánchez (3/3).

C.3 New Zealand d. Namibia (58~14)

24 September 2015, Olympic Stadium, London.
Attendance: 51,820; Referee: Romain Poite (France).
New Zealand: Try: Vito, Milner-Skudder (2), Fekitoa, Barrett, Savea (2), Smith, Taylor; Con: Barrett (4/8); Slade; Pen: Barrett.
Namibia: Try: Deysel; Pen: Kotzé (3/3).

C.4 Argentina d. Georgia (54~9)

25 September 2015, Kingsholm, Gloucester.
Attendance: 14,256; Referee: JP Doyle (England).
Argentina: Try: Lavanini, Cubelli, Imhoff (2), Cordero (2), Landajo; Con: Sánchez (3/4), Bosch (2/3); Pen: Sánchez (2/2); Drop: Sánchez.
Georgia: Pen: Kvirikashvili (3/3).

C.5 Tonga d. Namibia (35~21)

29 September 2015, Sandy Park, Exeter.
Attendance: 10,103; Referee: Glen Jackson (New Zealand).
Tonga: Try: Veainu (2), Ram (2), Fosita; Con: Lilo (2/5); Pen: Lilo (1/2), Morath.
Namibia: Try: Tromp, Burger (2); Con: Kotzé (3/3).

C.6 New Zealand d. Georgia (43~10)

2 October 2015, Millennium Stadium, Cardiff.
Attendance: 69,187; Referee: Pascal Gaüzère (France).
New Zealand: Try: Naholo, Savea (3), Coles 22, Read, Fekitoa; Con: Carter (4/7).
Georgia: Try: Tsiklauri; Con: Malaghuradze; Pen: Malaghuradze (1/1).

C.7 Argentina d. Tonga (45~16)

4 October 2015, Leicester City Stadium, Leicester.
Attendance: 29,124; Referee: Jaco Peyper (South Africa).
Argentina: Try: Tuculet, Imhoff, Sánchez, Montoya, Cordero; Con: Sánchez (4/5); Pen: Sánchez (4/5).
Tonga: Try: Morath, Tonga'uiha; Pen: Morath (2/4).

C.8 Georgia d. Namibia (17~16)

7 October 2015, Sandy Park, Exeter.
Attendance: 11,156; Referee: George Clancy (Ireland).
Georgia: Try: Gorgodze, Malaghuradze; Con: Kvirikashvili (2/2); Pen: Kvirikashvili.
Namibia: Try: Kotzé; Con: Kotzé; Pen: Kotzé (3/3).

C.9 New Zealand d. Tonga (47~9)

9 October 2015, St. James' Park, Newcastle.
Attendance: 50,985; Referee: John Lacey (Ireland).
New Zealand: Try: B. Smith, Woodcock, Milner-Skudder (2), Williams, Cane, Nonu; Con: Carter (6/7).
Tonga: Pen: Morath (3/3).

C.10 Argentina d. Namibia (64~19)

11 October 2015, Leicester City Stadium, Leicester
Attendance: 30,198; Referee: Pascal Gaüzère (France).
Argentina: Try: Hernández, Moroni, Agulla, Isa, Noguera Paz, Alemanno, Senatore, Montoya, Cubelli; Con: González Iglesias (4/5), Socino (4/4); Pen: González Iglesias (1/2).
Namibia: Try: Tromp, Greyling, Jantjies; Con: Kotzé (2/2).

Pool C Matches

The nations in Pool C with their respective world rankings consisted of **Argentina (8), Georgia (16), Namibia (20), New Zealand (1)** and **Tonga (11)**.

Going into this tournament, the number one ranked All Blacks looked almost invincible. However, the Argentinians rubbed off some of that shine in their group match as the Puma's led until the final 20 minutes before New Zealand finally steadied and pushed through for a narrow win (26~16). As expected, both these teams qualified for the quarter finals. The performance of Georgia and their brilliant flanker, Gorgodza was also a tournament highlight.

Results	P	W	D	L	PF	PA	BP	Pts
New Zealand	4	4	0	0	174	49	3	19
Argentina	4	3	0	1	179	70	3	15
Georgia	4	2	0	2	53	123	0	8
Tonga	4	1	0	3	70	130	2	6
Namibia	4	0	0	4	70	174	1	1

8. Millenium Stadium, Cardiff, Wales.

POOL D - TEAMS

D	CANADA	FRANCE	IRELAND	ITALY	ROMANIA
Coaches:	Kieran Crowley	Philippe Saint-André	Joe Schmidt	Jacques Brunel	Lynn Howells
Players:	Ray Barkwill	Guilhem Guirado	Rory Best	Leonardo Ghiraldini	Eugen Căpăţână
	Aaron Carpenter	Benjamin Kayser	Sean Cronin	Davide Giazzon	Andrei Rădoi
	Benoit Piffero	Dimitri Szarzewski	Richardt Strauss	Andrea Manici	Otar Turashvili
	Hubert Buydens	Uini Atonio	Nathan White	Matías Agüero	Mihai Lazăr
	Jason Marshall	Eddy Ben Arous	Tadhg Furlong	Martin Castrogiovanni	Ion Paulică
	Djustice Sears-Duru	Vincent Debaty	Cian Healy	Dario Chistolini	Horaţiu Pungea
	Andrew Tiedemann	Nicolas Mas	Jack McGrath	Lorenzo Cittadini	Alexandru Ţăruș
	Doug Wooldridge	Rabah Slimani	Mike Ross	Michele Rizzo	Andrei Ursache
	Brett Beukeboom	Alexandre Flanquart	Iain Henderson	Valerio Bernabò	Marius Antonescu
	Jamie Cudmore	Yoann Maestri	Paul O'Connell (c)	Joshua Furno	Valentin Popîrlan
	Evan Olmstead	Pascal Papé	Donnacha Ryan	Marco Fuser	Valentin Ursache
	Nanyak Dala	Thierry Dusautoir (c)	Devin Toner	Quintin Geldenhuys	Johannes van Heerden
	Kyle Gilmour	Bernard Le Roux	Chris Henry	Mauro Bergamasco	Stelian Burcea
	John Moonlight	Yannick Nyanga	Jordi Murphy	Simone Favaro	Viorel Lucaci
	Jebb Sinclair	Fulgence Ouedraogo	Seán O'Brien	Francesco Minto	Mihai Macovei (c)
	Tyler Ardron (c)	Damien Chouly	Peter O'Mahony	Samuela Vunisa	Daniel Carpo
	Richard Thorpe	Louis Picamoles	Jamie Heaslip	Alessandro Zanni	Ovidiu Toniţa
	Phil Mack	Rory Kockott	Conor Murray	Sergio Parisse (c)	Tudorel Bratu
	Jamie Mackenzie	Morgan Parra	Eoin Reddan	Edoardo Gori	Valentin Calafeteanu
	Gordon McRorie	Sébastien Tillous-Borde	Paddy Jackson	Guglielmo Palazzani	Florin Surugiu
	Nathan Hirayama	Frédéric Michalak	Ian Madigan	Marcello Violi	Dănuţ Dumbravă
	Liam Underwood	Rémi Tales	Jonathan Sexton	Tommaso Allan	Michael Wiringi
	Nick Blevins	Mathieu Bastareaud	Darren Cave	Carlo Canna	Csaba Gál
	Connor Braid	Alexandre Dumoulin	Keith Earls	Tommaso Benvenuti	Paula Kinikinilau
	Ciaran Hearn	Gaël Fickou	Robbie Henshaw	Michele Campagnaro	Florin Vlaicu
	Conor Trainor	Wesley Fofana	Jared Payne	Gonzalo Garcia	Adrian Apostol
	Jeff Hassler	Sofiane Guitoune	Tommy Bowe	Luca Morisi	Ionuţ Botezatu
	Phil Mackenzie	Yoann Huget	Luke Fitzgerald	Leonardo Sarto	Florin Ioniţă
	DTH. van der Merwe	Noa Nakaitaci	David Kearney	Giovanbattista Venditti	Mădălin Lemnaru
	Matt Evans	Brice Dulin	Simon Zebo	Andrea Masi	Cătălin Fercu
	Harry Jones	Scott Spedding	Rob Kearney	Luke McLean	Sabin Strătilă

D.1 Ireland d. Canada (50~7)

19 September 2015, Millennium Stadium, Cardiff.
Attendance: 68,523; Referee: Glen Jackson (New Zealand).
Ireland: Try: O'Brien, Henderson, Sexton, D. Kearney, Cronin, R. Kearney, Payne; Con: Sexton (3/4), Madigan (3/3); Pen: Sexton.
Canada: Try: Van der Merwe; Con: Hirayama.

D.2 France d. Italy (32~10)

19 September 2015, Twickenham Stadium, London.
Attendance: 76,232; Referee: Craig Joubert (South Africa).
France: Try: Slimani, Mas; Con: Michalak (2/2); Pen: Michalak (5/7), Spedding.
Italy: Try: Venditti; Con: Allan; Pen: Allan (1/2).

D.3 France d. Romania (38~11)

23 September 2015, Olympic Stadium, London.
Attendance: 50,626; Referee: Jaco Peyper (South Africa).
France: Try: Guitoune (2), Nyanga, Fofana, Fickou; Con: Parra (3/3), Kockott (2/2); Pen: Parra.
Romania: Try: V. Ursache; Pen: Vlaicu (2/3).

D.4 Italy d. Canada (23~18)

26 September 2015, Elland Road, Leeds.
Attendance: 33,120; Referee: George Clancy (Ireland).
Italy: Try: Rizzo, Garcia; Con: Allan (2/2); Pen: Allan (3/3).
Canada: Try: Van der Merwe, Evans; Con: Hirayama (1/2); Pen: Hirayama (2/3).

D.5 Ireland d. Romania (44~10)

27 September 2015, Wembley Stadium, London.
Attendance: 89,267; Referee: Craig Joubert (South Africa).
Ireland: Try: Bowe (2), Earls (2), Kearney, Henry; Con: Madigan (4/6); Pen: Madigan (2/2).
Romania: Try: Toniţa; Con: Vlaicu; Pen: Calafeteanu.

D.6 France d. Canada (41~18)

1 October 2015, Stadium 'mk', Milton Keynes.
Attendance: 28,145; Referee: JP Doyle (England).
France: Try: Fofana, Guirado, Slimani, Papé, Grosso; Con: Michalak (4/4), Parra; Pen: Michalak (2/2).
Canada: Try: Van der Merwe, Carpenter; Con: Hirayama (1/2); Pen: Hirayama (2/2).

D.7 Ireland d. Italy (16~9)

4 October 2015, Olympic Stadium, London.
Attendance: 53,187; Referee: Jérôme Garcès (France).
Ireland: Try: Earls; Con: Sexton; Pen: Sexton (3/5).
Italy: Pen: Allan (3/3).

D.8 Romania d. Canada (17~15)

6 October 2015, Leicester City Stadium, Leicester.
Attendance: 27,153; Referee: Wayne Barnes (England).
Romania: Try: Macovei (2); Con: Vlaicu (2/2); Pen: Vlaicu (1/3).
Canada: Try: Van der Merwe, Hassler; Con: Hirayama; Pen: McRorie (1/4).

D.9 Italy d. Romania (32~22)

11 October 2015, Sandy Park, Exeter.
Attendance: 11,450; Referee: Romain Poite (France).
Italy: Try: Sarto, Gori, Allan, Zanni; Con: Allan (3/4); Pen: Allan (2/2).
Romania: Try: Apostol (2), Popîrlan; Con: Vlaicu (2/3); Pen: Vlaicu.

D.10 Ireland d. France (24~9)

11 October 2015, Millennium Stadium, Cardiff.
Attendance: 72,163; Referee: Nigel Owens (Wales).
Ireland: Try: R. Kearney, Murray; Con: Madigan (1/2); Pen: Sexton (2/2), Madigan (2/2).
France: Pen: Spedding (2/3), Parra.

Pool D Matches

The nations in Pool D with their respective world rankings consisted of **Canada (18)**, **France (7)**, **Ireland (6)**, **Italy (14)** and **Romania (17)**.

Ireland and France were the standout teams in pool D and scored relatively easy wins over the other three opponents. However, the final match to determine the places in the pool resulted in a resounding win for Ireland (24~9), who in the process recorded the equal best (with Australia) defensive figures of the tournament. Italy played well to hold onto third place in the pool, with both Romania and Canada demonstrating that they were definitely developing by showing occasional flourishes of superb rugby.

Results	P	W	D	L	PF	PA	BP	Pts
Ireland	4	4	0	0	134	35	2	18
France	4	3	0	1	120	63	2	14
Italy	4	2	0	2	74	88	2	10
Romania	4	1	0	3	60	129	0	4
Canada	4	0	0	4	58	131	2	2

171

9. James Park Stadium, Newcastle, England.

THE PLAYOFFS

Quarter Finals

The quarter final matches were all highly entertaining encounters. In the first two quarter finals, Wales lost narrowly to South Africa (19~23), and New Zealand crushed a hapless France to end any French hopes of a tournament victory (62~13).

Argentina held off a determined fight back from an injury depleted Ireland (43~20), to advance to their second Rugby World Cup semi final. Scotland had their match won with

QUARTER FINALS

QF1 South Africa d. Wales (23~19)

17 October 2015, Twickenham Stadium, London.
Attendance: 79,572; Referee: Wayne Barnes (England).
South Africa: Try: Du Preez; Pen: Pollard (5/7); Drop: Pollard.
Wales: Try: G. Davies; Con: Biggar; Pen: Biggar (3/4);
Drop: Biggar.

QF2 New Zealand d. France (62~13)

17 October 2015, Millennium Stadium, Cardiff.
Attendance: 71,619; Referee: Nigel Owens (Wales).
New Zealand: Try: Retallick, Milner-Skudder, Savea (3),
Kaino, Read, Kerr-Barlow (2); Con: Carter (7/9); Pen: Carter.
France: Try: Picamoles; Con: Parra; Pen: Spedding, Parra (1/2).

QF3 Argentina d. Ireland (43~20)

18 October 2015, Millennium Stadium, Cardiff.
Attendance: 72,316; Referee: Jérôme Garcès (France).
Argentina: Try: Moroni, Imhoff (2), Tuculet; Con:
Sánchez (4/4); Pen: Sánchez (5/6).
Ireland: Try: Fitzgerald, Murphy; Con: Madigan (2/2);
Pen: Madigan (2/4).

QF4 Australia d. Scotland (35~34)

18 October 2015, Twickenham Stadium, London.
Attendance: 77,110; Referee: Craig Joubert (South Africa).
Australia: Try: Ashley-Cooper, Mitchell (2), Hooper,
Kuridrani; Con: Foley (2/5); Pen: Foley (2/2).
Scotland: Try: Horne, Seymour, Bennett; Con:
Laidlaw (2/3); Pen: Laidlaw (5/5).

two minutes left, but a controversial penalty to Australia allowed Foley to squeeze a goal and a slim Wallaby victory (35~34).

Semi Finals

The first-ever all southern hemisphere domination of the 2015 Rugby World Cup semi finals was a hotly discussed issue by the establishment, but that didn't stop some excellent rugby.

The first semi-final was played in front of 80,090 fans at Twickenham Stadium in London. The All Black fans sat in silence as South Africa pulled away to a handy half-time lead, but New Zealand were the better team and came back to win and book their place in the final (20~18).

SEMI FINALS

Semi Final 1
New Zealand d. South Africa (20~18)

24 October 2015, Twickenham Stadium, London.
Attendance: 80,090; Referee: Jérôme Garcès (France).
New Zealand: Try: Kaino, Barrett; Con: Carter (2/2);
Pen: Carter (1/2); Drop: Carter 46'
South Africa: Pen: Pollard (5/5); Lambie.

Semi Final 2
Australia d. Argentina (29~15)

25 October 2015, Twickenham Stadium, London.
Attendance: 80,025; Referee: Wayne Barnes (England).
Australia: Try: Simmons, Ashley-Cooper (3); Con: Foley (3/4);
Pen: Foley (1/2).
Argentina: Pen: Sánchez (5/5).

Argentina had been playing so well that many predicted the second semi-final would be a cracker, but despite Sanchez kicking five from five penalties, a four try to none performance by the Wallabies ensured the victory (29~15) and a historic crack at the Webb Ellis Cup against the All Blacks.

10. Twickenham Stadium, London, England.

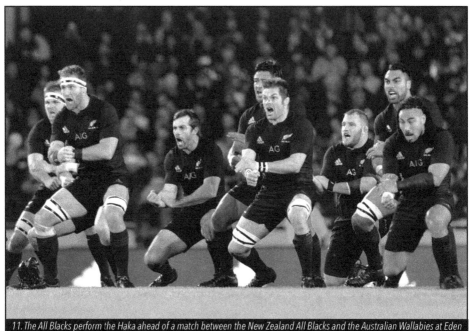

11. The All Blacks perform the Haka ahead of a match between the New Zealand All Blacks and the Australian Wallabies at Eden Park on August 15, 2015 in Auckland, New Zealand.

3rd Place Playoff

The playoff for third place was contested between South Africa and Argentina at Olympic Stadium in London, in front of 55,925 spectators on the 30th October 2015.

Having missed out on their opportunity to contest the Webb Ellis Cup, both sides were playing for pride. Pietersen commenced the scoring for South Africa in the 6th minute and Pollard followed up with the conversion and three penalties, for the Springboks to lead at the half (16~0).

The Boks raced out to lead by 24~3 before the Puma's launched an all too late recovery, scoring in injury time to wind up the match and finish in fourth place. South Africa took out the bronze medal (24~13), and farewelled their retiring warriors in Schalk Burger, Victor Mattfield, Brian Habana and Fourie du Preez.

THE FINAL

The first ever Rugby World Cup final featuring New Zealand against Australia was held in front of 80,125 excited fans at Twickenham Stadium, London. After performing their intimidating 'haka', the All Blacks got down to business and completely dominated the first half, although the Wallabies were only just slightly down on the scoreboard. But a New

Zealand try just before half time saw them lead 16~3 at the break.

Another All Black try just after the resumption had the Australians reeling at 17 points down! However, with tries by Pocock and Kuridrani, and three goals by Foley, the Wallabies gradually clawed themselves back into the match to be just slightly adrift at the 65th minute mark. Millions of Wallaby and All Black fans on the other side of the world held their breath with New Zealand being only four points ahead (21~17). However, a 45 metre drop goal from Dan Carter and a runaway try from Beauden Barrett with one minute remaining sealed another historic Kiwi victory (34~17).

In winning the 2015 Rugby World Cup the New Zealand All Blacks became the first nation ever to win the tournament back to back, and they also became the first nation to win the Rugby World Cup on three occasions.

FINALS

FINAL
New Zealand d. Australia (34~17)
31 October 2015, Twickenham Stadium, London.
Attendance: 80,125; Referee: Nigel Owens (Wales).
New Zealand: Try: Milner-Skudder, Nonu, Barrett; Con: Carter (2/3); Pen: Carter (4/4); Drop: Carter.
Australia: Try: Pocock, Kuridrani; Con: Foley (2/2); Pen: Foley.

3rd/4th Playoff
South Africa d. Argentina (24~13)
30 October 2015, Olympic Stadium, London.
Attendance: 55,925; Referee: John Lacey (Ireland).
South Africa: Try: Pietersen, Etzebeth; Con: Pollard (1/2); Pen: Pollard (4/5).
Argentina: Try: Orlandi; Con: Sánchez; Pen: Sánchez; Drop: Sánchez.

AFTERMATH

Tournament Awards

During the 2015 Rugby World Cup tournament, Japan's brilliant final try and victory against South Africa in the opening round was named the World Cup best match moment. Also, the Rugby World Cup sponsors 'Société Générale' from France unveiled their 'Dream Team', which consisted of their best performing players of the tournament.

Criticism Of The Draw

The timing of the draw drew criticism due to its distance from the actual tournament. By the time of the pool match between

Société Générale's 'Dream Team'			
Position	#	Player	Nation
Full Back	15	Ayumu-Goromaru	Japan
Right Wing	14	Nehe Milner-Skudder	New Zealand
Outside Centre	13	Conrad Smith	New Zealand
Inside Centre	12	Matt Giteau	Australia
Left Wing	11	Julian Savea	New Zealand
Fly Half	10	Dan Carter	New Zealand
Scrum Half	9	Greig Laidlaw	Scotland
Number 8	8	David Pocock	Australia
Open Flanker	7	Schalk Burger	South Africa
Blind Flanker	6	Mamuka Gorgodza	Georgia
Right Lock	5	Leone Nakarawa	Fiji
Left Lock	4	Eben Etzebeth	South Africa
Tighthead Prop	3	Ramiro Herrera	Argentina
Hooker	2	Stephen Moore	Australia
Loosehead Prop	1	Marcos Ayerza	Argentina

England and Wales on 26th September, pool A contained the 2nd, 3rd, 4th and 9th ranked teams in the world (Australia, England, Wales and Fiji).

Following England's exit at the pool stage after defeats by Australia and Wales, making them the first sole host nation and the first former champion not to reach the knockout stage, there was much criticism. Wales coach Warren Gatland said it all:

"Everyone is making a thing about the first home country to hold a World Cup to miss out on the quarter finals, but the stupid thing, as we all know, is why was the World Cup draw done three years ago? That's just ridiculous

as far as I am concerned. If they had followed the football model, then we wouldn't be in this position. There are other people outside this who need to have a look at themselves and why those decisions were made, and you have got to feel sorry for the people involved and who this has affected."

The chief executive of World Rugby Brett Gosper subsequently acknowledged the criticisms, adding...

"We'll look at that next time to see if it's possible to stage the draw closer to the tournament."

The attendance at Rugby World Cup 2015 broke all records reaching 2,477,805, with an average attendance of 51,621 spectators at each of the 48 matches.

CREDITS

2019
IX RUGBY WORLD CUP
Japan

1. Japan v Hong Kong in Tokyo.

2. Japanese 2019 Rugby World Cup Mascots

The 2019 Rugby World Cup is scheduled to be the 9th Rugby World Cup, the quadrennial rugby union world championship. The tournament will be hosted by Japan from the 20th September to 2nd November. This will be the first time the tournament is to be held in Asia, the first time that a different logo (based on the World Rugby logo, rather than a stylised rugby ball) will be used, and also the first time that the event will take place outside the traditional heartland of rugby union nations. The Opening Ceremony is scheduled for 20 September 2019 in Tokyo Stadium.

THE HOST

The IRB requested that any member unions wishing to host

the 2015 or 2019 Rugby World Cup should indicate their interest by the 15th August 2008. This was purely to indicate interest and no details had to be provided at that stage. The 2019 tournament received interest from nine different nations.

Russia initially announced plans to bid for both the 2015 and 2019 World Cups, but withdrew both bids in February 2009 in favour of what proved to be a successful bid for the 2013 Rugby World Cup Sevens. Australia withdrew from the bidding process on the 6th May 2009.

The last three potential hosts in Italy, Japan and South Africa were announced on the 8th May 2009. At a special meeting held in Dublin on 28th July 2009, the International Rugby Board (IRB) confirmed that Japan would host the 2019 event.

THE TEAMS

The top three teams in each of the four pools at the 2015 Rugby World Cup automatically qualified for the 2019 tournament. Japan finished third in Pool B during the 2015 Rugby World Cup and so finished in a qualifying position, however by virtue of hosting the tournament, Japan were assured qualification for the tournament even before the 2015 Rugby World Cup took place. The remaining

3. Kumagaya Rugby Stadium, Kumagaya, Japan.

eight spaces were decided by existing regional competitions (e.g. the Rugby Europe International Championships) followed by a few cross regional play-offs.

Seeded Teams

Twelve teams qualified as a result of finishing in the top three in each of their respective pools during the 2015 Rugby World Cup tournament. This meant that **New Zealand, South Africa, Australia, England, France, Georgia, Ireland, Argentina, Wales, Italy** and **Scotland** all automatically qualified for the event, and were joined by **Japan** as the host nation.

Qualifying Teams

All other nations vying for a place in the tournament had to qualify for the remaining eight places through a series of qualification matches, which were contested by 81 teams.

Namibia won the single African Zone slot over teams from Kenya, Zimbabwe, Ivory Coast, Morocco, Mauritius, Nigeria, Zambia, Tunisia, Cameroon, Senegal, Uganda, Botswana and Madagascar.

Uruguay and the **United States** won the two American Zone places over teams from Trinidad & Tobago, Brazil, Venezuela, Colombia, Guyana, Ecuador, Bermuda, Cayman Islands, Jamaica, Mexico, Bahamas, Barbados, Chile,

4. Shizuoka Stadium 'ECOPA' Fukuroi-shi, Shizuoka-ken, Japan

5. Kyusyu-Sekiyu Dome, Bigeye, otherwise known as Oita Stadium, Oita, Japan.

Peru, St Vincent & Grenadines, Guatemala and Paraguay.

The European Zone had one place up for grabs, which was keenly contested across six separate rounds by 32 nations. **Russia** eventually qualified over teams from Croatia, Cyprus, Russia, Denmark, Latvia, Moldova, Norway, Romania, the Netherlands, Ukraine, Poland, Belgium, Serbia, Switzerland, Israel, Austria, Bosnia & Herzegovina, Portugal, Estonia, Finland, Germany, Czech Republic, Slovenia, Andorra, Sweden, Hungary, Spain, Turkey, Malta, Lithuania and Luxembourg.

Asian Zone teams competed from Malaysia, Sri Lanka, Kazakhstan, South Korea,

Guam, Hong Kong, the Philippines, Thailand, Singapore, Uzbekistan and the United Arab Emirates. **Fiji** and **Tonga** won the two Oceania Zone places over teams from the Cook Islands, Samoa and Tahiti.

Repechage Teams

The repechage was a great initiative, essentially giving a few unlucky teams a second chance. There were two repechage positions available in the 2019 Rugby World Cup. **Samoa** defeated Germany in a Europe/Oceania play-off for direct qualification to the World Cup. The final spot was decided by a repechage tournament in Marseille in

November 2018, which saw **Canada** claim the final berth.

THE DRAW

The pool draw for 2019 Rugby World Cup took place on 10th May 2017 in Kyoto, Japan. The draw was moved from its traditional time of December in the year following the previous World Cup, after the November internationals, so that nations had a longer period of time to increase their World Rankings ahead of the draw.

The seeding system from previous Rugby World Cups was retained with the 12 automatic qualifiers from 2015 being allocated to their respective bands based on their World Rugby Rankings on the day of the draw:

- *Band 1: The four highest-ranked teams*
- *Band 2: The next four highest-ranked teams*
- *Band 3: The final four directly qualified teams.*

The remaining two bands were made up of the eight qualifying teams, with allocation to each band being based on the previous Rugby World Cup playing strength:

- *Band 4: - Oceania 1, Americas 1, Europe 1, Africa 1*
- *Band 5: - Oceania 2, Americas 2, Play-off Winner, Repechage Winner.*

As each team was drawn from the pot, they were allocated to Pool A, then Pool B, the third to Pool C and the fourth Pool D.

6. Inside view of Kobe Stadium, Kobe, Hyogo Prefecture, Japan.

7. Fans watch a rugby match at Ajinomoto Stadium, also known as Tokyo Stadium, Chofu, Japan.

THE POOL STAGE

In the first round or pool stage, the twenty teams were divided into four pools of five teams. Each pool will be a single round-robin of ten games, in which each team plays one match against each of the other teams in the same pool. Teams are awarded four league points for a win, two for a draw and zero for a defeat by eight or more points. A team scoring four tries in one match is awarded a bonus point, as is a team that loses by fewer than eight points, and both bonus points are awarded if both situations apply.

The teams finishing in the top two of each pool advance to the quarter-finals. The top three teams in each pool will receive automatic qualification into the 2023 Rugby World Cup in France. If three teams are tied on points, the below criteria will be used to decide pool placings, and then the criteria will be repeated.

Tie-breaking Criteria

If two or more teams are tied on match points, the following tiebreakers apply:

- *Difference between points scored for and points scored against in all pool matches.*
- *Difference between tries scored for and tries scored against in all pool matches.*
- *Points scored in all pool matches.*
- *Most tries scored in all pool matches.*
- *Official World Rugby Rankings as of 14th October 2019.*

Pool A Schedule

The nations in Pool A with their respective current world rankings consist of **Ireland (3), Japan (11), Russia (20), Samoa (17)** and **Scotland (7).**

The front runners of this group are Ireland and Scotland, but Samoa and Russia are capable of playing great rugby, and Japan will be pumped in front of their home crowd.

A.1 Japan v Russia (-   )
20 September 2019, Tokyo Stadium, Chofu.
Attendance: _____
Referee: _____
Japan:_____
_____
Russia:_____
_____

A.2 Ireland v Scotland (-   )
22 September 2019, Int'l Stadium, Yokohama.
Attendance: _____
Referee: _____
Ireland:_____
_____
Scotland:_____
_____

A.3 Samoa v Russia (-   )
24 September 2019, Kumagaya Stadium, Kumagaya.
Attendance: _____
Referee: _____
Samoa:_____
_____
Russia:_____
_____

A.4 Japan v Ireland (-   )
28 September 2019, Shizuoka Stadium, Fukuroi
Attendance: _____
Referee: _____
Japan:_____
_____
Ireland:_____
_____

A.5 Scotland v Samoa (-   )
30 September 2019, Kobe Misaki Stadium, Kobe
Attendance: _____
Referee: _____
Scotland:_____
_____
Samoa:_____
_____

A.6 Ireland v Russia (-   )
3 October 2019, Kobe Misaki Stadium, Kobe.
Attendance: _____
Referee: _____
Ireland:_____
_____
Russia:_____
_____

A.7 Japan v Samoa (-   )
5 October 2019, City of Toyota Stadium, Toyota.
Attendance: _____
Referee: _____
Japan:_____
_____
Samoa:_____
_____

A.8 Scotland v Russia (-   )
9 October 2019, Shizuoka Stadium, Fukuroi.
Attendance: _____
Referee: _____
Scotland:_____
_____
Russia:_____
_____

A.9 Ireland v Samoa (-   )
12 October 2019, Fukuoka Stadium, Fukuoka.
Attendance: _____
Referee: _____
Ireland:_____
_____
Samoa:_____
_____

A.10 Japan v Scotland (-   )
13 October 2019, Int'l Stadium, Yokohama.
Attendance: _____
Referee: _____
Japan:_____
_____
Scotland:_____
_____

Pool B Schedule

The nations in Pool B with their respective current world rankings consist of **Canada (21)**, **Italy (14)**, **Namibia (23)**, **New Zealand (1)** and **South Africa (5)**. The form of South Africa has been moderate, but Namibia will struggle. Canada and Italy should be exciting, however no one will match the power of the All Blacks.

B.1 New Zealand v South Africa (-)
21 September 2019, Int'l Stadium, Yokohama.
Attendance: _____
Referee: _____
New Zealand: _____
_____
South Africa: _____
_____

B.2 Italy v Namibia (-)
22 September 2019, Hanazano Stadium, Higashiosaka.
Attendance: _____
Referee: _____
Italy: _____
_____
Namibia: _____
_____

B.3 Italy v Canada (-)
26 September 2019, Fukuoka Stadium, Fukuoka.
Attendance: _____
Referee: _____
Italy: _____
_____
Canada: _____
_____

B.4 South Africa v Namibia (-)
28 September 2019, City of Toyota Stadium, Toyota.
Attendance: _____
Referee: _____
South Africa: _____
Namibia: _____
_____

B.5 New Zealand v Canada (-)
2 October 2019, Oita Stadium, Oita.
Attendance: _____
Referee: _____
New Zealand: _____
_____
Canada: _____
_____

B.6 South Africa v Italy (-)
4 October 2019, Shizuoka Stadium, Fukuroi.
Attendance: _____
Referee: _____
South Africa: _____
_____
Italy: _____
_____

B.7 New Zealand v Namibia (-)
6 October 2019, Tokyo Stadium, Chofu.
Attendance: _____
Referee: _____
New Zealand: _____
_____
Namibia: _____
_____

B.8 South Africa v Canada (-)
8 October 2019, Kobe Misaki Stadium, Kobe.
Attendance: _____
Referee: _____
South Africa: _____
_____
Canada: _____
_____

B.9 New Zealand v Italy (-)
12 October 2019, City of Toyota Stadium, Toyota.
Attendance: _____
Referee: _____
New Zealand: _____
_____
Italy: _____
_____

B.10 Namibia v Canada (-)
13 October 2019, Memorial Stadium, Kamaishi.
Attendance: _____
Referee: _____
Namibia: _____
_____
Canada: _____
_____

Pool C Schedule

The nations in Pool C with their respective current world rankings consist of **Argentina (10), England (4), France (8) Tonga (13)** and **United States (15).** Tonga and the USA are always entertaining, but England and France should dominate the group. Watch out for Argentina, who are capable of anything on their day.

C.1 France v Argentina (-)
21 September 2019, Tokyo Stadium, Chofu.
Attendance: _____
Referee: _____
France:_____
_____
Argentina:_____
_____

C.2 England v Tonga (-)
22 September 2019, Sapporo Dome, Sapporo
Attendance: _____
Referee: _____
England:_____
_____
Tonga:_____
_____

C.3 England v USA (-)
26 September 2019, Kobe Misaki Stadium, Kobe.
Attendance: _____
Referee: _____
England:_____
_____
USA:_____
_____

C.4 Argentina v Tonga (-)
28 September 2019, Hanazano Stadium, Higashiosaka.
Attendance: _____
Referee: _____
Argentina:_____
_____
Tonga:_____
_____

C.5 France v USA (-)
2 October 2019, Fukuoka Stadium, Fukuoka.
Attendance: _____
Referee: _____
France:_____
_____
USA:_____
_____

C.6 England v Argentina (-)
5 October 2019, Tokyo Stadium, Chofu.
Attendance: _____
Referee: _____
England:_____
_____
Argentina:_____
_____

C.7 France v Tonga (-)
6 October 2019, Kumamoto Stadium, Kumamoto.
Attendance: _____
Referee: _____
France:_____
_____
Tonga:_____
_____

C.8 Argentina v USA (-)
9 October 2019, Kumagaya Stadium, Kumagaya.
Attendance: _____
Referee: _____
Argentina:_____
_____
USA:_____
_____

C.9 England v France (-)
12 October 2019, Int'l Stadium, Yokohama.
Attendance: _____
Referee: _____
England:_____
_____
France:_____
_____

C.10 USA v Tonga (-)
13 October 2019, Hanazano Stadium, Higashiosaka.
Attendance: _____
Referee: _____
USA:_____
_____
Tonga:_____
_____

Pool D Schedule

The nations in Pool D with their respective current world rankings consist of **Australia (6), Fiji (9), Georgia (12) Uruguay (16)** and **Wales (2).** Georgia and Uruguay will find it hard going, but Fiji are unpredictable. The D.5 match between Australia, who are down on form and 'Six Nations' champions Wales will be a cracker.

D.1 Australia v Fiji (-)
21 September 2019, Sapporo Dome, Sapporo.
Attendance: _____
Referee: _____
Australia:_____
_____
Fiji:_____
_____

D.2 Wales v Georgia (-)
23 September 2019, City of Toyota Stadium, Toyota.
Attendance: _____
Referee: _____
Wales:_____
_____
Georgia:_____
_____

D.3 Fiji v Uruguay (-)
25 September 2019, Memorial Stadium, Kamaishi.
Attendance: _____
Referee: _____
Fiji:_____
_____
Uruguay:_____
_____

D.4 Georgia v Uruguay (-)
29 September 2019, Kumagaya Stadium, Kumagaya.
Attendance: _____
Referee: _____
Georgia:_____
_____
Uruguay:_____
_____

D.5 Australia v Wales (-)
29 September 2019, Tokyo Stadium, Chofu.
Attendance: _____
Referee: _____
Australia:_____
_____
Wales:_____
_____

D.6 Georgia v Fiji (-)
3 October 2019, Hanazano Stadium, Higashiosaka.
Attendance: _____
Referee: _____
Georgia:_____
_____
Fiji:_____
_____

D.7 Australia v Uruguay (-)
5 October 2019, Oita Stadium, Oita.
Attendance: _____
Referee: _____
Australia:_____
_____
Uruguay:_____
_____

D.8 Wales v Fiji (-)
9 October 2019, Oita Stadium, Oita.
Attendance: _____
Referee: _____
Wales:_____
_____
Fiji:_____
_____

D.9 Australia v Georgia (-)
11 October 2019, Shizuoka Stadium, Fukuroi.
Attendance: _____
Referee: _____
Australia:_____
_____
Georgia:_____
_____

D.10 Wales v Uruguay (-)
13 October 2019, Kumamoto Stadium, Kumamoto.
Attendance: _____
Referee: _____
Wales:_____
_____
Uruguay:_____
_____

8. Japan on the attack against Canada on the 6th August 2013.

QUARTER FINALS

QF1 1st Pool C v 2nd Pool D
_____v_____ (-   )
19 October 2019, Oita Stadium, Oita.
Attendance: _____
Referee: _____
        :_____
_____
        :_____
_____

QF3 1st Pool D v 2nd Pool C
_____v_____ (-   )
20 October 2019, Oita Stadium, Oita.
Attendance: _____
Referee: _____
        :_____
_____
        :_____
_____

QF2 1st Pool B v 2nd Pool A
_____v_____ (-   )
19 October 2019, Tokyo Stadium, Chofu.
Attendance: _____
Referee: _____
        :_____
_____
        :_____
_____

QF4 1st Pool A v 2nd Pool B
_____v_____ (-   )
20 October 2019, Tokyo Stadium, Chofu.
Attendance: _____
Referee: _____
        :_____
_____
        :_____
_____

SEMI FINALS

SF1 - Winner QF1 v QF2 Winner
_____v_____ (-   )
26 October 2019, Int'l Stadium, Yokohama.
Attendance: _____
Referee: _____
        :_____
_____
        :_____
_____

SF2 - Winner QF3 v QF4 Winner
_____v_____ (-   )
27 October 2019, Int'l Stadium, Yokohama.
Attendance: _____
Referee: _____
        :_____
_____
        :_____
_____

FINALS

3rd - Losers of SF1 v SF2
_____v_____ (-   )
1 November 2019, Tokyo Stadium, Chofu.
Attendance: _____
Referee: _____
        :_____
_____
        :_____
_____

Final - Winners of SF1 v SF2
_____v_____ (-   )
2 November 2019, Int'l Stadium, Yokohama.
Attendance: _____
Referee: _____
        :_____
_____
        :_____
_____

9. Passionate Japanese rugby team supporters known as the Dresden Hillbillies!

CREDITS

Text

This article uses material from the Wikipedia article https://en.wikipedia.org/wiki/2019_Rugby_World_Cup which is released under the http://creativecommons.org/licenses/by-sa/3.0/ Creative Commons Attribution-Share-Alike License 3.0.

Images

1. '2014 Asian Five Nations, Japan v. Hong Kong (National Olympic Stadium, Japan)' by D𝜏 (25 May 2014). Available at https://commons.wikimedia.org/wiki/File:A5N_2014_National_Anthem_of_Japan_01.jpg under the Creative Commons Attribution 4.0 International license.

2. 'Japanese: Rugby World Cup 2019 Mascot [日本語: ラグビーワールドカップ 2019 マスコット]' by 江戸村のとくぞう (24 Feb 2018). Available at https://commons.wikimedia.org/wiki/File:Rugby_World_Cup_2019-25.jpg under the Creative Commons Attribution-Share Alike 4.0 International license.

3. 'Kumagaya Rugby Stadium [日本語: 熊谷ラグビー場]' by Waka77 (19 Jan 2019). Available at https://commons.wikimedia.org/wiki/File:Kumagayarugby-07.JPG The copyright holder of this work, releases this work into the public domain. This applies worldwide.

4. 'Shizuoka-stadium 'ECOPA' Fukuroi-shi, Shizuoka-ken, Japan' by WAKA77 (21 Mar 2003). Available at https://commons.wikimedia.org/wiki/File:Ecopa030304.jpg The copyright holder of this work, releases this work into the public domain. This applies worldwide.

5. 'Kyusyu-Sekiyu dome,Bigeye [日本語: 九州石油ドーム　ビッグアイ]' by 撮影者自身による投稿 (14 May 2006). Available at https://commons.wikimedia.org/wiki/File:Ooita_Stadium20090514.jpg The copyright holder of this work, releases this work into the public domain. This applies worldwide.

6. 'Inside view of Kobe Wing Stadium, Kobe, Hyogo Prefecture, Japan. Its rectangle roof was opened' by yuk (6 Dec 2008). Available at https://commons.wikimedia.org/wiki/File:Inside_View_of_Kobe_Wing_Stadium.jpg under the Creative Commons Attribution-Share Alike 3.0 Unported license.

7. 'Ajinomoto Stadium, Tokyo [日本語:味の素スタジア]' by 江戸村のとくぞう (3 Nov 2018). Available at https://commons.wikimedia.org/wiki/File:Ajinomoto_Stadium_2018-13.jpg under the Creative Commons Attribution-Share Alike 4.0 International license.

8. Canada VS Japan rugby' by caleb j from Kelowna, Canada (6 Aug 2013). Available at https://commons.wikimedia.org/wiki/File:Rugby_Canada_vs_Japan_DSC_7283-Edit_(14374998791).jpg under the Creative Commons Attribution 2.0 Generic license.

9. 'Japanese Rugby Team Supporters and Dresden Hillbillies' by tonal decay (20 Sep 2007). Available at https://www.flickr.com/photos/realname/2038873882/ under the Attribution-ShareAlike 2.0 Generic (CC BY-SA 2.0) license.

Full terms at http://creativecommons.org/licenses/by/2.0.

2023
X RUGBY WORLD CUP
France

1. *World Rugby returns to France.*

X Rugby World Cup

8th September to 21st October, 2023

2. Grand Stade de Bordeaux, France (42,000 spectators).

The 2023 Rugby World Cup will be the tenth Rugby World Cup. At a special meeting of the sport's governing body on the 15th November 2017, World Rugby chose the French Rugby Federation bid ahead of bids by the South African Rugby Union and the Irish Rugby Football Union. France had launched its bid on 9th February 2017. On 17th March, 12 host cities were selected, but this list was later reduced to nine cities (excluding Paris, Montpellier and Lens).

The event will take place in the 200th anniversary year of the 'invention' of the sport of rugby as demonstrated by William Webb Ellis. The 2023 Rugby World Cup will run from the 8th September to 21st October 2023 with the final match taking place at the Stade de France in Paris.

THE BID

Three bids to host the 2023 Rugby World Cup were submitted to World Rugby headquarters by the June 2017 deadline, with France being selected on the 15th November 2017 ahead of bids from both Ireland and South Africa. Italy withdrew its bid in September 2016, while Argentina and the United States had initially expressed interest, but ultimately decided against a formal bid. Rugby World Cup 2023 will be France's first time as sole host, having already been principal host in 2007, co-host in 1991, and subsidiary host in 1999.

THE TEAMS

Some 20 teams are set to compete at the 10th Rugby World Cup. A total of 12 teams will have gained automatic qualification to the tournament after finishing in the top three of their respective pools at the 2019 Rugby World Cup, while France automatically qualifies as host. The remaining seven or eight spaces will be decided by existing regional competitions (e.g. the Rugby Europe Int'l Championships) followed by a few cross regional play-offs. The final spot will be decided by a repechage tournament in November 2022.

3. Grand Stade de Lille Métropole, France (50,000 spectators).

4. Stade Vélodrome, Marseille, France (67,000 spectators).

THE VENUES

To prepare for the event, the French Rugby Federation has negotiated the use of the following football venues:

- **Stade de France**,Saint-Denis (Paris) (80,698 spectators) is the national stadium of France, located just north of Paris in the commune of Saint-Denis.

- **Stade Vélodrome**, Marseille (67,394 spectators) known as the Orange Vélodrome for sponsorship reasons, is a multi-purpose stadium in Marseille, France.

- Parc Olympique Lyonnais, Décines-Charpieu (Lyon) (59,186 spectators) known for sponsorship reasons as Groupama Stadium is a large stadium in Décines-Charpieu, in the Lyon Metropolis.

- Stade Pierre-Mauroy, Villeneuve-d'Ascq (Lille) is a multi-use (Arena), retractable roof stadium (50,186 seats) in Villeneuve-d'Ascq, Lille (European Metropolis of Lille), Hauts-de-France, opened in August 2012.

- Matmut Atlantique, Bordeaux (42,115 spectators) The Nouveau Stade de Bordeaux, currently also known as the Matmut Atlantique for sponsorship

purposes, is a football stadium in Bordeaux, France.

- Stade Geoffroy Guichard, Saint-Étienne (41,965 spectators) is a multi-purpose stadium in Saint-Étienne, France.

- Allianz Riviera, (35,624 spectators) is a multi-use stadium in Nice, France, used mostly for football matches of host OGC Nice and also for occasional home matches of rugby union club Toulon.

- Stade de la Beaujoire, Nantes (40,000 spectators) is a stadium in Nantes, France. It is the home of the FC Nantes football club.

- Stadium de Toulouse, Toulouse is the largest multi-purpose stadium in Toulouse, France (33,150 spectators). It is the home of Toulouse Football Club and hosts the big games of rugby for Stade Toulousain in the European Rugby Champions Cup or Top 14.

The tournament planners are in full swing, have developed an event website and are already disseminating news at:

https://www.rugbyworldcup.com/france2023

5. Inauguration of the Allianz Riviera Stade, Nice on the 23 September 2013.

CREDITS

Text

This article uses material from the Wikipedia article https://en.wikipedia.org/wiki/2023_Rugby_World_Cup which is released under the http://creativecommons.org/licenses/by-sa/3.0/ Creative Commons Attribution-Share-Alike License 3.0.

Images

1. 'Information Ballon de rugby sous la Tour Eiffel à l'occasion de la coupe du monde de rugby 2007 en France' by PRA (7th Sep 2007). Available at https://upload.wikimedia.org/wikipedia/commons/b/b4/Coupe_du_monde_rugby_-_tour_Eiffel.JPG under the Creative Commons Attribution-Share Alike 3.0 Unported, 2.5 Generic, 2.0 Generic and 1.0 Generic license.

2. 'Grand Stade de Bordeaux' by PA (16 Nov 2014). Available at https://commons.wikimedia.org/wiki/File:Grand_Stade_de_Bordeaux_2014-11-16.jpg under the Creative Commons Attribution-Share Alike 4.0 International license.

3. 'Grand Stade Lille Métropole' by Liondartois (17 Aug 2012). Available at https://commons.wikimedia.org/wiki/File:Grand_Stade_Lille_Métropole_LOSC_first_match.JPG under the Creative Commons Attribution-Share Alike 3.0 Unported license.

4. 'Stade Vélodrome, Marseille' by Zakarie Faibis (16 Aug 2015). Available at https://commons.wikimedia.org/wiki/File:Stade_Vélodrome_f.jpg under the Creative Commons Attribution-Share Alike 4.0 International license.

5. 'L'Allianz Riviera, Nice le jour de son inauguration.' by Mirasol (23 Sep 2013). Available at https://commons.wikimedia.org/wiki/File:Allianz_inauguration.jpg under the Creative Commons Attribution-Share Alike 3.0 Unported license.

Full terms at http://creativecommons.org/licenses/by/2.0.

SUMMARY OF
NATIONS IN RUGBY WORLD CUP

NATIONS	1987	1991	1995	1999	2003	2007	2011	2015	2019
	16 teams	16 teams	16 teams	20 teams	20 teams	20 teams	20 teams	20 teams	20 teams
Argentina	13th	14th	13th	QF 8th	9th	3rd	QF 8th	4th	
Australia	4th	1st	QF 5th	1st	2nd	QF 6th	3rd	2nd	
Canada	9th	QF 8th	10th	12th	14th	17th	13th	17th	
England	QF 5th	2nd	4th	QF 5th	1st	2nd	QF 6th	9th	
Fiji	QF 8th	13th	DNQ	10th	10th	QF 7th	14th	12th	
France	2nd	QF 7th	3rd	2nd	4th	4th	2nd	QF 8th	
Georgia	DNQ	DNE	DNQ	DNQ	19th	13th	15th	16th	
Ireland	QF 7th	QF 6th	QF 8th	9th	QF 6th	11th	QF 7th	QF 5th	
Italy	12th	10th	11th	20th	12th	11th	11th	11th	
Ivory Coast	DNE	DNQ	15th	DNQ	DNQ	DNQ	DNQ	DNQ	DNQ
Japan	15th	9th	16th	17th	17th	16th	17th	10th	
Namibia	DNE	DNE	DNQ	19th	20th	20th	20th	18th	
New Zealand	1st	3rd	2nd	4th	3rd	QF 5th	1st	1st	
Portugal	DNE	DNQ	DNQ	DNQ	DNQ	19th	DNQ	DNQ	DNQ
Romania	11th	12th	14th	14th	15th	15th	19th	15th	DNQ
Russia	DNQ	DNE	DNQ	DNQ	DNQ	DNQ	18th	DNQ	
Samoa	DNE	QF 7th	QF 7th	11th	11th	14th	10th	13th	
Scotland	QF 6th	4th	QF 6th	QF 6th	QF 8th	QF 8th	9th	QF 6th	
South Africa	DNE	DNE	1st	3rd	QF 5th	1st	QF 5th	3rd	
Spain	DNE	DNQ	DNQ	18th	DNQ	DNQ	DNQ	DNQ	DNQ
Tonga	14th	DNQ	12th	15th	18th	10th	12th	14th	
United States	10th	15th	DNQ	16th	13th	18th	16th	19th	
Uruguay	DNE	DNE	DNQ	13th	16th	DNQ	DNQ	20th	
Wales	3rd	11th	9th	QF 7th	QF 7th	9th	4th	QF 7th	
Zimbabwe	16th	16th	DNQ	DNQ	DNQ	DNQ	DNQ	DNQ	DNQ

NB: *Placings from 1st to 4th are self-evident. All other placings are calculated on the difference between Points For (PF) and Points Against (PA), which include For and Against points for Quarter Finalists.*
DNE = Did Not Enter; DNQ = Did Not Qualify.

CPSIA information can be obtained
at www.ICGtesting.com
Printed in the USA
BVHW021215120822
644454BV00006B/184